Contents

PART IV
FROM THE UNDERSIDE OF HISTORY

GUSTAVO GUTIERREZ

THE POWER OF THE POOR IN HISTORY

SELECTED WRITINGS

SCM PRESS LTD

For
Hugo Echegaray,
unforgettable friend
and
brother in hope,
witness to the gladness of Easter

Translated by Robert R. Barr from the Spanish
La Fuerza historica de los pobres
published 1979 by Centro de Estudios y Publicaciones,
Lima Peru

English translation © 1983 by Orbis Books, Maryknoll,
NY 10545

334 01279 1

First British edition published 1983
by SCM Press Ltd
26–30 Tottenham Road, London N1
Second impression 1986

Photoset in the United States
and printed in Great Britain by
Richard Clay (The Chaucer Press) Ltd
Bungay, Suffolk

Foreword

The Centro de Estudios y Publicaciones and Orbis Books are pleased to publish this compilation of eight works by Gustavo Gutiérrez, the pioneer of liberation theology in Latin America.

The eight selected texts represent complementary moments and focuses in his theological reflection from 1969 to the present. What these moments and focuses have in common is their point of departure, their presence "from within"—their author's continuous attention to the particular set of problems being encountered and worked on in the Latin American church throughout the course of those so rich and demanding years.

Christians in increasing numbers are responding to challenges of every stripe and strain. Groups and communities of Christians battle in the midst of their people, bearing witness, celebrating and deepening a faith incarnate in the agonizing and rapid evolution of Latin America. And the theologian shares the struggle. He or she gathers up these experiences and seeks to express them, together with their ever new and living message.

Within a framework furnished by the theology of liberation, themes unfold that have matured now, through their contact with new facts, new deeds, new reflections. This leads to confrontations and breaches, of course—and not only with preconciliar theologies, but with "progressivist" developments as well, whose point of departure falls short of the living experience and struggle of the "poor of the earth."

Part I presents a biblical overview of some of the major sources of the theology of liberation. Part II contains three articles that were milestones in the evolution of Christian commitment and reflection in the decade from 1969 to 1979. Part III treats of the third plenary session of the Latin American Bishops' Conference, held in Puebla de los Angeles, Mexico, in 1979. Part IV explores a penetrating insight into a new point of departure for theology—the underside of history.

The author has reviewed all these texts for publication as a single collection, making numerous revisions and updatings. More detailed notes on the individual texts are furnished at the beginning of each chapter. We trust that a certain amount of repetition—unavoidable in articles written for separate publication by an author eager to share his interconnected insights with others—will be more than adequately compensated for by the advantage of having all these complementary texts under one cover.

—*Centro de Estudios y Publicaciones, Lima, Peru*
—*Orbis Books, Maryknoll, N.Y.*

Preface:
After Ten Years

Some ten years ago—in early 1973—a book by Gustavo Gutiérrez, a Roman Catholic theologian at that time virtually unknown in the English-speaking world, was published in English.[1] It was the account of a new theological way of thinking and doing, also virtually unknown outside of Latin America, with the then strange name of "liberation theology." Deeply challenging and disturbing to its new audience, the book was almost immediately recognized as a groundbreaking event in the theological world.

In the succeeding decade, dozens of other books have appeared in English dealing with liberation themes, many of them by other Latin American theologians, but increasingly by their counterparts in Asia and Africa as well. In North America, the concerns of black theology, feminist theology, and those speaking for Hispanics, Asian-Americans, Native Americans, homosexuals, and other groups serve as an ongoing reminder to the theological establishment that liberation is not only something sought far away, but near at hand as well.

The tenth anniversary of the publication of Gutiérrez's first volume in English is a propitious occasion on which to receive his latest volume in English and to reflect briefly not only on what has been happening in the interval, but to highlight emphases that Gutiérrez himself has chosen to stress in essays written during that time and here collected together for our further conscientization.

A PEOPLE'S THEOLOGY

By way of retrospect we need only remind ourselves that Gutiérrez would be the first to insist that he is not the creator of liberation theology. As he has insisted from the beginning, and as he repeats in the pages below, liberation theology is a theology of the people, a by-product of the ongoing struggle of the poor to overcome oppression, rather than a theology of the experts crafted in quiet libraries and then offered to "the masses." If his earlier book was the first full-scale (and still the best) statement of the position, that fact only reflects that he has been in active solidarity with the people, and that his book is, in effect, the product of an assiduous note-taker, who gathered together what people were thinking about their acting and provided support out of Scripture and the tradition of the church. Theology, as he insists again and again in the pages below, is always the "second act." The "first act" is commitment, commitment to the struggle of "the wretched of the earth"; as people live out and reflect on that commitment, a theology emerges. The word used to describe this ongoing give-and-take between action and reflection is *praxis*, and theology is consequently described as "critical reflection on praxis in the light of the Word of God."

So this is a people's theology, not a textbook theology, and it is appropriate that the initial essay below is addressed not to professional theologians but to lay people, who gather every summer for a two-week course in Lima, where they reflect together, with people like Gutiérrez, on what they are doing and thinking the rest of the year. Gutiérrez himself, although a professional theologian, is of "the people," a *mestizo* born and raised in Peru, who, after getting a first-rate theological education in Europe, returned to minister to working-class people in Lima and found that the first-rate education didn't "fit" his situation. As a result, he had to start learning all over again, in the midst of his involvement with the people in Rimac, a slum area of Lima in which he still lives and works.[2]

The informal structures in Latin America, through which this people's theology has come into being, are called *comunidades de base*, "grassroots communities" that have grown up by the tens of thousands all over the continent. Often lay-initiated, functioning sometimes with and sometimes without priests, these groups have joined their Bible study and liturgical life to everyday concerns for transformation of the unjust economic order, challenges to the political dictators, interventions on behalf of the thousands who have "disappeared," and so on. The *comunidades* are emerging as the arena of real power for significant change in Latin America, and their commitment to struggle has been the seedbed of the theology that Gutiérrez and others have shared with the rest of us.[3]

It is the reality of this involvement of the poor that explains the vigor and tenacity of the Latin American struggle within the church and upon the society. Put another way, this reality is but a further instance of what Gutiérrez means, particularly in his next-to-last essay, by doing theology "from the underside of history." The phrase is a key to understanding what is going on. This is not theology created by the intelligentsia, the affluent, the powerful, those on top; it is theology from the bottom, from "the underside," created by the victims, the poor, the oppressed. It is not theology spun out in a series of principles or axioms of timeless truth that are then "applied" to the contemporary scene, but a theology springing up out of the poverty, the oppression, the heartrending conditions under which the great majority of Latin Americans live.

A DIFFERENT METHOD

As the essay just referred to insists, this distinguishes the theology of liberation from the theology of the dominant groups in the modern world who live in North America, Great Britain, and Europe. It is not so much a theology with a different *content* (the major Christian themes are amply affirmed in the following pages) as it is a theology with a different *method*, theology as the second act rather than the first. To be sure, the new method means that the specific content of time-honored Christian affirmations will be articulated in a different way; Jesus as "liberator" may mean something different to a Latin American who is starving, than notions of "Christian liberty" mean to comfortably-fed inhabitants of the northern hemisphere. The differences will force both groups back through tradition to the Scriptures and a new reading of the basic resources that all Christians share. (To the nature of this new reading, which Gutiérrez calls a "militant reading," we will shortly return.)

But there is another methodological difference between "our" way of doing theology and the liberation way, which Gutiérrez indicates many times in these essays; the two theologies respond to different interlocutors. Gutiérrez sees northern hemisphere theology as a sustained attempt to answer the questions of *nonbelievers*, the ones for whom, in the modern world, belief has become difficult because of the Enlightenment, or modern science, or technology. Such questions are primarily intellectual. But in the situation in which Gutiérrez lives, the questions are posed by those whom he calls *nonpersons*, the "marginated," those for whom society has no place, those pushed away from the responsibility of a fully human existence. This does not mean that they truly *are* "nonpersons," but only that they are treated as such by those with power in society and consequently are more and more prone so to regard themselves. Their question is not "How can we believe in God in the world of modern science?" but "How can we believe in a personal God in a world that denies our personhood?" The issue is not mainly intellectual; it affects the *whole* person, who is already wondering how liberation can come and how one can move from being a nonperson to a real person. And this means looking at the political, social, and economic structures of society as the context in which the theological issue is raised.

So to the charge that liberation theology includes political, social, and economic analysis, the response must be, "Of course it does! How else could it be faithful to the situation from which, and to which, it is trying to speak?" But if the charge is that it is *only* political, social, and economic analysis, one can confidently reply, buttressed by the following essays, that the charge is arrant nonsense.

So much was fairly clear by the time *A Theology of Liberation* appeared ten years ago, and all of it is fortified and strengthened by the essays below that have been written since that time. Reactions in the interval have been vigorous.

MEDELLÍN (1968) . . .

Many of the emerging themes of liberation concern were picked up and incorporated into the conference of Latin American bishops held at Medellín, Colombia, in 1968. Small wonder, since many of those espousing such concerns, Gutiérrez included, were present at Medellín as theological advisors to the bishops. The fine hand of our present author can be detected in several of the Medellín documents, especially the one with the innocuous-sounding title "Peace," in which a significant analysis of "institutional violence" makes clear that Latin America is already a continent of violence, the violence of the social structures that doom many to suffering and extinction even when no shots are being fired. The theme of the *dependency* of Latin American economies on the rich economies of the north is also stressed, and a commitment to the cause of those oppressed and destroyed by these presumably benign structures is pledged by the bishops.[4]

To be sure, not all the bishops were aware in 1968 that they were signatories to a revolutionary document, but revolutionary document it was, opening up not only a whole new way of looking at poverty and misery in Latin America, but giving substantial support to the then-emerging *comunidades de base* as vehicles for carrying on and implementing Medellín's concerns.

. . . AND PUEBLA (1979)

Indeed, so great was the impetus furnished by Medellín that within a few years many bishops had drawn back, dismayed at the power among the laity that they had unleashed. As plans were made for a follow-up of Medellín a decade later (finally held in Puebla, Mexico, in 1979), extraordinary pressures were exerted, both within the Conference of Latin American Bishops and from Rome, to take the teeth out of liberation theology and the *comunidades*. A Preliminary Document was circulated, written mainly from a European perspective, i.e., "from above," which was (from the point of view of the conservatives) mistakenly circulated among the *comunidades* for comment and refinement. Seldom in church history has an ecclesiastical document been so uniformly discredited. Objections by the planeload made their way to Rome and to the various episcopal centers in Latin America, and not a few Latin American bishops were among the most vocal opponents. The reaction offered by Gutiérrez, in Chapter 5 below, is a good example of the most trenchant of the critiques. The result of the ferment was that the Preliminary Document had to be virtually scrapped and a brand new text hammered out during the Puebla meetings themselves.[5]

So worried were the conservatives that the bishops at Puebla would be influenced by the liberation theologians that the latter were unceremoniously excluded from entering the seminary walls within which the conclave was held. They were present in the city of Puebla in great numbers, however, and, as is now well known, they rented a house, from which they submitted proposed drafts for the various sections through the hands of "friendly bishops." The result was that the final document, though very uneven and much too long, managed to reinsert most of the emphases that the conservatives wanted excised. Thus the *comunidades de base,* rather than having their wings clipped, emerged more significantly than before, and, in the document for which Puebla will surely longest be remembered, the bishops committed themselves to "a preferential option for the poor" as the main item on the church's agenda for the next decade.[6] Once again, it is now well known that Gutiérrez was a chief architect of the draft of this section. One can reflect, in the light of this fact, that it is important to have one's concerns disseminated, and if they can be disseminated above the signatures of bishops, that is a bit of extra help no Catholic in his or her right mind is going to disdain.

At the beginning of the Puebla meetings, the *New York Times* reported (wrongly) that Pope John Paul II had condemned liberation theology in his opening speech. Many lesser journals, piggybacking on the *Times'* reputation, followed suit. But the pope did no such thing, and if his opening allocution (probably written by other hands for him) was not magnanimous in praise of liberation concerns, his subsequent speeches during the week he spent in Mexico became, whether so intended or not, the most expansive papal endorsement one could have wished for. Not only did the pope come out firmly on behalf of the poor and oppressed, but he went on to assert that they had the right to immediate help, "neither a handout nor a few crumbs of justice," insisting that "for their sake we must act promptly and thoroughly; we must implement bold and thoroughly innovative transformations." He reminded his hearers that it is a clear path of church teaching that "there is always a social mortgage on all private property," and that if other measures fail to correct injustices arising out of maldistribution of property, "expropriation" is appropriate.[7]

What grew out of Medellín, in other words—the emergence of a "liberation" perspective and the reality of the *comunidades*—represented forces that not even the combined efforts of conservatives based in Latin America and Rome could thwart at Puebla. No longer can this theology, growing out of the agonies and aspirations of the poorest of the poor, be destroyed, deflected, or dismissed as a "fad."

AN ONGOING STRUGGLE

None of this, however, should suggest that some kind of "victory" has been achieved by liberation forces in Latin America. Not only are long-run signals from Rome always mixed, but the steady increase of martyrs to the cause of liberation continues: Latin American dictators continue to assassinate (usually after torture) or imprison (usually with torture) those who denounce the injustices of the status quo. Worse, in all of the mounting repression, the not-so-hidden hand of United States foreign policy can be detected, giving power, prestige, and guns to the dictators so that the repression continues. Amid ongoing flouting of human rights throughout the continent, the U.S. State Department still persuades the president to certify to Congress that "significant progress is being made," a progress thus far undetectable to the mounting number of victims and their families.

What is amazing, in the light of the ongoing persecution, sure to continue for the foreseeable future, is the fact that people like Gutiérrez are not downhearted. To be sure, they tell us, it is a grim time; there is suffering and hardship, and these will continue. But along with the suffering and hardship there is a great hope. For never before have the people of the continent felt that they could do anything about their situation. And now they do. They are persuaded that things need not remain as they are. The centuries of succumbing to fate, often disguised by the church as providence ("Accept your lot as God's will, avoid making trouble, and you will get a reward in paradise"), are yielding to a new determination to help bring about change. There is even, as Gutiérrez points out in one essay, a "joy" in contemplation of the future. For the struggle of the poor is being transformed into "the power of the poor in history," and the ultimate outcome is assured, since the God of the Bible is a God who sides with them and offers "good news to the poor."

THE CASE FOR "SUBVERSION"

In the light of the above comments, which set the context of these essays, it remains only to comment briefly on themes that are prominent in the following pages. The essays come from different situations, all but one (the second) having been written since *A Theology of Liberation*, and the special circumstances of each essay are indicated in the appropriate places. To the extent that there is some repetition (as is inevitable in such a collection), let that be counted a plus, for we can thereby detect the concerns to which Gutiérrez insistently returns.

The lay emphasis in Gutiérrez's theology is exemplified by the fact, already noted, that the initial essay is addressed to lay people, and its style is such that it can provide a clear summary of the nature of the Christian faith for us as well as its original hearers. The "summer sessions" in Lima at which Gutiérrez speaks every year are designed for hundreds of people who have already made the "first act," i.e., commitment to the human struggle for liberation, and gather annually to explore the "second act," which we now know to be theological reflection. A further value of this essay for those of us in the northern hemisphere is that it shows in clear-cut fashion that Gutiérrez is a *theologian* and that his theology is not, as the critics so often and so wrongly state, "mere" sociology or Marxist analysis. Here, and elsewhere throughout this volume, there is a strong emphasis on reading the Bible, what he later refers to as the necessity for "a militant reading," in which the Bible is read from the perspective of those dwelling on "the underside of history." This is a Bible that our middle-class perspectives have safely camouflaged for us, and there could be no more significant *entree* into liberation theology for the rest of us than to follow Gutiérrez through the biblical passages he exegetes in the present volume.[8]

Such comments prepare us for the rehabilitation of an unexpected word: *subversion*. If things need to be radically changed or overthrown (*vertir*), that can be attempted either from "above" (super-version) or from "below" (sub-version). But there is no doubt in Gutiérrez's mind that super-version won't work; any changes "from above" will be minimal and cosmetic, designed not to change things but only to make the present situation seem palatable enough to negate the need for change. The only significant change, the only change that will make a difference to the poor, will be change that comes "from below," i.e., change that is initiated and carried out by them, from "the underside of history." As though with intellectuals in mind, Gutiérrez reminds us that re-reading history, i.e., seeing it in a new way, is not enough. *The only significant re-reading involves a re-making*, and the re-making must be done by the victims or there will be no significant re-making:

> We shall not have our great leap forward, into a whole new theological perspective, until the marginalized and exploited have begun to become the artisans of their own liberation—until their voice makes itself heard directly, without mediations, without interpretors [p. 65].

As he tells us in a later essay, Puebla heard the word; the bishops wrote:

> We support the aspirations of laborers and peasants, who wish to be treated as free, responsible human beings. They are called to share in the decisions that affect their lives and their future [§1162 and see below p. 155].

This will not necessarily be good news to those in the "super" position, for, as Gutiérrez reminds us, "then we shall have a gospel that is no longer 'presentable' in society. It will not sound nice and it will not smell good" (p. 22). Reminiscent, perhaps, of those uncouth fisherman-turned-disciples from Galilee, whose speech was rough and who must have retained for a long time the odor of their original callings.

FROM "RENEWAL" TO "LIBERATION" TO "STRUGGLE AND HOPE"

The context of the three essays in the section "From Medellín to Puebla" is highly significant. In the period between Medellín and Puebla, Gutiérrez edited three collections of essays, articles, and position papers that were reflective of the times through which the church was going. The titles of these collections indicate the shifts in perspective.

The first of these was *Signos de renovación (Signs of Renewal)*, compiled shortly after Medellín, which was itself seen as a major sign of "renewal" in the church, building on the openings provided by Vatican II, and in particular its document on "The Church and the World Today" (*Gaudium et Spes*).

But a stronger word was soon needed to describe the subsequent activity that grew out of Medellín, so the second volume, published in 1973, was called *Signos de liberación (Signs of Liberation)*, as "renewal" swiftly pointed beyond itself to more radical change, for which "liberation" was the only appropriate term, calling less for repairing the present structures of society than challenging their adequacy to create a just world for all peoples.

The costs of participating in a liberation struggle so defined are indicated by the title of the third collection in the series, published in 1978 just before

Puebla, *Signos de lucha y esperanza (Signs of Struggle and Hope)*, in which it is seen both that liberation is costly and will entail *struggle*, and yet that there are resources available for the degree of engagement that is demanded, so that *hope* is also (as we earlier discovered) a reality on the scene. Indeed, this simultaneous affirmation of "struggle" and "hope" is a key to understanding the kind of commitment out of which "second act" theology is sustained. To struggle without hope would be futile, leading to cynicism or despair; to hope without struggling would be irrelevant, cheap, and self-defeating. But *to struggle while affirming hope* is to have a future and to be empowered by it for the present.

THE AVOIDANCE OF "REDUCTIONISM"

In the course of the essays representing the stages just described, Gutiérrez emphasizes a number of points of ongoing significance for those engaged in the liberation struggle. The theme that *to know God is to do justice* is reiterated as a way of emphasizing the indissolubility of theology and ethics. The real center for liberation theology is the *deed*, and it is the quality of the deed that defines the nature and authenticity of the theological affirmation. To "do justice" is a way of affirming the God of justice. To fail to do justice is to deny the God of justice and worship an idol. Example: General Pinochet claims to believe in God and is frequently photographed at Mass. But General Pinochet orders the torturing of political prisoners, which is *not* to "do justice," and therefore *not* to "know God." The one who is complicit in the torturing of prisoners is denying the God of the Bible; such a one is a nonbeliever, and atheist, no matter what the profession of the lips may be.

Gutiérrez likewise distinguishes the theology of "liberation" from what he calls the theology of "revolution," because of the Achilles' heel of the latter, which is to "baptize the revolution" (p. 44), as though there were certain things beyond criticism. Co-existent with this repudiation of uncritical blessing of every and all means of securing social change is Gutiérrez's frequent disavowal of what he calls "reductionism," i.e., reducing theology to sociology or politics or economics. It takes a good theology to avoid this:

> Only an appreciable degree of political maturity will enable us to get a real grasp of the political dimension of the gospel and keep us from reducing it to a system of social service, however sophisticated, or to a simple task of "human advocacy." Such maturity will likewise enable us to avoid reducing the task of evangelization to some form of political activity, which has laws and exigencies of its own [p. 68].

Even more strongly and positively:

> The gospel message is a message that can never be identified with any concrete social formula, however just that formula may seem to us at the moment. The word of the Lord is a challenge to its every historical

incarnation and places that incarnation in the broad perspective of the radical and total liberation of Christ, the Lord of history [p. 69, cf. also p. 98].

For Gutiérrez, however, the encounter with "Christ, the Lord of history" takes places in the encounter with the poor person—a very biblical insight, particularly in the light of Matthew 25:31–46. The theme is picked up again at the end of Chapter 7, on "Theology from the Underside of History," an excursion that "will lead us along paths where we shall not meet the great ones of this world. Instead we shall meet the Lord. We shall meet him in the poor of Latin America and of other continents" (p. 214). These poor, whom God loves, are loved by God simply because they are poor, and not because they are morally superior or have greater spiritual insight (cf. p. 95). There is no false romanticism about poverty and how it ennobles those whom its tentacles grasp. The task of solidarity with the poor is not to exalt their poverty but to find ways to do battle with them so that it may be overcome.

A NEW VIEW OF HUMAN RIGHTS

In the most recent period of "struggle and hope," the issue of human rights has assumed a new urgency in Gutiérrez's thought. There are at least two reasons for this, not unrelated: (1) the swelling list of martyrs in every country, as dictators fearful of popular uprisings use any pretext (or none) to destroy those suspected of participation in potential uprisings, and (2) the greater attention given to the issue by the outside world. The Carter administration, for example, at least paid lip service to concern for human rights, and in a few cases actually cut aid to countries guilty of flagrant violations—a posture the Reagan administration promptly repudiated by not only restoring such aid, but by tacitly assuring dictators that they need not worry about U.S. "interference," a fact that cannot help but encourage dictators receiving arms and support from the United States to disregard world opinion that is outraged by torture and indiscriminate mass killings.

But for Gutiérrez such discussion, important as it is, does not get to the heart of the basic issue. Attention must certainly be called to the suppression of the right of dissent, of freedom of expression, of the holding of unpopular opinions, but such attention runs the danger of leaving untouched the further issue of what can be called *social* human rights, i.e., the right of people to food, clothing, education, shelter, health care, employment. In the northern hemisphere, such "rights" are usually defined as privileges, available to those who can pay for them. But the whole discussion of human rights aborts, Gutiérrez feels, if the latter "rights" are not center stage. Doing away with torture, admirable and important as a goal in itself, need not affect the denial of the other rights mentioned, and when torture is abolished a government is likely to assert that the human rights problem has been "solved." But as long as children are growing up in a society where their parents cannot get jobs, so that children grow up undernourished, as long as people cannot get decent housing or education and health care for their children, human rights are being violated, and such rights must be the focal point of human endeavor in this area (cf. pp. 87–88). Measured against such a yardstick, there is a long way to go.

ACTING THROUGH THE CHURCH

As far as the essays concerning Puebla are concerned (Part III below), enough has already been said to indicate the themes central to them. Here we need note only that the very fact of Gutiérrez's deep involvement in both Medellín (where he was a theological consultant) and Puebla (where he was denied admittance and had to work "off the scene") demonstrates an important commitment to the church that is central to practitioners of liberation theology. Many of those espousing liberation causes have gotten scant thanks, and often much grief, from the church, and there must often be an impulse to throw in the towel, leave the institution, and work more effectively (perhaps) with groups not so tied to a cautious way of doing things. But, not only because of his own commitment to the church as Christ's body in the world, but also because of the sociological realities in Latin America where the church and the church's symbols play a significant cultural role, Gutiérrez not only remains within the church but actively within the church. His assiduous work before, during, and after both Medellín and Puebla bespeaks a loyalty and commitment for which he receives little official thanks and much public challenge. But the church is, and remains, the locus of his activity.

THE IMPORTANCE OF THE DEED

The last two essays in this collection represent a special effort on Gutiérrez's part to reach out toward those of us who live, think, and act elsewhere than in Latin America. Without here recapitulating the whole of a long and sophisticated argument, we can be reminded once more by these essays of the fundamental difference in method between our own ways of theologizing and those of the Latin Americans. Just as Gutiérrez really seeks to enter into our ways of thinking in order to understand them, so he invites and even impels us to do the same thing with his convictions. The concluding brief essay on Bonhoeffer is a helpful coda to the highly orchestrated pamphlet-length essay preceding it. For in it he notes that it can occasionally be true that someone conditioned by the "dominant" theology of the northern hemisphere can be so influenced by contemporary events (in Bonhoeffer's case the rise of Hitler), that a lifetime of theological training can be questioned and a new perspective sought, since there is a new situation within which the faith must be re-thought and re-lived. The example of Bonhoeffer is particularly telling, since Bonhoeffer was a bourgeois of the bourgeois, nurtured in an affluent, comfortable, untroubled home and culture. If he, with every reason to cling to all that was a part of his formation, could so radically challenge all that and begin to see things from what he called "the view from below" (not too far from what Gutiérrez calls "the underside of history), then there is hope for all of us.

The title of this preface, "After Ten Years," is identical with the title Eberhard Bethge gave to an essay of Bonhoeffer's, written in 1942, "after ten years" of the rule of Hitler. The paragraph within that essay dealing with "the view from below" is cited twice by Gutiérrez in the pages below, and I risk its inclusion yet a third time, because it states so clearly the *beginning* of a road down which northern hemisphere Christians are going to have to begin to walk, if we are going to come within hailing distance of what Gutiérrez and his companions are about in Latin America:

> There remains an experience of incomparable value. We have for once learnt to see the great events of world history from below, from the perspective of the outcast, the suspects, the maltreated, the powerless, the oppressed, the reviled—in short, from the perspective of those who suffer.[9]

Perhaps that will enable us to hear Gutiérrez—who must have the last word—more clearly, when he tells us:

> All the political theologies, the theologies of hope, or revolution, and of liberation, are not worth one act of genuine solidarity with exploited social classes. They are not worth one act of faith, love, and hope, committed—in one way or another—in active participation to liberate persons from everything that dehumanizes them and prevents them from living according to the Word of God.[10]

—Robert McAfee Brown

NOTES

1. Gutiérrez, *A Theology of Liberation* (Maryknoll, N.Y.: Orbis Books, 1973).

2. There is fuller information about Gutiérrez's life and thought in my *Gustavo Gutiérrez* (Atlanta: John Knox Press, 1980), especially Chapter Two.

3. For more on the *comunidades*, see Alvaro Barreiro, *Basic Ecclesial Communities* (Maryknoll, N.Y.: Orbis Books, 1982).

4. The Medellín documents are available in Louis Colonnese, ed., *The Church in the Present-Day Transformation of Latin America in the Light of the Council* (Bogotá: CELAM, 1970), Volume II. The document on "Peace" is on pp. 71–82.

5. For details of this period, see Penny Lernoux, "The Long Path to Puebla," in John Eagleson and Philip Scharper, eds., *Puebla and Beyond* (Maryknoll, N.Y.: Orbis Books, 1979), pp. 3–27.

6. The document is contained in *Puebla and Beyond*, pp. 264–67.

7. Ibid., p. 82.

8. Extensive help in this task is provided in Gutiérrez's most recent work, *El Dios de la vida* (*The God of Life*) (Lima: Pontificia Universidad Católica del Perú, 1982), a volume of Bible studies first shared by Gutiérrez at the "summer course" for lay people in Lima in 1981.

9. Dietrich Bonhoeffer, *Letters and Papers from Prison*, new greatly enlarged edition (New York: Macmillan, 1972), p. 17.

10. Gutiérrez, *Theology of Liberation*, p. 308, slightly altered.

PART I
BIBLICAL OVERVIEW
OF THE SOURCES
OF LIBERATION THEOLOGY

1

God's Revelation and Proclamation in History

Ask any Christian what the Bible is, and the answer you receive will seem clear and simple: the Bible is the word of God. And yet for many persons actual contact with the Bible is no simple matter at all. The Bible does not present the good news in systematic form. It is not a theology book, or a catechism, or a collection of conciliar texts. We find ourselves face to face with an ensemble of books that tell the history of a people—without being a history book. There are factual accounts, almost anecdotal in style, there are interpretations of events recounted and meditations on them, there are biographical sketches, there are accounts of the preaching of the prophets and of Jesus (in various versions), there are theological analyses. The Bible is a collection of books, different books of different kinds.

What ties them together is that they all tell of a people's faith. And that is why we can read there the certainties, the perplexities, the deficiencies, and the gladness of our own faith in God. For we too are his people. This is why it is so easy to grasp the meaning of the Bible—and why it is at the same time so difficult.

Today all believers consider frequent contact with the Bible important. The Bible is our prayer book par excellence. Reading it and hearing it explained permit us to rediscover the deep meaning of our life and our commitments. And yet we tend to approach the Bible with a certain sense of insecurity. We feel out of our element. We are on unfamiliar ground. We are afraid of not knowing what we are talking about. We have the idea that serious Bible reading demands historical, philological, theological, and geographical knowledge that most of us do not have.

Presentation made at the opening of the summer session offered by the Department of Theology of the Catholic University of Lima, Peru, in 1975. The Spanish text was first published as a Supplement to *Páginas*, 2/1 (Lima: Centro de Estudios y Publicaciones [CEP], March 1976).

So we look to the specialists, the exegetes, and we depend on their "scientific interpretation of the text" to tell us what the Bible means. And now, alas, we see that not many believers have what it takes to be a scientific exegete. And so now we are more insecure than ever about our contact with the Bible. Exegetes, as someone once said, are members of a very exclusive, expensive club. To become a member of this club you have to have assimilated Western culture—German and Anglo-Saxon culture, actually—because exegesis in the Christian churches of today is so closely tied in with it. (What must an African, an Oriental, a Latin American make of this exegesis, especially on some of the fine points?) I am not suggesting that scientific interpretation is invalid. But we do have to be careful not to exaggerate its importance. We have to remember that its purpose is the proclamation of the good news to the poor.

For some, the effort to read the Bible may be directed toward simply adapting its message and language to men and women of today. For others, however, it is a matter of reinterpretation. We reinterpret the Bible, from the viewpoint of our own world—from our personal experience as human beings, as believers, and as church. This approach is more radical. It goes more to the roots of what the Bible actually is, more to the essence of God's revelation in history and of God's judgment on it.

Let us try to understand the Bible—or, as the evangelist puts it, to "believe the full message of the prophets" (Luke 24:25)—in the following pages using this second approach. And let us start out with Christ, the fulfillment of the promise of the Father, for this is the only way to grasp the profound unity of the Old and New Testaments. Our reading, then, will be *christological*.

But it will also be a reading *in faith*. It will not be a reading done by trained specialists, but by a community that knows itself to be the subject of the word's intercession, that recognizes Christ as Lord both of history and its own life.

Hence, thirdly, our reading will be *historical*. God reveals himself in the history of the people that believed and hoped in him—and this leads us to rethink his word from the viewpoint of our own history. But because ours is a true history, crisscrossed by confrontation and conflict, we can enter into it consciously and effectively only by steeping ourselves in the popular struggles for liberation.

Hence, finally, our reading of the Bible will be a *militant* reading. The great questions about the word of the Lord arise out of Christian practice. It is time to reclaim this militant reading of the word of God in faith. It is time to open the Bible and read it from the perspective of "those who are persecuted in the cause of right" (Matt. 5:10), from the perspective of the condemned human beings of this earth—for, after all, theirs is the kingdom of heaven. It is for them that the gospel is destined, it is to them that the gospel is preferentially addressed. But they will receive it only insofar as they carry it with them.

GOD REVEALS HIMSELF IN HISTORY

Faith and History

The faith of the Jewish people is not based on theories about a supreme being who created the world and now keeps it running and orderly. This sort of reflection is there, but only later, and secondarily. Nor does Old Testament faith arise out of the affirmation of a prehistorical (and therefore ahistorical), mythical occurrence. The earthly paradise chronicled in the book of Genesis, itself a late composition, could run the risk of just such a misunderstanding.

Word and Happening. The Bible *tells a story*. Human beings began to write history, say some historians, with the Bible. Biblical faith means knowing history and believing in the God who reveals himself in it. God makes himself known in his works. Right from the start, then, works are important for a faith in accord with the Bible. "Yahweh is a living God" is a concept that recurs again and again in the Bible (see, for example, Judg. 8:19; 1 Kings 17:1; 1 Sam. 17:26–36). He is a God who acts. He is a God who speaks, this God of Israel. The Bible ridicules gods who "have mouths, but never speak" (Ps. 115:5). The word of God, on the contrary, is efficacious:

Yes, as the rain and the snow come down from the heavens and do not return without watering the earth, making it yield and giving growth to provide seed for the sower and bread for the eating, so the word that goes from my mouth does not return to me empty, without carrying out my will and succeeding in what it was sent to do [Isa. 55:10–11].

Yahweh's word is *dabar*: word and happening, both at the same time.

Historical Creeds. Professions of faith in God by Israel always refer to historical facts. These are the so-called historical creeds. I give two examples:

In times to come, when your son asks you, "What is the meaning of the decrees and laws and customs that Yahweh our God has laid down for you?" you shall tell your son, "Once we were Pharaoh's slaves in Egypt, and Yahweh brought us out of Egypt by his mighty hand. Before our eyes Yahweh worked great and terrible signs and wonders against Egypt, against Pharaoh and all his House. And he brought us out from there to lead us into the land he swore to our fathers he would give to us. And Yahweh commanded us to observe all these laws and to fear Yahweh our God, so as to be happy for ever and to live, as he has granted us to do until now. For us right living will mean this: to keep and observe all these commandments before Yahweh our God as he has directed us" [Deut. 6:20–25].

The Lord frees the Jewish people from slavery and oppression. And he makes sure he does it through signs that will make his activity visible. But this breach with a situation of exploitation will be real only thanks to the fulfillment of a promise: that the people would be settled in a "land where milk and honey flow"—the Promised Land, which in its own turn is the promise of future fulfillments. This liberating deed of Yahweh is the basis of the Jewish people's behavior: the people's "right living" will consist in putting Yahweh's commandments into practice:

> My father was a wandering Aramaean. He went down into Egypt to find refuge there, few in numbers; but there he became a nation, great, mighty, and strong. The Egyptians ill-treated us, they gave us no peace and inflicted harsh slavery on us. But we called on Yahweh the God of our fathers. Yahweh heard our voice and saw our misery, our toil and our oppression; and Yahweh brought us out of Egypt with mighty hand and outstretched arm, with great terror, and with signs and wonders. He brought us here and gave us this land, a land where milk and honey flow [Deut. 26:5-9].

Here again we find basically the same ideas. The reference to Jacob (the "wandering Aramaean") expresses the people's historical origin and modest beginnings. Once more, everything centers on liberation from the oppression that had been suffered in Egypt. It is in that liberation that the God of biblical faith is revealed.

The same "creed" is found, more briefly, in other books of the Bible—for example, in Amos 2:10, 3:2. They can all be summed up the same way: "Yahweh delivered us from Egypt." The God of Israel is the God who delivers, the God who liberates.

The cultural context of these "historical creeds" should be noted. They constitute a profession of faith within the framework of a celebration of Yahweh's liberating deed. The covenant theme does not yet appear. We find only the foundation, only the basic historical fact—liberation from Egypt. The covenant itself has its roots in this fact. Israel's faith rests on both.

Open-Ended History. The history from which biblical faith springs is an open-ended history, a history open to the future. Liberation from Egypt is an event that will be reread again and again, to shed light on other historical interventions of Yahweh (see Pss. 105 and 106, for example). The land where he leads this people fulfills a promise, a promise made to their ancestors; but the land in turn is itself a promise, opening history to still other fulfillments.

Faith is transmitted not by remembering a past event, but by rereading it in the light of the present—in the light of Yahweh's new promises. "I Am who I Am," Yahweh had said (Exod. 3:14); I am the one I shall be, the one you shall discover me to be. The God of biblical faith launches that faith into the future. Knowledge of Yahweh is an eschatological stance. God is love—love in the present and, fully, at the end of time. Hope is an essential element of a faith in accord with the Bible.

Liberation for the Establishment of Justice and Right

It is not enough, however, to say that God reveals himself in history, and that therefore the faith of Israel fleshes out a historical framework. One must keep in mind that the God of the Bible is a God who not only governs history, but who orientates it in the direction of establishment of justice and right. He is more than a provident God. He is a God who takes sides with the poor and liberates them from slavery and oppression.

Liberation. This is the meaning of Yahweh's interventions in history. The purpose of his activity is not to demonstrate his power, but to liberate, and make justice reign:

> Father of orphans, defender of widows,
> such is God in his holy dwelling;
> God gives the lonely a permanent home,
> makes prisoners happy by setting them free,
> but rebels must live in an arid land [Ps. 68:5-6].

This is Yahweh. His might is at the service of justice. His power is expressed in the defense of the rights of the poor (see Ps. 146:7-9). The real theophany, or revelation of God, is in the liberation of the person who is poor.

To Know God Is to Do Justice.

> Doom for the man who founds his palace on anything but integrity,
> his upstairs rooms on anything but honesty,
> who makes his fellow man work for nothing,
> without paying him his wages,
> who says, "I will build myself an imposing palace
> with spacious rooms upstairs,"
> who pierces lights in it,
> panels it with cedar, and paints it vermilion.
> Are you more of a king
> for outrivaling others with cedar?
> Your father ate and drank, like you,
> but he practiced honesty and integrity,
> so all went well for him.
> He used to examine the cases of poor and needy,
> then all went well.
> Is not that what it means to know me?—
> it is Yahweh who speaks [Jer. 22:13-16].

Knowledge of God is love of God. In the language of the Bible, "to know" is not something purely intellectual. To know means to love. Sin is the absence of the knowledge of Yahweh, and it is on this that the people will be judged: "Sons of Israel, listen to the word of Yahweh, for Yahweh indicts the inhabitants of the country" (Hos. 4:1).

To know God as liberator *is* to liberate, *is* to do justice. For the Bible, the root of behavior that can be called "just" is in the historical fact that constitutes a resumé of its faith: God delivered us from Egypt:

> You must not pervert justice in dealing with a stranger or an orphan, nor take a widow's garment in pledge. Remember that you were a slave in Egypt and that Yahweh your God redeemed you from there. That is why I lay this charge on you [Deut. 24:17-18].

To deal with a poor man or woman as Yahweh dealt with his people—this is what it is to be just: "He who looks down on his neighbor sins, blessed is he who takes pity on the poor" (Prov. 14:21; cf. Exod. 22:20-23).

God and the Poor. Our relationship with God is expressed in our relationship with the poor. Proverbs puts it aphoristically: "To mock the poor is to insult his creator" (Prov. 17:5).

God reveals himself in history, yes, but history is full of conflicts. The prophet Amos is fierce on this point:

> Listen to this word, you cows of Bashan
> living in the mountain of Samaria,
> oppressing the needy, crushing the poor,
> saying to your husbands, "Bring us something to drink!"
> The Lord Yahweh swears this by his holiness:
> The days are coming to you now
> when you will be dragged out with hooks,
> the very last of you with prongs.
> Out you will go, each by the nearest breach in the wall,
> to be driven all the way to Hermon.
> It is Yahweh who speaks [Amos 4:1-3].

Thus the reciprocal relationship between God and the poor person is the very heart of biblical faith. Here the two essential, ongoing dimensions of faith are inextricably intertwined:

> The word that was addressed to Jeremiah by Yahweh, "Go and stand at the gate of the temple of Yahweh and there proclaim this message. Say, 'Listen to the word of Yahweh, all you men of Judah who come in by these gates to worship Yahweh. Yahweh Sabaoth, the God of Israel, says this: Amend your behavior and your actions and I will stay with you here in this place. Put no trust in delusive words like these: This is

the sanctuary of Yahweh, the sanctuary of Yahweh, the sanctuary of Yahweh! But if you do amend your behavior and your actions, if you treat each other fairly, if you do not exploit the stranger, the orphan and the widow (if you do not shed innocent blood in this place), and if you do not follow alien gods, to your own ruin, then here in this place I will stay with you, in the land that long ago I gave to your fathers for ever [Jer. 7:1-7].

Touchstone of Injustice. To sin—not to love, not to know, Yahweh—is to create relationships of injustice, to make an option for oppression and against liberation. Still worse, if persons feign a belief in Yahweh, and proclaim that he is in their midst, the truth will come out in their practice with regard to the poor:

> Now listen to this, you princes of the House of Jacob,
> rulers of the House of Israel,
> you who loathe justice
> and pervert all that is right,
> you who build Zion with blood,
> Jerusalem with crime.
> Her princes pronounce their verdict for bribes,
> her priests take a fee for their rulings,
> her prophets make divinations for money.
> And yet they rely on Yahweh. They say,
> "Is not Yahweh in our midst?
> No evil is going to overtake us."
> Because of this, since the fault is yours,
> Zion will become plowland,
> Jerusalem a heap of rubble,
> and the mountain of the Temple a wooded height [Mic. 3:9-12].

Knowledge of God is tested on the terrain of actual practice. Failure to know God means to make an option against the God who rescued Israel from Egypt in order to establish justice and right.

Covenant and Fidelity

"I shall be your God, and you shall be my people." This sums up the covenant that Yahweh strikes with his people. The covenant implies a *double belonging*—of God to the Jewish people and of the Jewish people to God. The guarantee of this mutual possession is Yahweh's love, as expressed in the deed by which he liberated the people from servitude in Egypt. Yahweh demands in exchange that the people bear witness to him in history (see Ezek. 36). The exodus affords a grasp of the perspective in which the covenant is situated, and the covenant in turn gives full meaning to the liberation from

Egypt. Liberation leads to communion. This is the process by which the "people of God" is built.

To be just is to be faithful to the covenant. *Fidelity* is at once *justice* and *holiness*. Justice in the Bible is what unites one's relationship with the poor to one's relationship with God. Only thus does justice mean holiness. To be faithful to the covenant means to practice the justice implied in God's liberating activity on behalf of the oppressed.

This practice of justice as an expression of fidelity is found in the promise that precedes the covenant struck with Abraham:

> Now, Yahweh had wondered, "Shall I conceal from Abraham what I am going to do, seeing that Abraham will become a great nation with all the other nations of the earth blessing themselves by him? For I have singled him out to command his sons and his household after him to maintain the way of Yahweh by just and upright living. In this way Yahweh will carry out for Abraham what he has promised him " [Gen. 18:17–19].

To be faithful is to establish justice and right. This is what true holiness consists in. This is what the prophets are calling for when they demand fidelity to the covenant. They are calling for the concrete historical actualization of the promise made to Abraham.

Faith in a Situation of Exile

Crisis of Faith. The Babylonian captivity provoked a profound crisis of faith in the Jewish people. Finding themselves once more in servitude, they began to wonder about the God who had liberated them from Egypt. The situation now was even worse than it had been before, worse than in Egypt. The oppression was more cruel now. Their homeland had been destroyed, their temple leveled. Their national consciousness of being a free people had been humiliated. How could Yahweh permit this? Was he a God of liberation or was he not? Why was he allowing them to fall into slavery all over again? Israel confesses itself to be a sinful people, deserving of punishment. But this is not enough. The psalmist asks the painful question: "How could we sing one of Yahweh's hymns in a pagan country?" (Ps. 137:4).

How can one sing the praises of a God of liberation in the midst of a situation of oppression? The searing question goes straight to the bottom of the faith-crisis of the people of Israel. The great theologian of the exile, Second Isaiah, will digest the situation and meditate on it. The experience and reflection of the exiled people will afford it the opportunity to take a step forward. Now it grasps what a great leader of our own time put this way: "There is only one way out. Forward." And so the exile, instead of turning the people in upon itself, prompts it to make a quantum leap.

Universalism. This leap will follow a double trajectory. The first will be that of a new universalistic consciousness. Beginning with the exile, Israel understands that its God is not only its God—he is the God of all the peoples of the earth. At the heart of their faith-crisis the Jewish people begins to divest itself of something. It begins to renounce private ownership of God. God begins to be understood as the liberator of all peoples (see Isa. 41:1-7, 43:10, 44:8). Even in the preexilic prophets there is a kind of rough draft of this universalism, as they remind the Jews that God rescued other peoples, too; that after all, their escape from Egypt was only one exodus among many:

> Are not you and the Cushites all the same to me,
> sons of Israel?—it is Yahweh who speaks.
> Did not I, who brought Israel out of the land of Egypt,
> bring the Philistines from Caphtor,
> and the Aramaeans from Kir? [Amos 9:7].

But this notion of a universal God entails two other important considerations as well. First, this God of liberation is so powerful, he must also be the creator of all things; and so there arises the theme of creation as the first of God's salvific deeds. Secondly, Yahweh must ultimately be the liberator of human existence in its totality; Israel starts to discover that life does not end, that resurrection vanquishes death.

The second avenue of escape from the clutches of the exilic faith-crisis lies in the Jewish people's inkling of a *new covenant*. Now we have a new point of departure. From the exile forward, the Jewish people is on its way again. Jeremiah and Ezekiel give us basic texts here:

See, the days are coming—it is Yahweh who speaks—when I will make a new covenant with the House of Israel (and the House of Judah), but not a covenant like the one I made with their ancestors on the day I took them by the hand to bring them out of the land of Egypt. They broke that covenant of mine, so I had to show them who was master. It is Yahweh who speaks. No, this is the covenant I will make with the House of Israel when those days arrive—it is Yahweh who speaks. Deep within them I will plant my Law, writing it on their hearts. Then I will be their God and they shall be my people. There will be no further need for neighbor to try to teach neighbor, or brother to say to brother, "Learn to know Yahweh!" No, they will all know me, the least no less than the greatest—it is Yahweh who speaks—since I will forgive their iniquity and never call their sin to mind [Jer. 31:31-34].

I mean to display the holiness of my great name, which has been profaned among the nations, which you have profaned among them. And the nations will learn that I am Yahweh—it is the Lord Yahweh who speaks—when I display my holiness for your sake before their eyes. Then I am going to take you from among the nations and gather you together from all the foreign countries, and bring you home to your own land. I shall pour clean water over you and you will be cleansed; I shall cleanse you of all your defilement and all your idols. I shall give you a new heart, and put a new spirit in you; I shall remove the heart of stone from your bodies and give you a heart of flesh instead. I shall put my spirit in you, and make you keep my laws and sincerely respect my observances. You will live in the land which I gave your ancestors. You shall be my people and I will be your God [Ezek. 36:23–28].

Yahweh's continued, permanent fidelity demands a new fidelity on the part of his people. The new covenant will be one written on the heart of each and every individual. Now the law will be at once interior and universal, instead of exterior and particular.

Memory and Freedom

The Bible is historical. Memory is important. The memory of past historical deeds is evoked in order to draw attention to Yahweh's liberating action in the present. A beautiful and powerful text reads, "It was not with our fathers that Yahweh made this covenant, but with us, with us who are here, all living today" (Deut. 5:3). The covenant has been struck today. It is not a fact confined to the past.

Biblical faith, however, besides being memory, is freedom: *openness to the future*. Recalling the liberating deed of Yahweh is not the nostalgia of bygone days. All great love contains the memory of the first moment. In strong moments it is the font of gladness; in difficult moments it is the reaffirmation of hope. In either case the gaze is to the fore. The future is the task. Memory thus has the function of conditioning a creative liberty. What we were saying about the exile is a vigorous example of memory (of the flight from Egypt) and openness (to new paths of liberation).

The faith of Israel moves in this dialectic of memory and liberty. This is what is celebrated in its *worship*. We have already pointed out that it is worship that is the context of the "historical creeds"—this evoking of the past in function of the future. Israel celebrates its rituals not in order to appease the divine wrath but to give thanks for the liberation and the covenant, and to take cognizance of God's new interventions in its history. Israel's fidelity—doing justice to the poor—is the condition of authentic worship, say the prophets.

JESUS CHRIST, THE FATHER'S TRUTH

It is in this framework that the revelation in Jesus Christ is situated—in continuity with the revelation of God in history, but also as an absolute beginning. Jesus Christ is the full manifestation of the God who is love: the

Father. He is the fulfillment, and the new departure, of the promise of love. He is the one who bears witness that God is truth. He is the truth of the Father and the key of Scripture.

Jesus Is Christ

Being a Christian does not mean, first and foremost, believing in a message. It means believing in a person. Having faith means believing that a certain human being of our own history, a Jew named Jesus, who was born of Mary, who proclaimed the Father's love, the gospel, to the poor, and liberation to those in captivity, who boldly confronted the great ones of his people and the representatives of the occupying power, who was executed as a subversive, is the Christ, the Messiah, the Anointed One, the Son. "These [signs] are recorded so that you may believe that Jesus is the Christ, the Son of God, and that believing this you may have life through his name" (John 20:31; cf. Rom. 10:9). The gospel is the good news because it comes from Jesus the Christ—"Here begins the gospel of Jesus Christ, the Son of God" (Mark 1:1; NAB).

The God we believe in is the Father of Jesus. Not only do we know Jesus as a person of our history, but we recognize in him the Son. In Jesus God not only reveals himself in history, he becomes history. He "pitches his tent" in the midst of history (John 1:14). Because it is Jesus who announces it, the gospel is the good news. The message must not hide the fact that our faith goes beyond it, transcends it. Our faith goes through the gospel straight to Christ. Jesus has already come into the world; this is true. He is a historical fact. But far from closing history, this fact opens it to unsuspected thoroughfares. Christ is not only come, he is the one who is to come. He is in the future of our history.

This is what we call the parousia (Greek for presence, advent, or arrival), the second coming. Over and above what it may have to offer of the marvelous or the miraculous, the parousia has a meaning: it means this openness of history to Christ—in the "today" of the Christian community and of humankind.

Christ the Liberator

The nub, the nucleus, of the biblical message, we have said, is in the relationship between God and the poor. Jesus Christ is precisely *God become poor*. This was the human life he took—a poor life. And this is the life in and by which we recognize him as Son of his Father.

He was poor indeed. He was born into a social milieu characterized by poverty. He chose to live with the poor. He addressed his gospel by preference to the poor. He lashed out with invective against the rich who oppressed the poor and despised them. And before the Father, he was poor in spirit.

Christ came to proclaim the kingdom of God to us. Matthew and Mark say so at the beginning of their gospels. Kingdom signifies globalization. Nothing escapes it. "Kingdom of God" means, God reigns—that is, that his love, his fatherhood, and a community of brothers and sisters, is going to reign among all human beings. This is the mystery hidden until this moment and now revealed (Rom. 16:25).

Luke specifies that the kingdom is a kingdom of justice:

> He came to Nazareth, where he had been brought up, and went into the synagogue on the sabbath day as he usually did. He stood up to read, and they handed him the scroll of the prophet Isaiah. Unrolling the scroll he found the place where it is written:
>> The spirit of the Lord has been given to me,
>> for he has anointed me.
>> He has sent me to bring the good news to the poor,
>> to proclaim liberty to captives
>> and to the blind new sight,
>> to set the downtrodden free,
>> to proclaim the Lord's year of favor.
> He then rolled up the scroll, gave it back to the assistant and sat down. And all eyes in the synagogue were fixed on him. Then he began to speak to them, "This text is being fulfilled today even as you listen" [Luke 4:16–21; citing Isa. 61:1–2].

He is proclaiming a kingdom of justice and liberation, to be established in favor of the poor, the oppressed, and the marginalized of history.

This proclamation of the kingdom, this struggle for justice, leads Jesus to death. His life and his death give us to know that the only possible justice is definitive justice. The only justice is the one that goes to the very root of all injustice, all breach with love, all sin. The only justice is the one that assaults all the consequences and expressions of this cleavage in friendship. The only justice is the definitive justice that builds, starting right now, in our conflict-filled history, a kingdom in which God's love will be present and exploitation abolished:

> For now I create new heavens and a new earth, and the past will not be remembered, and will come no more to men's minds. Be glad and rejoice for ever and ever for what I am creating, because I now create Jerusalem "Joy" and her people "Gladness." I shall rejoice over Jerusalem and exult in my people. No more will the sound of weeping or the sound of cries be heard in her; in her, no more will be found the infant living a few days only, or the old man not living to the end of his days. To die at the age of a hundred will be dying young; not to live to be a hundred will be the sign of a curse. They will build houses and inhabit them, plant vineyards and eat their fruit. They will not build for others

to live in, or plant so that others can eat. For my people shall live as long as trees, and my chosen ones wear out what their hands have made [Isa. 65:17–22].

A New Covenant

Jesus Christ is himself the new covenant. In him God becomes the Father of all nations, and all men and women see that they are his children and one another's sisters and brothers. "However many the promises God made, the Yes to them all is in him," Paul tells us (2 Cor. 1:20). And along these same lines the book of Revelation will say that Christ is the "Amen" to God's glory (Rev. 7:12). Thus Jesus Christ comes forward as the principle, the point of departure, of the interpretation of Scripture. In Jesus we meet God. In the human word we read the word of God. In historical events we recognize the fulfillment of the promise.

This is the basic circle of all hermeneutics: from the human being to God and from God to the human being, from history to faith and from faith to history, from love of our brothers and sisters to the love of the Father and from the love of the Father to the love of our brothers and sisters, from human justice to God's holiness and from God's holiness to human justice, from the poor person to God and from God to the poor person.

In Jesus a new creation is accomplished:

From now onward, therefore, we do not judge anyone by the standards of the flesh. Even if we did once know Christ in the flesh, that is not how we know him now. And for anyone who is in Christ, there is a new creation; the old creation has gone, and now the new one is here [2 Cor. 5:16–17].

It is a new beginning, and its norm will be the ever new commandment, "Love one another, as I have loved you" (John 15:12). This is what will make the faithful of the new covenant "friends" and no longer "servants." The universality of the new covenant passes by way of Christ's death and is sealed by his resurrection. Jesus' death is the consequence of his struggle for justice, his proclamation of the kingdom, and his identification with the poor. His death, like the exile of old, will be the occasion of a great discovery: it will occasion a faith-crisis for his disciples, because it was the collapse of many a hope that had fed on Jesus' life. But it was also the opportunity to overleap the limits of their understanding of Jesus' person and mission.

We might say the resurrection uproots him, rips him up out of a particular date and space, forces upon us an understanding of the universality of the status of the children of God, and the community of brothers and sisters, that he announced. His disciples will reread the deeds and words of Jesus in the light of Easter; then their eyes will be opened, as were those of the disciples on the way to Emmaus (Luke 24:31). There is no other road to the Father but that of Jesus Christ. "You have been buried within him, when you were baptized; and by baptism, too, you have been raised up with him through your belief in the power of God who raised him from the dead" (Col. 2:12).

The Lord's Supper

The Eucharistic celebration, too, moves within the dialectic of memory and freedom. It is the memorial of the death and resurrection of Jesus, a memorial couched in the context of the passover supper that celebrates Yahweh's liberating deed in rescuing the Jewish people from Egypt.

The Eucharist is thanksgiving for all the historical deeds in which God's love is revealed. But it is also the act of taking upon ourselves today, creatively and freely, the sense and meaning that Jesus sought to give his own life. It is not a simple memorial. It is not confined to the past, a sort of sorrowful and nostalgic recollection of the Lord. It is openness to the future, full of trust and gladness. It is the reception of the Spirit of Christ, for "where the Spirit of the Lord is, there is freedom" (2 Cor. 3:17).

The celebration of the Lord's Supper presupposes a communion and solidarity with the poor in history. Without this solidarity, it is impossible to comprehend the death and resurrection of the Servant of Yahweh.

THE POOR PROCLAIM THE GOSPEL

To believe in the God who reveals himself in history, and pitches his tent in its midst, means to live in this tent—in Christ Jesus—and to proclaim from there the liberating love of the Father.

Deed and Word

The God who rescues his people in history, just as the Christ who is poor, can be proclaimed only with works, with deeds—in the practice of solidarity with the poor. This was the basic demand of the covenant. The fact is that Jesus Christ makes this demand even more imperative. "The man who lives by the truth comes out into the light," the gospel says (John 3:21). Truth is made. It is not automatic. Faith without works is dead, says St. James, in a text that bears reading in its entirety:

> Take the case, my brothers, of someone who has never done a single good act but claims that he has faith. Will that faith save him? If one of the brothers or one of the sisters is in need of clothes and has not enough food to live on, and one of you says to them, "I wish you well; keep yourself warm and eat plenty," without giving them these bare necessities of life, then what good is that? Faith is like that: if good works do not go with it, it is quite dead.

This is the way to talk to people of that kind: You say you have faith and I have good deeds; I will prove to you that I have faith by showing you my good deeds—now you prove to me that you have faith without any good deeds to show. You believe in the one God—that is creditable enough, but the demons have the same belief, and they tremble with fear. Do realize, you senseless man, that faith without good deeds is useless. You surely know that Abraham our father was justified by his deed, because he *offered his son Isaac on the altar* [Gen. 22:9]. There you see it: faith and deeds were working together; his faith became perfect by what he did. This is what scripture really means when it says: *Abraham put his faith in God, and this was counted as making him justified* [Gen. 15:6]; and that is why he was called "the friend of God."

You see now that it is by doing something good, and not only by believing, that a man is justified. There is another example of the same kind: Rahab the prostitute, justified by her deeds because she welcomed the messengers and showed them a different way to leave. A body dies when it is separated from the spirit, and in the same way faith is dead if it is separated from good deeds [James 2:14–26].

Practice is the locus of verification of our faith in God, who liberates by establishing justice and right in favor of the poor. It is also the locus of verification of our faith in Christ, who laid down his life for the proclamation of the kingdom of God and the struggle for justice. Easter life is the life of practice: "We have passed out of death and into life, and of this we can be sure because we love our brothers" (1 John 3:14). The only faith-life is the one the Scriptures call "witness." And witness is borne in works. To believe is to practice.

Only from a point of departure at the level of practice, only from deed, can the proclamation by word be understood. In the deed our faith becomes truth, not only for others, but for ourselves as well. We become Christians by acting as Christians. Proclamation in word only means taking account of this fact and proclaiming it. Without the deed, proclamation of the word is something empty, something without substance.

Deed is self-subsistent—and yet word expresses it, completes it. Without the word, the deed is open to different interpretations. And to speak out a lived experience, to speak out about a deed, leads one to live it and perform it more consciously and more profoundly.

Nevertheless, the relationship between deed and word is asymmetric. What basically counts is the deed. Of course it will not do to overemphasize this or push it to extremes; its only purpose is the better to express a complex reality. Jesus Christ, the heart of the gospel message, is the Word made flesh, the Word become deed. Only in this unity of deed and word is there any sense in the distinctions we make in the task of proclaiming liberation in Jesus Christ.

From among the Poor

Taking Sides. Evangelization, or the proclamation of the good news, is the proclamation of Christ's liberation. It is a total liberation, which goes straight to the root of all injustice and exploitation, straight to the root of the breach in friendship and love. But it is a liberation that dare not be interpreted "spiritually," spiritualistically—though there is a strong penchant for such interpretation in certain Christian circles. Love and its antithesis, sin, are historical realities. They are experienced and lived in concrete circumstances. Hence it is that the Bible speaks of liberation and justice as opposed to slavery and the humiliation of the poor.

The gift of the status of child of God is experienced only in historical contexts. It is in making our neighbors into sisters and brothers that we receive this gift, for it is a gift not of word but of work. This is what it means to experience the Father's love and to bear him witness. The proclamation of a God who loves all human beings in equal fashion must be enfleshed, incarnated, in history—must become history.

The proclamation of this liberating love in the midst of a society characterized by injustice and the exploitation of one social class by another social class is what will make this emergent history something challenging and filled with conflict. This is how we bring to pass the truth of God at the very heart of a society in which social classes confront one another with hostility. For we shall be taking sides with the poor, with the populous classes, with the ethnic groups others scorn, with cultures that are marginalized. It is from here that we must strive to live and proclaim the gospel of the love of God. Its proclamation to the exploited, the laborers and *campesinos* of our lands, will lead them to perceive that their situation is contrary to the will of the God who makes himself known in events of liberation. It will help them come to a consciousness of the profound injustice of their situation.

Unmasking Misuse of the Gospel. It must not be forgotten that the Bible has been read and communicated from the viewpoint of the dominating sectors and classes, abetted by a good part of exegesis that is thought of as "scientific." In this way what is "Christian" has been forced to play a role, within the dominant ideology, that affirms and consolidates a society divided into classes. The masses will arrive at an authentic political consciousness only in direct participation in the popular struggles for liberation.

In the immensity and complexity of the social process that must crush a system of oppression and lead to a classless society, ideological struggle too has an important place. Hence it is that the communication of the message as reread from the point of view of the poor and oppressed, and from the point of view of militant cooperation with them in their struggles, will have the function of unmasking all intent and effort to make the gospel play the role of justifying a situation at odds with what the Bible calls "justice and right."

Not the Same God

This is what we mean by a liberating proclamation of the gospel, a liberating evangelization. Only from the viewpoint of the poor are we going to understand the radical nature of Christ's liberation. As José María Arguedas put it, "the God of the masters is not the same"—is not the God of the poor, not the God of the Bible. The biblical God is the one who proclaims the good news to the poor. The concrete implications are many:

> The spirit of the Lord Yahweh has been given to me,
> for Yahweh has anointed me.
> He has sent me to bring good news to the poor,
> to bind up hearts that are broken;
> to proclaim liberty to captives,
> freedom to those in prison;
> to proclaim a year of favor from Yahweh,
> a day of vengeance for our God [Isa. 61:1–2].

This is the God who has taken sides with the poor, who considers the rich blasphemers because they speak of God in order to better oppress the poor:

> Listen, my dear brothers: it was those who are poor according to the world that God chose, to be rich in faith and to be the heirs to the kingdom which he promised to those who love him. In spite of this, you have no respect for anybody who is poor. Isn't it always the rich who are against you? Isn't it always their doing when you are dragged before the court? Aren't they the ones who insult the honorable name to which you have been dedicated? [James 2:5–7].

Faith in God

The God who reveals himself in history is a God irreducible to our manner of understanding him, to our theology, even to our faith itself. It is impossible to appropriate to oneself this God who becomes present in events, this God who becomes history.

God is a love that ever surpasses us, a love that encompasses us all around, "since it is in him that we live, and move, and exist, as indeed some of your own writers have said: We are all his children" (Acts 17:28).

He is the utterly Other, the Holy One: "For I am God, not man: I am the Holy One in your midst" (Hos. 11:9; cf. Isa. 6:3).

God manifests himself in awe as a God of power (Exod. 19:18), or makes himself heard gently and discreetly in a breath of the wind (1 Kings 19:12). But ultimately he is a God who dwells within the human being of a contrite heart (Isa. 57:15), in the bosom of his people. From there he demands an attitude of confidence in himself, of receptivity to his Word, his Son. To all who accept him he gives the power to be "children of God" (John 1:12).

Faith is an attitude of commitment, of confidence in the other. It presupposes a leaving of oneself, it presupposes a collective projection. It presupposes a contemplative attitude—an *ex-stasy*, a going out of oneself; without the contemplative dimension there is no Christian life.

Faith implies breach. This is what was demanded of the one Paul calls the father of faith: "Yahweh said to Abram, 'Leave your country, your family and your father's house, for the land I will show you' " (Gen. 12:1). Faith is entry into a new world, one in a way unforeseeable. It is making a journey without knowing beforehand the route we shall be following (John 21:18).

Faith is confidence in love. It is faith in the Father who loved us first, without any merit of our own, and who fills our life with love and largess. Love is at the very wellspring of our existence. This is why we reach fulfillment only by loving. Love is our trademark, branded into our being by the hand of him who made us. Faith is more than merely *believing in* God; it is *believing that* God loves us. It is believing that God loves us by establishing justice and right in this conflict-charged history of ours. To believe is to love God and to be in solidarity with the poor and the exploited of this world in the midst of social confrontations and popular struggle for liberation. To believe is to proclaim the kingdom as Christ does—from the midst of the struggle for justice that led him to his death.

To evangelize, to proclaim the gospel, is to communicate this faith in an irreducible God, who demands an attitude of trust, and whom we recognize in his works of rescue and liberation—in his Son become human history.

The Subversion of History

The locus of our encounter with the Father of Jesus Christ is the concrete history of men and women. And in Jesus Christ we proclaim to all men and women that Father's love. We have called this history one of conflict. But there is more to it than that. We have also to insist that history—where God reveals himself, and where we proclaim him—must be reread from the viewpoint of the poor, from a point of departure among "the condemned of the earth."

The history of humanity, as someone has said, has been "written with a white hand." History has been written from the viewpoint of the dominating sectors. We have a clear example of this in the history of Latin America and Peru. The perspective of history's vanquished is something else again. But history's winners have sought to wipe out their victims' memory of the struggles, so as to be able to snatch from them one of their sources of energy and will in history: a source of rebellion.

As it has been lived in history, Christianity has largely been, and still is, closely linked with one culture (Western), one ethnic strain (white), and one class (the dominant). Its history, too, has been written from a white, occidental, bourgeois bias.

We must recover the memory of the "scourged Christs of America," as Bartolomé de las Casas called the Indians of our continent. This memory never really died. It lives on in cultural and religious expressions, it lives on in resistance to ecclesiastical apparatus. It is a memory of the Christ who is present in every starving, thirsting, imprisoned, or humiliated human being, in the despised minorities, in the exploited classes (see Matt. 25:31–45). It is the memory of a Christ who not only "freed us, he meant us to remain free" (Gal. 5:1).

But *rereading* history means *remaking* history. It means repairing it from the bottom up. And so it will be a subversive history. History must be turned upside-down from the bottom, not from the top. What is criminal is not to be *sub*versive, struggling against the capitalist system, but to continue being "*super*versive"—bolstering and supporting the prevailing domination. It is in this subversive history that we can have a new faith experience, a new spirituality—a new proclamation of the gospel.

A Church of the People*

The gospel read from the viewpoint of the poor, the exploited classes, and their militant struggles for liberation, convokes a church of the people. It calls for a church to be gathered from among the poor, the marginalized. It calls for the kind of church that is indicated in Jesus' predilection for those whom the great ones of this world despise and humiliate (see Matt. 22:1–10; Luke 14:16–24). In a word, it calls together a church that will be marked by the faithful response of the poor to the call of Jesus Christ. It will spring from the people, this church. And the people will snatch the gospel out of the hands of their dominators, never more to permit it to be utilized for the justification of a situation contrary to the will of the God who liberates. For this God is a God who "reincorporates himself," as Arguedas says—reincorporates himself into a history that bears the mark of the poor, into the popular struggles for liberation, into hope for the exploited.

This reincorporation of God will come about only when the poor of the earth effectuate a "social appropriation of the gospel"—when they dispossess those who consider it their private property. The gospel tells us that the sign of the arrival of the kingdom of God is that the poor have the gospel proclaimed to them. The poor are those who believe and hope in Christ. That is to say the poor are the Christians. Strictly speaking, the Christians are, or should be, the poor who receive the gospel—those in solidarity with the interests, aspirations, and combats of the oppressed and repressed of the world today.

*We are using this expression (*iglesia popular*) in the sense of "the church of the poor."

Evangelization, the proclamation of the gospel, will be genuinely liberating when the poor themselves become its messengers. That is when we shall see the preaching of the gospel become a stumbling block and a scandal. For then we shall have a gospel that is no longer "presentable" in society. It will not sound nice and it will not smell good. The Lord who scarcely looks like a human at all (cf. the songs of the Servant of Yahweh in Isaiah) will speak to us then, and only at the sound of his voice will we recognize him as our liberator. That voice will convoke the *ek-klesia*, the assembly of those "called apart," in a new and different way.

Long has the church been built *from within*, in function of Christendom and its extension and preservation in the world—"ecclesiocentrism." A more recent perspective has led some to think of the church *from without*, from the world, from a world that does not believe, a world that often is hostile. This is the world in which the church was to be a sign of salvation according to Vatican Council II.

Today we understand even better. We are called to build the church *from below*, from the poor up, from the exploited classes, the marginalized ethnic groups, the despised cultures. This is what we call the project of a popular church, a church that, under the influence of the Spirit, arises from within the masses.

How can you sing to God in a strange land? The sorrowful quandary of the exilic psalmist is ours anew today. Without "singing" to God, without celebrations of God's liberating love, there is no Christian life. But how can we sing to God in a continent, in a country, of oppression and repression? This is a serious faith-question.

It leads us to a kind of new covenant, one that God makes "with us who are here, all living today" (Deut. 5:3). And we rip up the treaty struck by history with the culture and classes that have dominated us. It leads us to a covenant with the poor of this world. It leads us to a new sort of universality. Some will feel genuine terror. And all of us will feel a disquiet, as we are deprived of our age-old securities. For this is a path along which—to cite Arguedas once more—"what we know is much less than the great hope we feel."

PART II
FROM MEDELLIN TO PUEBLA

2

Involvement in the Liberation Process

INTRODUCTION

The Latin American church is in crisis. Some may try to tone down this fact or offer various interpretations of it, but that does not change the essential fact. The reality is clear enough and it cannot be hidden away or talked out of existence. We must face up to it boldly if we do not want to live in an imaginary world.

The scope and seriousness of the situation is of enormous proportions. Long gone is the era when the church could handle questions and problems by appealing to its doctrines and distinctions. Today it is the church itself that is being called into question. It is being called into question by many Christians who experience in their daily lives the terrible distance that separates the church from its roots in the gospel and its lack of harmony with the real world of Latin America. It is also being called into question by many who are far away from it—many more than our traditional pastoral outlook is willing to admit—who see it as an obstructive force in the effort to construct a more just society. And now it is even being called into question by those who are associated with the existing "order," and who look with discomfort on the initiatives being undertaken by some dynamic segments in the church.[1]

So let us grant that the church is living through a time of crisis and a moment of judgment (which is what crisis means). The ecclesial community is confronted with "happenings" and with Christ, the Lord of history, through them. And we might well raise Cardinal Suhard's old question: Does all this

---

Spanish text first published as the Prologue to *Signos de renovación: Recopilación de documentos post-conciliares de la Iglesia en América Latina* (Lima: Comisión Episcopal de Acción Social, 1969), pp. 6–16. The English translation first appeared as the Introduction to *Between Honesty and Hope* (Maryknoll, N.Y.: Orbis, 1970; now out of print). The text has been edited for inclusion in the present volume.

represent *growth* or *decline* for the church in Latin America? To pose this question aright, we must adjust our theological perspective and spell out what we really mean by "growth" and "decline" when it comes to the church. But even if we do that, there is a danger that our anxiety-ridden question will drive us to focus on the dry bones of numerical statistics or to dull our disquiet in some new form of triumphalism.

There is every indication that the coming years will provide us with very different ways of viewing the church, that we shall view its presence in ways that are quite different from those that we have been accustomed to in the past or that we might formulate today. But for the present we are faced with a more modest task: to recognize and acknowledge the emergence of a new situation that is full of promise and uncertainty, and that is leading us to a new ecclesial awareness under the impulse of the Spirit.

At the opening of the second session of Vatican II, when the shadow of John XXIII still cast a bright glow over the church, Pope Paul VI spoke of the church's desire and duty of coming at last to a full understanding of its true nature.[2] And a year later he spoke once again of the need for the church to deepen its awareness of the mission it must carry out in the world. The council faced up to this task; and the church has continued to do this, often in unexpected ways, in the years following the end of the council. Going beyond the strict letter of its documents, the council opened up perspectives that have not ceased to provoke wondrous surprise, fear, or alarm—depending on one's point of view.

In line with this spirit, the church of Latin America has sought to find its place. Accustomed to being a docile link in the chain of Christianity, the Christian community of Latin America has nevertheless begun to show an awareness of itself, to examine its presence on this continent, and to raise its voice above a whisper. There has been no lack of opposition and misunderstanding from those who regard this as insubordination pure and simple.

The documents issuing from Medellín and groups of involved bishops, priests, religious, and lay persons bear witness to this new development. Even clearer witness is provided by the gestures, initiatives, crises, experiences, and ferment of ideas that lie behind these same documents, as well as by the specific commitments they have prompted.

The church in Latin America is particularly rich in problems. But that is not a wholly negative state of affairs. If it shows the required courage, the very gravity of the problems it faces may enable it to get quickly to the heart of the matter. It can slough off the atavistic encumbrances that have plagued its gospel message and its ecclesial structures. It can frankly ask itself the most essential questions: What does being Christian mean? How can the church truly be the church in the new circumstances that surround it?

In coming to this new ecclesial awareness, we can distinguish two vital aspects. Inseparable in practice, they may be studied separately for the sake of greater clarity. These two aspects are (1) our new understanding of the Latin American situation, and (2) the quest for new ways in which the people of God might exert its presence therein.

CONFRONTING THE REAL SITUATION OF LATIN AMERICA

The self-awareness of the Christian community is conditioned historically by the world of which it is a part, and by its way of viewing this world.

Moving Out of the Ghetto

We need not begin from scratch to work up our own private vision of reality. In the case of Latin America, which is what concerns us here, we must rather become really involved in the way that the people of Latin America see themselves and their course in history. Thus we must start by opening our ears and listening to them—which presupposes that we are willing to move out of our own narrow world.

From the past right up to today, the Christian community in Latin America has lived largely in its own ghetto world. Born at a time when the Catholic Church was leading a Counter-Reformation movement, the Latin American church has always been marked by an attitude of defense. This defensive posture has led it to engage in silent retreat on numerous occasions, to act as a quiet refuge for all those who felt fearful and in need of protection as they tried to follow God's lead. This posture was reinforced by the occasional attacks from liberal and anticlerical factions during the period that followed political independence in the last century. It was further reinforced by the harsh criticism of more recent social movements, which have sought to introduce radical social change and which have regarded the church as an obstacle to such change.

All this led the church to solidify its ties with established authority, thus enjoying the latter's support and forming a common front against their presumed enemies. It also led it to create and maintain costly educational institutions, social services, and charitable works that were practically duplicates of those in the world around it. It was a futile, perhaps last-ditch effort to prolong an outdated brand of Christianity in a society that no longer evinced religious oneness and that had clearly and openly entered a period of ideological pluralism. The church thus became an easy and compliant prey for those who used it to protect their own selfish interests and the established order, in the name of the "Christian West."

Probing the Real Causes

Moving out of the ghetto is one aspect of a broader attitude: opening up to the world. It involves sharing, in a more positive and unreserved way, the vision that Latin Americans have of their situation. It also involves contributing in an effective way to the elaboration and development of this vision, and committing ourselves wholeheartedly to the activities it entails.

Recent years have been critical ones in this respect. We have come out of a long period when ignorance about the real Latin American situation prevailed, and we have also left behind the brief period when false optimism was promoted by vested interests. We are abandoning the sketchy and hazy views of the past for an overall, integrated understanding of our real situation.

The true face of Latin America is emerging in all its naked ugliness. It is not simply or primarily a question of low educational standards, a limited economy, an unsatisfactory legal system, or inadequate legal institutions. What we are faced with is a situation that takes no account of the dignity of human beings, or their most elemental needs, that does not provide for their biological survival, or their basic right to be free and autonomous. Poverty, injustice, alienation, and the exploitation of human beings by other human beings combine to form a situation that the Medellín conference did not hesitate to condemn as "institutionalized violence."[3]

This phrase might well seem strange in a pronouncement by the hierarchy.[4] But it should be emphasized that it is not something thrown in as an aside, for the whole Medellín document on peace is focused on this concept.[5] It is a commonplace for all experts on Latin America, and a reality that is known and experienced daily by most of those who live in Latin America. It is only within this real context that one can honestly raise the complex question of the moral rightness or wrongness of putting down violence. No double standard will do. We cannot say that violence is all right when the oppressor uses it to maintain or preserve "order," but wrong when the oppressed use it to overthrow this same "order."[6]

The most important change in our understanding of the Latin American situation, however, has to do with its deeper, underlying causes. These are now seen in the context of a broader historical process. It is becoming ever more clear that underdevelopment, in a total sense, is primarily due to economic, political, and cultural dependence on power centers that lie outside Latin America. The functioning of the capitalist economy leads simultaneously to the creation of greater wealth for the few and greater poverty for the many. Acting in complicity with these outside power centers, the oligarchies of each nation in Latin America operate through various mechanisms to maintain their dominion over the internal affairs of their own countries.

This new awareness of the Latin American situation shines through various documents in varying degrees of clarity. It finds authoritative and clear-cut expression in the Medellín document on peace, which forthrightly speaks of "internal colonialism" and "external neocolonialism."[7] In Latin America these are the ultimate causes of the violence that is committed against the most basic human rights.

Our new vision, attentive to structural factors, will help Christians to avoid the fallacy of proposing a personal change detached from concrete conditions, as a necessary prerequisite to any social transformation. If any of us remain wedded to this fallacy, in the name of some hazy humanism or disembodied spiritualism, we shall only prove to be accomplices in the continuing postponement of the radical changes that are necessary. Such changes call for simultaneous work on both persons and structures, for they condition each other mutually.

Involvement in the Liberation Process

When we characterize the Latin American situation as one of dependence and unfair domination, we are naturally led to talk about liberation, and to participate in the process that will lead to it. We are in fact dealing with a term that expresses the new stance adopted by Latin Americans, a stance that is gradually taking concrete shape in official documents. It is recapitulated forcefully in the Medellín conference and in the Thirty-Sixth Episcopal Assembly of Peru. Expressions such as "development" and "integration," with their attendant retinue of international alliances, agencies, and experts, are relegated to the shadows; for they involve a different vision of the Latin American situation.

But to stress the need for liberation presupposes far more than simply differences in our analyses of the situation. At a deeper level, it means that we see the ongoing development of humanity in a particular perspective, and in terms of a specific philosophy and theology of history. It means that we see it as a process of human emancipation, aiming toward a society where men and women are truly free from servitude, and where they are the active shapers of their own destiny. Such a process does not lead us simply to a radical transformation of structures—to a revolution. It goes much further, implying the perduring creation of a wholly new way for men and women to be human.

There is an urgent need for Christians to involve themselves in the work of liberating this oppressed continent, by establishing real solidarity with the oppressed persons who are the chief victims. The first step is for the church as a whole to break its many ties with the present order, ties that it has maintained overtly or covertly, wittingly or unwittingly, up to now. This will not be an easy task, for it will mean abandoning outworn traditions, suspicions, viewpoints, advantages, and privileges, as well as the forces of inertia. It will also mean accepting the fact that the future cast of the church will be radically different from the one we know today. It will mean incurring the wrath of the groups in power—with all the risks that entails. Above all, it will mean believing in the revolutionary and liberating power of the gospel—believing in the Lord—and authentic faith, a faith that goes beyond the mere recitation and acceptance of codified truths. This will not be easy. We know it, of course, and we have said it countless times. But perhaps we have not been sufficiently aware of the fears and vacillations of the vast majority of the Christian community in Latin America. Perhaps we have not realized how much they bore ironic witness to this truth.

One manifestation of our break with injustice and exploitation, which the present economic and social structures foist upon the vast majority of our people under the guise of law, should come from the bishops. They must turn to the oppressed, declaring their solidarity with them and their desire to join with them in their struggle. This is what they must do instead of what they have done in the past, when they turned to those in power and called for necessary reforms while implying that their own position need not be affected by such change.[8]

CREATING A NEW ECCLESIAL PRESENCE

At Vatican II the church affirmed a desire to render service. The concrete forms that this pledge takes must necessarily be based on the world in which the Christian community is present.

Present Inadequacies

A better awareness of the harsh realities in Latin America goes hand in hand with a clearer realization that the church's structures are inadequate for the world in which it lives. They show up as outdated and lacking in vitality when confronted with new questions, and in one way or another seem to be tied up with the unjust order we wish to eradicate. This fact is the chief source of the misunderstandings, frictions, crises, and desertions that we witness.

Those who want to shape their lives to the demands of the gospel find it increasingly difficult to accept vague, romantic appeals to "fellowship" and "Christian unity" that do not take account of the causes underlying the present state of affairs, or of the concrete conditions required for the construction of a just society. Such vague appeals forget that the catholicity, the universality, of the church is not something attained once for all time, or something to be maintained at any price. It must be won continuously, by courageous effort and open-eyed struggle. Wittingly or unwittingly, these appeals seem designed to palliate the real tensions that do and should exist, and ultimately to maintain the status quo. The frank and decisive stands taken by the hierarchy and other sectors of the church in the last few years have been welcome breaths of fresh air. They will undoubtedly help to separate the wheat from the chaff. They will identify the real Christian among all those who call themselves Christians.

Vatican II proclaims that the church, like Christ, must carry out its work of redemption "in poverty and under oppression." But this is not the image presented by the Latin American church as a whole. Quite the contrary. Once upon a time we may not have been clearly aware of this, but that time is past. Today the church feels the sharp pangs of its tragic inconsistency; it is aware of its disloyalty to the gospel, its failure to confront the real situation in Latin America.

This has given rise to letters, declarations, new forms of commitment, and even "protest movements" in the church. All these things can easily become grist for the sensation-seeking media. But altogether apart from their transitory news value, their sometimes ambiguous doctrinal roots, and the misleading commentaries they provoke, they have a much deeper significance, and we must try to probe it. They betoken the concern many Christians have with the form that the church's presence in Latin America now takes. They reveal a hidden vitality, a spirit that refuses to be bound to the cold letter of the law. If we do not pay heed to the message they contain, we may one day find ourselves in an atmosphere of general indifference, longing wistfully for those "hotheads" who had used unconventional means to express their desire for change in the church and for fidelity to the gospel.

The most vital sectors of the people of God in Latin America are thus committed to a search for two things: (1) the theological bases that will ground their activity on a continent caught up in a process of liberation; and (2) new ecclesial structures that will allow them to live a true life of faith in accordance with Latin Americans' growing awareness of their own specific historical destiny.

A Theology of Human Liberation

We have suggested that an authentic presence in Latin America presupposes a concern on the part of the church for the specifically political dimensions of that presence. Would such a concern mean the church were falling prey to some sort of aberrant temporalism, and abandoning its spiritual mission? After all, this is what frightens many persons of good will (and ill will).

The gospel, these persons say, is first and foremost a message of eternal salvation; building the earth is a task for human beings on this earth. The first task belongs to the church, the second task belongs to temporal society. The most they will admit is that the church may lay down certain ethical dictates for the work of building civil society—so long as they do not openly question the interests of those who hold the reins of economic and political power.

But a closer look at reality, such as I have outlined above, has wrought a profound change in the life and outlook of the whole church. Although I cannot discuss the process in detail here, I can point out that the church has restored its ties with the Christian tradition of antiquity and has rediscovered that salvation embraces all humanity, and each individual. It will be worth our while to spell out briefly the theological notions that form the basis for this new outlook on the part of the church.

Concrete reflection on human existence has carried contemporary theology far beyond the scholastic and essentialist outlook that was based on distinguishing various orders and levels. At the same time that it was renewing its contact with its roots in the Bible, theology was moving toward the notion that humankind had but one vocation; or, to put it more exactly, that all human beings shared the same single vocation. Thus we do not have two juxtaposed histories, one sacred and the other profane. There is only one single process of human development, definitively and irreversibly assumed by Christ, the Lord of history. His salvific work embraces all the dimensions of human existence. Two major biblical themes clearly illustrate this viewpoint: the relationship between creation and salvation, and the messianic promises.

In the rather simplistic catechetics of the past, creation was presented as the explanation for the existing world. This is not incorrect, but it is incomplete. In the Bible, creation is not a stage prior to the work of salvation; it is the first salvific activity. "Before the world was made, he chose us in Christ" (Eph. 1:4). Creation is inserted in the salvation process, in God's self-communication. The religious experience of Israel is primarily history, but this history is simply the prolongation of God's creative activity. That is why the Psalms praise Yahweh simultaneously as Creator and Savior (see Ps. 136). The God who transformed chaos into cosmos is the same as the one who acts in salvation history. The redemptive work of Christ, in turn, is presented in the context of creation (see John 1). Creation and salvation have a christological import; in Christ all have been created and all have been saved (see Col. 1:15–20).

Thus when we say that men and women fulfill themselves by carrying on the work of creation through their own labors, we are asserting that they are operating within the framework of God's salvific work from the very first. Subduing the earth, as Genesis bids them do, is a salvific work. To work in the world and transform it is to save it. Inasmuch as it is a humanizing factor that transforms nature, work tends to build a society that is more just and more worthy of humankind—as Marx clearly saw. The Bible helps us to appreciate the deeper reaches of this effort. Building the earthly city is not simply a humanizing phase prior to evangelization, as theology used to put it. Building the earthly city actually immerses human beings in the salvation process that touches all humanity. Every obstacle that degrades or alienates the work of men and women in building a humane society is an obstacle to the work of salvation.

A second major theme of the Bible echoes this same thinking. The messianic promises, the events that announce and accompany the coming of the Messiah, are not isolated happenings. Like the first theme, the thread of messianism runs through the whole Bible. It is actively present in the history of Israel, and thus has its proper place in the historical development of God's people.

The prophets proclaim a reign of peace. But peace presupposes the establishment of justice, the defense of the rights of the poor, the punishment of oppressors, and a life free from the fear of enslavement. A benighted spiritualization has often caused us to forget the human power imbedded in the messianic promises and the transforming effect they might have on unjust social structures. The conquest of poverty and the abolition of exploitation are signs of the Messiah's arrival and presence. According to the book of Isaiah, the kingdom will become a reality when "they shall not build for others to live in, or plant for others to eat" (Isa. 65:22)—when everyone profits from their own labor. To work for a just world where there is no servitude, oppression, or alienation is to work for the advent of the Messiah. The messianic promises establish a close tie between the kingdom of God and living conditions that are worthy of human beings. God's kingdom and social injustice are incompatible.

The message to be gleaned from these two biblical themes is clear. Salvation embraces all, as *Populorum Progressio* (21) reminds us. Preaching the gospel message is not preaching escape from the world. On the contrary, the word of God deepens and fortifies our involvement in history. Concretely, this involvement means solidarity with the oppressed of Latin America and participation in their struggle for emancipation. And this solidarity and participation involve the realization that salvation history is a continuing process of liberation. It is through encounters with the poor and the exploited that we shall encounter the Lord (see Matt. 25:31 ff.). To be a Christian in our day is to involve ourselves creatively in the different phases of humanity's liberation process. Faith opens up infinite horizons to our human effort, giving dynamic vitality to our active presence in history.

These are some of the theological notions that implicitly or explicitly underlie the new Christian statements coming from Latin America. Only against this backdrop can we properly understand the efforts of certain Christian groups to be authentically present in the world of Latin America. Theirs is not a suspect temporalism; theirs is a desire, though undoubtedly flawed and imperfect, to be wholly loyal to the word of the Lord.

New Ecclesial Structures

There was a time when the vitality or decrepitude of the Latin American church was measured by the number of its priests. You simply calculated the number of faithful per priest and made your analysis on that basis. If you were at all in touch with the actual situation, you made mention of the disturbing geographical distance between the priests and most of their faithful. The scarcity of vocations seemed to be the major obstacle to be overcome if the underdeveloped church were to grow. Today, few still view the matter that way. The problem of priests has other, more delicate, facets. Everything seems to indicate that the lifestyle of the priest, which had remained static for centuries, is about to undergo a profound transformation in the near future. But even more important is the fact that it is merely one symptom of the broader and graver crisis afflicting the Christian community.

The older approach to this whole problem had a markedly clerical cast, which tended to minimize the problematical nature of the situation. Its gravest error was undoubtedly the type of solution it suggested for the church's problems. It was felt we could move out of the past by making efforts to modernize certain ecclesiastical structures or to inaugurate certain pastoral adaptations. Basically it is that whole approach that is today being called into question.

From now on we shall have to attack this issue with greater boldness, with the fortitude that Scripture enjoins on Christ's disciples (see Acts 4:31). That fortitude must induce us to carry out not halfway reforms that gloss over our fears and trepidations, but a transformation far more radical than anything we know today. The times demand of us a creative spark that will allow us to work up and create new ecclesial structures and new ways for the Christian community to be present to the world. The alarmed reaction of certain factions in the church that rise up in protest against those who would explore the signs of the times is no solution.

One solid line of endeavor for the Latin American church in this quest will be for it to assert its own distinctive personality. We have lived in a state of dependence that has not allowed us to fully develop our own qualities up to now. As a church, we have been a mirror image rather than a fountainhead, in the terms of Father de Lima Vas. We have been mirroring the European church—uncritically borrowing our theology, institutions, canon law, spirituality, and lifestyle. We have not been a creative fountainhead for new activities that would fit in with a world in revolution, for ecclesial structures that would be appropriate for a Third World church, or for ideas that would allow us to strike deep roots in our own reality. Working free of the colonial mentality is undoubtedly one of the major tasks confronting the Christian community of Latin America. It will also be one way in which we can make a genuine contribution to the universal church.

Another solid line of endeavor will be our commitment to genuine poverty. This is an area where Christians offer ample witness to the contrary. We often confuse making a vow of poverty with living a life of poverty. We often confuse possession of absolute essentials with comfortable ensconcement in the world. We often confuse instruments for service with power leverage. We need an honest, clear-headed reform that will put an end to the discrepancy between our preaching and our practice. We must live in a church that is not only open to the poor but poor itself. Only in this way can we radically change the present face of the Christian community.

In this context, the episcopal conference at Medellín may represent for the Latin American church what Vatican II was for the whole church. It was not an end point but a point of departure. It was not only a forum for documents that sum up the ecclesial community's present awareness of this moment in history, but also a stimulus to push on further and to put life into our words. All this will not be done without difficulty. We shall always feel light-headed impulses that will prompt us to sensation-seeking postures rather than deep commitments. But the greatest threat will be the temptation to immobility and a preference for changes that do not really change the existing situation. We are more bound to the old structures than we realize.

Vatican II, and, one hopes, the Medellín conference, opened up the floodgates and allowed long-dammed waters to flow freely. When the flood is over, we shall realize that it has done more cleansing than destroying. Right now, however, our task is not to anxiously protect the texts of Vatican II and Medellín from erroneous interpretations, or to provide erudite commentaries. The important thing for us is to expound them in our deeds—to verify their truth in our daily Christian life.

The church is experiencing the effects of living in a world that is undergoing profound and decisive changes. The church itself must set out on uncharted roads, turn down new byways, without knowing what risks and obstacles will be encountered. It is not easy to believe that the Spirit will lead us to the whole truth (see John 16:13). It is not easy to set out without consulting a road map in advance. But today that is what the Christian community in Latin America must do.

Some may well complain that the positions expressed in these documents do not offer any responses or solutions. That may be true. But we must not forget that those who change the course of history are usually those who pose a new set of questions, rather than those who offer solutions.

NOTES

1. This alarm is clearly reflected in an article by Alberto Lleras Camargo that was published in the North American magazine *Vision* (Sept. 29, 1968). In line with a similar article on the Medellín conference that was published in a Peruvian periodical, Lleras Camargo pejoratively labels one group of participating bishops "progressivists" and "radicals."

2. Address at the opening of the second session of Vatican Council II (Sept. 29, 1965).

3. See the Medellín Document on Peace, in *Between Honesty and Hope* (Maryknoll, N.Y.: Maryknoll, 1970).

4. The expression was not retracted, as some uninformed commentators had hoped. Nor is it derived from Marxist sociology, as these same persons opined. The basic notion and the term itself can be found before Medellín in various statements issued by lay apostolic groups.

5. The idea is present at the very beginning of the Document on Peace and is developed throughout (see nos. 1 and 14, for example).

6. See the interesting article by Gonzalo Arroyo, "Violencia institucionalizada en América Latina," *Mensaje,* Nov. 1968. The author concludes on a forceful note: "Have we Christians, who profess belief in the rewards of peace, done more than talk about global structural changes? Have we devoted all our energy to eliminating institutionalized injustice? If we are not doing that today, we have no right to cast the first stone!" (p. 544).

7. See the Document on Peace.

8. In this connection it is interesting to note the section directed to "our fellow peasants and laborers" in a statement of the Peruvian Episcopal Assembly, Jan. 1969. Citing the Medellín document on peace, they state that they "will do everything in our power to foster and promote your grassroots organizations, so that you may reclaim your rights and obtain authentic justice" (Justice and Peace Commission, 2.4.2). In another section they stress that their forthright denunciation of abuses and injustices will be accompanied by "concrete action in solidarity with the poor and the oppressed" (ibid., 2.4.6).

3

Liberation Praxis and Christian Faith

Theology is an understanding of the faith. It is a rereading of the word of God as that word is lived in the Christian community. But it is a reflection directed toward the communication of the faith, toward the proclamation of the good news of the Father's love for all humankind. To evangelize, to preach the gospel, is to bear witness to this love and say that it is revealed to us, and becomes flesh, in Christ.

Reflection on the faith occurs between this experience and this communication. The theological task strikes root in our human and Christian being, and springs up in function of the proclamation of the good news. For this reason, the theological undertaking is at once changing and constant. One is a Christian at the heart of history—a concrete history, continuously transforming the conditions of human life. The gospel must be proclaimed to women and men who fulfill themselves as human beings in the measure that they forge their own destiny.

Theological reasoning is uttered upon a truth that is a way, upon a Word who has pitched his tent in the midst of history. The unending labor of theology takes different forms, in function of the Christian experience and of the proclamation of the gospel at a given moment in emergent history.

Hence we can separate theological reflection neither from the Christian community nor from the world in which that community lives. Theology is an expression of the awareness that a Christian community has of its faith at a

---

This article originally appeared as the Introduction to *Signos de liberación: Testimonios de la Iglesia en América Latina, 1969–1973* (Lima: CEP, 1973). The author has developed and expanded it here, incorporating parts of two other articles published the following year: "Movimientos de liberación y teología," *Concilium*, Spanish ed., no. 93 (March 1974), pp. 448–56; and "Praxis de liberación y anuncio," *Concilium*, Spanish ed., no. 96 (June 1974), pp. 353–74. In its reworked form it was first published in English by the Mexican-American Cultural Center, San Antonio, Texas, 1974, under the title *The Praxis of Liberation and Christian Faith*. The present text is a fresh translation from the Spanish.

given moment in history. This moment, dated and sealed, is a *locus theologicus* of the first importance. For theology is an attempt to do a reading of the faith from a point of departure in a determined situation, from an insertion and involvement in history, from a particular manner of living our encounter with the Lord in our encounter with others. Theology is a reading of the faith from the cultural universe that corresponds to this involvement in history and this religious experience.

Faith is always given in concrete gestures and precise conditions. "To have faith" is precisely to live in the tent God has pitched in the midst of history. It is to die with the crucified Christ and know that we are born again "because we love our brothers" (1 John 3:14).

The theology of liberation is an attempt to understand the faith from within the concrete historical, liberating, and subversive praxis of the poor of this world—the exploited classes, despised ethnic groups, and marginalized cultures. It is born of a disquieting, unsettling hope of liberation. It is born of the struggles, the failures, and the successes of the oppressed themselves. It is born of a manner of seeing oneself and one another as daughters and sons of the Father, as a deep and demanding community of brothers and sisters. This is why theology comes later. This is why it is a second moment, after faith—a "faith that makes its power felt through love" (Gal. 5:6). This, over and above the real and fruitful demands of other contemporary thought, is the reason why the theology of liberation, as reflection, takes a different approach to the relationship of practice with theory.

But this understanding of the faith from within concrete historical praxis leads to a proclamation of the gospel at the very heart of this praxis. It is a proclamation that is at once voice and vigilance, active deed, in concrete solidarity with the interests and struggles of the populous classes. It is *word* concretized in *gesture*: it determines attitudes, and is celebrated in thanksgiving.

Recent years in Latin America have been marked by a real and demanding discovery of the world of the other—the poor, the oppressed, the exploited. In a social order that has been set up financially, politically, and ideologically by a few for their own benefit, the "others" of this society are beginning to make their voices heard. They are speaking less and less through intermediaries now and are beginning to have their direct say. They are starting to rediscover themselves and to make the system aware of their unsettling presence. They are beginning to be less and less the objects of demogogical manipulation, or thinly disguised social services, and are gradually becoming the agents of their own history, forgers of a radically different society.

But this discovery is made only in a revolutionary struggle that questions the existing social order in its very roots and insists on the involvement of popular power in the construction of a society of genuinely equal and free persons. It insists on a society in which private ownership of the means of production is eliminated, because private ownership of the means of production allows a few to appropriate the fruits of the labor of many, and generates the division of society into classes, whereupon one class exploits another. It insists on a society in which, by appropriating the means of production, the masses appropriate their own political management as well, and definitive freedom, thereby occasioning the creation of a new social consciousness.

For years, a growing number of Christians have been participating in this revolutionary process, and, through it, in the discovery of the world of the exploited of Latin America—which for most of them only means a new awareness of their own milieu. This involvement constitutes the *most important fact* in the life of the Latin American Christian community. It gives rise to a new way of being a human being and believer, a new way of living and thinking the faith, a new way of being summoned, and summoning, into *ek-klesia*, church, the assembly of those called together for mission.

This new Christian participation in the liberation process has various degrees of radicality and different nuances in different Latin American countries. It is expressed in languages that are still tentative, that grope their way forward by trial and error. Sometimes these modes of expression become lost in byways along the route, and sometimes they quicken their pace as the result of a particular occurrence.

The radical novelty this route holds for theological reflection and a celebration of faith in community has only gradually come to light. For it is a new way of understanding and celebrating faith from within a praxis—from within the liberating praxis through which so many Latin Americans, stubbornly struggling with all the difficulties, are seeking to build a different social order and a new way of being men and women in Latin America, where oppression is so familiar and repression is on the increase.

In the following pages I shall limit myself to a consideration of certain aspects of this liberating praxis in Latin America and Christian involvement in it. Such a consideration will unveil the nature of the matrix that this practice provides us for reflection on the faith—a reflection we undertake with a view to speaking the word of the Lord to every human being from a position of solidarity with the praxis of liberation.

The irruption of the "other" onto one's own scene, the perception of the world of the poor, leads one to an active solidarity with that other's interests and struggles. It leads to an involvement, a commitment, which translates into a pledge: to transform a social order that generates marginalized and oppressed persons. Participation in the praxis of liberation places us at the very heart of a concrete, conflictual history, in which we meet the Christ who reveals God to us as Father and reveals our neighbors to us as our sisters and brothers.

FROM WITHIN THE PRAXIS OF LIBERATION

A Long Itinerary

The phenomenon we have identified as the most important fact in the Latin American Christian community is both a stage along the way and the fruit of a process. Perhaps the most practical way to penetrate this process and demonstrate its consequences will be to follow the route that many Christians, driven by the demands of the actual, concrete praxis of liberation, have taken in Latin America.

First Steps. For a long time—a time that is still going on, as far as many are concerned—Latin American Christians demonstrated a mighty indifference to the problems of this world. Their religious formation considered "heaven" as the place where true life was to be expected and made of this present life a kind of play, a drama, in which their manner of acquitting themselves of their assigned role would constitute the "test" to decide their eternal destiny. To boot, the play was acted out in a religious world—supposedly the only real one—that was self-contained and purely tangential to the daily life of flesh-and-blood persons. It was a world with all its own norms, behavior, and worship, all self-contained and sufficient unto itself. Outside it, or rather beneath it, was the world of the profane—for instance, the political realm. This was the transitory world, hence somehow unreal.

Of course its unreality did not prevent those who claimed to live only for the world "up there" from solidly installing themselves in the world "down here." Such installation was necessary, it would seem, as the platform from which to proclaim to others that *they* ought not to become attached to anything ephemeral and corruptible.

Eternal life was seen exclusively as a future life and not as present in an active and creative form within our concrete historical involvement as well. It was a contracted, partialized view of human existence, the product of a gospel carefully reduced to suitably narrow, myopic dimensions.

The good will of some of those who sought in such hobbled fashion to safeguard the absolute character of the kingdom of God was to no avail in focusing their objectives. The great ones of this world had nothing to fear, and everything to gain, from a gospel thus converted into such a harmless lapdog, and they promptly became its protectors.

During this period Christian categories and values were adopted or reinterpreted by the ideology of the prevailing social order, and thus the domination of one social class by another was reinforced still further. Today the dominant groups continue to offer their support—for the defense of "Western Christian civilization"—and often their offer is accepted. But today a series of events within the Latin American church has motivated the lords of this world to append a threat to their offer: if their support is rejected, hostility and repression wait in the wings.

The historical antecedents of a theology of liberation had modest beginnings. For some decades, certain elements in Latin American Christianity had been concerned with what they called "the social problem." This occasioned the importation into Latin America of the European socio-Christian current of thought, where it played a role in awakening the social awareness of certain Christian groups. The situation of misery in which the vast majority of the Latin American people were living ceased to be seen simply as their fate and destiny, and the human beings who lived in this misery ceased to be considered simply as recipients of works of charity. Social injustice began to be seen as the basic cause of the imbalance.

How could one be a Christian without becoming involved in remedying this state of affairs? Everyone felt called and challenged by the harsh reality, but few perceived that it was the whole of society, and its system of values, that had to be called into question in their very roots—along with what it meant to be Christians.

In the socio-Christian perspective of that time, however, to create a more just and more Christian society meant merely to improve the same society—assimilate the marginalized, put an end to the more flagrant injustices. Sometimes a project might go further. But socio-economic analysis, lacking as it was in scientific method, in the final instance and in spite of all good intentions, managed to produce only a vague and general "defense of the dignity of the human person." All this was situated in the framework of the "concrete historical ideal," to use Maritain's term, of a society inspired by Christian values—now perceived as compatible with the more moderate claims of democratic liberties and social justice.

When a more scientific understanding of reality began to appear, language became more assertive and action more effective, but the point of departure remained essentially the same: doctrinal declarations and abstract principles. The upshot, as political experience demonstrated and continues to demonstrate, was that these positions, initially rejected as subversive by the prevailing system, maintained an ambiguity that made it possible for them to be reabsorbed by the social order they had intended to modify—to the point of becoming, in certain countries, a political mainstay of the most conservative and reactionary elements of all. In this context, theological reflection noisily proclaimed its "social concerns," but never did anything about them.[1]

The socio-Christian outlook did not carry the same weight in all the countries of Latin America. In some countries, in circles close to lay apostolate groups, the shortcomings and ambiguities of the Christian label in political activity quickly came under fire. Here Christian involvement in partisan politics took place through various other organizations, to which Christians, along with members of other spiritual families, openly belonged. Examples would be Brazil, Peru, and Uruguay. Christians *as* Christians joined together on another level instead, that of the forthright profession of their faith, as they formed communities in which they could share the experience of Christian life they had had in their various political commitments.

Looked upon with disfavor by those who preferred, if somewhat less traditionally and conservatively than had been customary, to see the Christian element as a politico-religious bloc behind a "Christian humanist" facade, frequently drawn into political parties of Christian inspiration, these Christians gradually became stronger and more numerous in several Latin American countries. Thus they battled the mentality that all Christian elements belonged to a single political approach. They opened themselves up to other points of view. They have been waging a struggle for more than a decade now against certain ideological expropriations of the Christian label, by conservative sectors and by socio-Christian political groups.

This expansive effort was accompanied by a theology that placed the accent on the area of faith itself, distinguishing it from the plane of temporal action. This was a contribution of capital importance and permitted another step forward, but it was still rigidly intraecclesial and the "worldy," the concrete historical, the political, did not really come into view as a way of living and understanding the Christian faith. Still, the "distinction of planes" had its effect—later, when the process of political radicalization was ready to begin. For not only did this radicalization take place earlier in countries where the distinction of planes was better received, but the arrival on the scene of this new political attitude did not at once occasion conflicts with temporal institutions of the immediate past whose inspiration had likewise been Christian. (This latter did occur, as it should, in other cases).[2]

Whichever path one took, the eventual outcome was that ever larger groups of both persuasions, at first mainly among agrarian leadership and youth, began to abandon positions that, when all was said and done, failed to go beyond a political developmentalism under the aegis of a more or less explicit spirit of reform. But the socialist revolution in Cuba put things political in a new light. The year 1965 marks a high point in the pitch of armed conflict in Latin America and hastened the political radicalization even of those who had thought other avenues ought to be explored for revolutionary activity.

The figures of Camilo Torres and "Che" Guevara set an indelible seal on the process of liberation in Latin America and had a decisive influence in certain Christian circles. In most Latin American countries the repressive character of the prevailing system now worsened, and "institutionalized violence," to use Medellín's felicitous term, became the order of the day. The indiscriminate use of force, in the form of arrests, massacre, and torture, was now the way to maintain "order" in the popular movements.

The case of Brazil deserves special mention. There a particularly cruel internal system of law, order, and security overflowed into hegemonic pretensions with respect to neighboring nations. Acting as an effective agent of imperialist capitalism, Brazil exported a model of economic development based on the most calculating and refined exploitation—valiantly denounced by the Brazilian bishops[3]—of the popular classes and less fortunate regions. It thereby managed to bring or return to power, in some of these countries, the most conservative segments of the dominant groups.

The political radicalization of Latin America was now inclining groups of Christian believers to revolutionary positions. Commitment was now more radical, the questioning of the established social order more global, and political analysis more incisive and penetrating, than it had been in the previous approach. Some Christians even began to acquire the perception of the fact of class struggle. But before we continue tracing this journey and its eventual result, let us examine more in detail the theological efforts that accompanied the radicalization, and new political commitments, of these Christian groups.

Theology and Politics. This new political awareness has occasioned a renewal of the theological debate on Christian faith and political activity. The theme is an old one, yet as valid and meaningful today as it ever was—for the gospel was proclaimed to human beings, and it is still meaningful. Treatment of the theme has varied down through the centuries of evolution of the Christian community, and some of its vectors have been isolated and studied and today constitute a legacy for theological reflection. But, like every problem as complex and full of implications as this one, it is continually being refocused. It is continually breaking with its past and opening new paths to the future.

We are living in a critical moment in the ongoing Christian assessment of the relationship between gospel message and political world. It is a polemical issue. It questions positions that once had seemed solidly established, and now it impinges on the social practice of Christians even more than before.

The new political theology from Germany moves along these lines of thought.[4] It does not propose to create a new theological discipline,[5] but does take a profoundly critical approach, rooted in the problematic of the Enlightenment, to the notion of the political as the proper locus of liberty and freedom. Accordingly, it speaks of a "new" political theology, in contradistinction to earlier theological approaches, which, disarmed by an Enlightenment (and Marxist) critique of religion, sought refuge in a faith lived in the sphere of the private. Hence the necessity of a "deprivatizing of theology," which "is the primary critical task of political theology."[6] With its new positioning of the problem of the impingement of faith on emergent history, political theology invites a critique of the very foundations of our contemporary theology.

Metz goes to the heart of what is really at stake in theology today when he writes:

> Properly speaking, the so-called hermeneutic problem of theology is not the problem of how systematic theology stands in relation to historical theology, how dogma stands in relation to history, but what is the relation between theory and practice, between understanding the faith and social practice.[7]

Political theology has occasioned polemics that have led it to refine its positions. Then too, conditioned though it may be by the political and cultural milieu in which is has arisen, demands made on it from beyond that milieu have opened it to new perspectives. This developing openness is possible because political theology goes straight to the root of certain questions that are basic for theology, and urgent for the human being and believer of today.

Two other efforts, of lesser scope, but emphasizing certain facets not taken into account, at least initially, by political theology, are to be found in the so-called theology of development and theology of revolution.

Beginning with the Bandung Conference of 1955, the term "development" began to be used as the compendious expression of the aspirations of human beings today for more humane conditions of life. It was the miserable circumstances of the so-called underdeveloped nations that posed the problem in the urgency it had now acquired. All this appeared in the papal encyclicals and Vatican Council II and occasioned considerable theological reflection.[8] Theology now sought to validate the effort to transform nature and to create a more just and more humane world. Appeal was made to the biblical view of work and to the Christian vocation to subdue the earth in order to make it more habitable for human beings. It was an optimistic and dynamic approach, emphasizing that human progress is a biblical requirement and a necessary condition for a fuller life of faith.

However, it was too dependent on the concept of "development," and especially on the political implications of "development." It did not adequately grasp the true causes of the misery and injustice in which poor peoples live. Nor did it appreciate the conflictual character of human history.[9] Certain passages in *Populorum Progressio* constituted an important theological advance along these lines, explicitly positing efforts to build a better society within the framework of total salvation in Christ.[10] This intimate relationship, which the encyclical calls "integral development," later became a bone of contention, occasioning debate on biblical terms and sources.

In 1966 another line of theological reflection emerged, again with strong biblical overtones. It was known as the theology of revolution. It included, as a segment, a theology of violence, and this was the tree that often hid the forest. The theology of revolution had been developed initially by theologians who were very familiar with certain countries then engaged in a process of revolution. But it was eventually removed from its context and found a sounding board in certain currents of thought in Germany. In this latter form it was reintroduced into Latin America.[11] The basic datum of this approach is that:

> It is in the revolutionary context that decisions concerning the great questions of civilization will have to be made, by those who have responsibility for the welfare and the future of human beings.[12]

The theological task, then, is to identify the place of the Christian faith in this challenge. This approach taken by the revolutionary commitment was radical. It called into question the established social order, and its political analysis began to perceive the reality of class confrontation. Here, then, faith comes into view as motive and justification for the involvement of Christians in a revolutionary process. Stripped of all the ideological interpretations calculated to dissimulate a cruel and conflictual social reality, these theologians claimed, the gospel is not only not at odds with revolution, but actually calls for revolution.

The merit of this theology was that it began to dismantle the image of a faith bound up with an unjust social order. Its shortcoming was that it ran the risk of having to pay the high price of becoming a "revolutionary Christian ideology." It was well received in certain Christian circles taking their first steps toward an involvement in the revolutionary process. But its Achilles' heel soon appeared in its attempt to "baptize the revolution," sometimes in spite of itself and the intentions of its original proponents. Its theological inadequacy also came to light. It was a simple ad hoc revolutionary thematization of certain biblical texts, especially from the Old Testament, in a somewhat fundamentalist interpretation.

Further—and this is important for our purposes—in the theology of development as well as in the theology of revolution, the point of departure, and consequently the mode of theological reflection, was the same as it had been in all the theologies before. The development enterprise, or revolutionary activity, was still merely the field of *application* of a given theological reflection, this time one concerned with certain facets of the political world. It was still not a theological reflection *from within* the liberation process. It was not a critical reflection from within, and upon, the concrete historical praxis of liberation. It was not theology done from within and upon faith as liberating praxis. When theology is finally done in this locus, perspectives will change.

The World of the Other

This was the path, retraced by us in giant steps, that took many Christians to the point where they could take one last step, and now gradually enter into a new world: the world of the other, the world of the poor, the oppressed, the exploited.

"Which of These Proved a Neighbor?" (Luke 10:36). Love of one's neighbor is an essential component of Christian existence. But as long as I define my neighbor as the person next door, the one I meet on *my* way, the one who comes to me for help, my world will remain the same. All spirit of individual "aid and assistance," all social reformism, is a "love" that stays on its own front porch. ("If you love those who love you, what thanks can you expect?"—Luke 6:32.) But if, on the contrary, I define neighbor as the one whose way *I* take, the person afar off whom I approach ("Which of these three, do you think, proved himself a neighbor to the man who fell into the brigands' hands?"—Luke 10:36), if I define my neighbor as the one I must go out to look for, on the highways and byways, in the factories and slums, on the farms and in the mines—then my world changes. This is what is happening with the "option for the poor," for in the gospel it is the poor person who is the neighbor par excellence. This option constitutes the nub and core of a new way of being human and Christian in Latin America today.[13]

But the poor person does not exist as an inescapable fact of destiny. His or her existence is not politically neutral, and it is not ethically innocent. The poor are a by-product of the system in which we live and for which we are responsible. They are marginalized by our social and cultural world. They are the oppressed, exploited proletariat, robbed of the fruit of their labor and despoiled of their humanity. Hence the poverty of the poor is not a call to generous relief action, but a demand that we go and build a different social order.

But first we have to remove the debris that blocks our vision and look at the question more closely. The option for the poor, taken in the commitment to liberation, has brought us to an understanding that the oppressed cannot be considered apart from the social class to which they belong. This would only lead us to "pity their situation."

The poor, the oppressed, are members of one social class that is being subtly (or not so subtly) exploited by another social class. This exploited class, especially in its most clear-sighted segment, the proletariat, is an active one. Hence, an option for the poor is an option for one social class against another. An option for the poor means a new awareness of class confrontation. It means taking sides with the dispossessed. It means entering into the world of the exploited social class, with its values, its cultural categories. It means entering into solidarity with its interests and its struggles.

This is the world into which various Christian circles are beginning to move, more and more rapidly now. Popular strata are coming to a more acute awareness of their own class interests. Other sectors are entering into solidarity with these interests, too, and with the struggles necessary to defend them. They have expressed this solidarity in numerous documents from various milieus, both before and after Medellín. In fact this is Medellín's immediate, exacting context. It has been expressed most of all in the involvement of small Christian groups, following different paths, all over Latin America.

The first and main question here is a radical one. It is a question of the prevailing social order. Latin American misery and injustice go too deep to be responsive to palliatives. Hence we speak of social revolution, not reform; of liberation, not development; of socialism, not modernization of the prevailing system. "Realists" call these statements romantic and utopian. And they should, for the rationality of these statements is of a kind quite unfamiliar to them. It is the rationality of a concrete, historical undertaking that heralds a different society, one built in function of the poor and the oppressed, and that denounces a society built for the benefit of a few. It is an undertaking "in progress," based on studies of the most rigorous scientific exactitude, from a point of departure in the exploitation of Latin America's great majorities by the dominant classes—and the perception that we live on a continent that is economically, socially, politically, and culturally dependent on power centers outside it, in the affluent countries.

External dependency and internal domination are the marks of the social structures of Latin America. Hence only class analysis will show what is really at stake in the opposition between oppressed lands and dominant peoples. Merely to consider the confrontation among nations is to dissimulate the real situation and of course render it more tolerable. The theory of dependency would be mistaking its way, and betraying the truth, if it did not situate its analysis in the framework of a class struggle taking shape all over the world. All these considerations enable us to grasp the Latin American social configuration as one of a dependent capitalism, and to anticipate the strategy that will be needed to extricate ourselves from this situation.

Only by overcoming a society divided into classes, only by installing a political power at the service of the great popular majorities, only by eliminating the private appropriation of the wealth created by human toil, can we build the foundation of a more just society. This is why the development of the concrete historical march forward of a new society is heading more and more in the direction of socialism in Latin America. But it is a socialism that is well aware of the deficiencies of many of its own concrete forms in the world today. It endeavors to break free of categories and clichés and creatively seek its own paths.

This effort to create a different society also includes the creation of a new human person, a human being that grows progressively free of all servitude preventing it from being the agent of its own lot in history. This leads us to question the dominant ideologies—in which certain religious elements are present—that today provide the model for the human being in our society. However, the construction of a different society, and a new human being, will be authentic only if it is taken on by the oppressed themselves. Hence the whole project must start out with their values. For it is from among the masses that this radical questioning of the prevailing social order, this effort for the abolition of the culture of oppressors, is arising. Only thus can a true social and cultural revolution be carried out.

Various political events that have profoundly modified history, the rapid development of science and the consequent mastery of nature, the use of new instrumentation for the understanding of social reality, as well as the cultural changes that all this has entailed, have hastened the maturation of political consciousness. Social praxis has become adult. Men and women are much more clear now about the conditions of their life in society, but also more conscious of being the active agents of their history.

This political awareness becomes acute when the contradiction is sharpened between growing aspirations for effective liberty and justice and a social order that recognizes them in law but denies them in fact, denies them in so many ways—to whole peoples, to social classes, to racial minorities. Hence the revolutionary, combative search for the genuine conditions for building a free and just society. Hence also a critical suspicion of any ideological justification of a cruel and conflictual situation.

A New Understanding of Politics. This option means taking a new position in the world of politics. It means, for many, taking a revolutionary, socialist option, and thus assuming a political task, in a global perspective, that turns out to be both more scientific and more conflictual than it appeared in the first stages of political involvement.

For a long time, the area of the political seemed an area apart, a sector of human existence subsisting alongside of, but distinct from one's family, professional, and recreational life. Political activity was something to be engaged in during the time left over from other occupations. Furthermore, it was thought, politics belonged to a particular sector of society specially called to this responsibility. But today, those who have made the option for commitment to liberation look upon the political as a dimension that embraces, and demandingly conditions, the entirety of human endeavors. Politics is the global condition, and the collective field, of human accomplishment. Only from a standpoint of this perception of the global character of politics, in a revolutionary perspective, can one adequately understand the legitimate narrower meaning of the term—orientation to political power.

All human reality, then, has a political dimension. To speak in this way not only does not exclude, but positively implies, the multidimensionality of the human being. But this conception rejects all socially sterile sectarianism that diverts our attention from the concrete conditions in which human existence unfolds. For it is within the context of the political that the human being rises up as a free and responsible being, as a truly human being, having a relationship with nature and with other human beings, as someone who takes up the reins of his or her destiny, and goes out and transforms history.

In the past, a stubbornly abstract and ahistorical education made Christians generally insensitive, and even hostile, to new ventures of scientific reason in the realm of the political. Nevertheless, Christians who were committed to the struggle for a different society did feel the urgency of as scientific an understanding as possible of the mechanisms of a capitalist society based on private profit and private ownership for profit. Without this understanding, their action would be ineffective. Vague, lyrical invitations to the "defense of the dignity of the human person," which ignored the in-depth causes of the prevailing social order and the concrete conditions for the construction of a just society, were totally effete and ineffectual. In fact in the long term they were but subtle forms of game-playing, rationalization.

Scientific reason presented a demanding but necessary challenge—an enterprise only barely underway then, but very real. Thanks to their new familiarity with the field of history and social studies, contemporary men and women had begun to be conscious of their economic and socio-cultural conditioning and to discern the in-depth causes of the situation of misery and spoliation in which the majority of the poor in the poor countries lived.

This new mentality had cost Christians very much, and continued to cost them very much. But it had enabled them to extricate themselves from the web of half-truths that had ensnared some Christian circles. For example, "What is the good of changing the structures without a change in the human heart?" This is only a half-truth, for changing social and cultural structures is a way of changing the human heart. There is a mutual dependency, and reciprocal demands, between the human heart and its social milieu, based on a radical unity. It is no more "mechanistic" to think that a structural change automatically makes for a new humanity, than to think that a "personal" change guarantees social transformations. Both assumptions are unreal and naive.

But perhaps what most shocks the Christian seeking to take sides frankly and decisively with the poor and exploited, and to enter into involvement with the struggles of the proletariat, is the conflictual nature of praxis in this context. Politics today involves confrontation—and varying degrees of violence—among human groups, among social classes with opposing interests. Being an "artisan of peace" not only does not dispense from presence in these conflicts, it demands that one take part in them, in order to pull them up by the roots.

There is no peace without justice. This is a hard, uncomfortable truth for those who prefer not to see these conflictual situations, or who, if they see them prefer palliatives to remedies. It is equally hard for those who, with all the good will in the world, confuse universal love with a fictitious harmony. But the gospel enjoins us to love our enemies. In the political context of Latin America, this means we have to recognize the fact of class struggle and accept the fact that we have class enemies to combat. There is no way not to have enemies. What is important is not to exclude them from our love.

In Christian circles, of course, we are not very much accustomed to thinking in conflictual, concrete terms. Instead of antagonism we prefer an eirenic spirit of conciliation. Instead of the provisional, we prefer our evasive "eternity." We have to learn to live peace, and think peace, in the midst of conflict. We have to learn to live and to think the definitive, the transhistorical, as something that happens in time.

Transforming History with a Liberating Love

For two centuries now, human beings have been beginning to experience their capacity to transform, with increased rapidity and control, the world they live in. The experience has changed the course of history, and it is the outstanding characteristic of our era. Undreamed-of possibilities have opened up for human life on earth. But these possibilities have been cornered, monopolized, by a minority of the human race, provoking frustration and exasperation on the part of the dispossessed masses.

The so-called industrial revolution ushered in an era of rapid and broad production of consumer goods, based on a previously unimaginable ability to transform nature.[14] The birth of the experimental sciences had already signaled the beginning of humanity's new dominion over nature, but this dominion reached consciousness and maturity only as scientific knowledge began to translate into technology—techniques for mastering the material world and satisfying the necessities of human life on a large scale.[15] The power of human productivity suddenly transcended all previously foreseeable limits, and the economic activity of society underwent all sorts of revolutionary changes. The process continued, and spiraled, and today we find ourselves on the threshold of what has been called a second industrial revolution.

All this has given contemporary men and women an awareness of their ability to modify radically the conditions of their life and has offered them a clear and exciting demonstration of their liberty with respect to nature. But it has also produced the most abysmal contrasts among the peoples of the earth that history has ever known.

One of the most uncontrollable results of the industrial revolution was the gradual replacement of the human being by the machine. This created a "marginal social excess" around the production of wealth—industry's so-called reserve army, marginalized members of the working class who were not absorbed by the system. The social price of this accelerated rhythm of industrialization, with its corresponding technological boom, began to be appreciated only late in the nineteenth century. Finally, in step with techno-logical progress and improved quality of life in the developed countries, an international division of labor was created that produced the huge contrasts among nations to which I have alluded.

Hence, although the industrial revolution has surely afforded the human race unprecedented capabilities and opportunities for transforming nature, it has just as surely aggravated contradictions within society. These contradic-tions are now at a point of international crisis that can no longer be dissimula-ted.

The consequences of the industrial revolution point up the scope of another historical process, one which dates from about the same time, but which demonstrates a different dimension of the transforming power of the human being. I refer to the dimension of politics. The French Revolution was an experience of humankind's ability to work a profound transformation in the existing social order. It proclaimed the right of every human being to participate in the conduct of the society to which he or she belonged. We are not concerned here with the immediate antecedents of this political revolu-tion, or with the largely declarative character of its proclamation. What is important is that, with all its ambiguities, it put an end to a certain type of society and instilled in the popular masses the desire for an effective share in the exercise of political power—the desire for an active role in history; in a word, the desire for a truly democratic society.

Here again we are confronted with a new affirmation of the freedom of the human being, this time with regard to social organization. But for this demo-cratic structure of society to be real, just economic conditions are necessary. If they are absent, both within the underdeveloped countries and in their external relationships with the developed countries, explosive tensions are created on the national and international level alike.

Europeans of two hundred years ago were acutely aware of standing on the threshold of a new era of history, an era of critical reason and the transform-ing freedom of human nature.[16] This new consciousness made new persons of them: men and women more in command of themselves and of their lot in history—a history that would never again see nature and society as discon-nected. Indeed, it became ever clearer that the industrial and the political revolution were not two haphazardly simultaneous, convergent processes, but truly interdependent movements. The more progress each of them made, the clearer their mutual involvement became. The transformation of history, then, would necessarily presuppose the simultaneous transformation of nature and society. There is, in this transforming praxis, more than simply a new awareness of the meaning of economic activity or political activity. There is an altogether new manner of being a human person in history.

But an approach to the transformation of history from the viewpoint of the dominated peoples and marginalized persons, from the viewpoint of the poor of this world, leads us to look on this transformation as a praxis of liberation. That is, we come to see something that perhaps escapes us when we view things from the standpoint of the minority of humankind that controls most of the science and technology, as well as most of the political power, in today's world. And suddenly this liberating praxis acquires *subversive* features—subversive of a social order in which the poor, society's "others," have only just begun to make their voices heard.[17]

What is really at stake, then, is not simply a greater rationality in economic activity, or a better social organization, but, over and above all this, justice and love. To be sure, these classic concepts do not often come up in the language of political science. But there is no avoiding them here. And this demonstrates the human depth and density of the matter with which we are dealing.

The use of the terms "justice" and "love" recalls to our minds that we are speaking of real human persons, whole peoples, suffering misery and exploitation, deprived of the most elemental human rights, scarcely aware that they are human beings at all. The praxis of liberation, therefore, inasmuch as it starts out from an authentic solidarity with the poor and the oppressed, is ultimately a praxis of love—real love, effective and concrete, for real, concrete human beings. It is a praxis of love of neighbor, and of love for Christ in the neighbor, for Christ identifies himself with the least of these human beings, our brothers and sisters. Any attempt to separate love for God and love for neighbor gives rise to attitudes that impoverish both.

It is easy to make a distinction between a heavenly and an earthly praxis—easy, but not faithful to the gospel of the Word who became a human being. It therefore would seem more authentic and profound to speak of a praxis of love as having its roots in the gratuitous and free love of the Father and as becoming concrete in solidarity with human beings—first with the poor and dispossessed, and then through them with all human beings.

BELIEVING IN ORDER TO UNDERSTAND

The option for the poor, for the oppressed strata of society, and for the struggles of the proletariat of Latin America, comports a whole new political outlook and calls for a concrete praxis of liberation. This outlook and this praxis place us in a different universe. All these things lead to a new spiritual experience, at the very heart of this praxis. That experience is the matrix of a new understanding of the word of God, of God's free gift bursting into human existence and transforming it.

God and the Poor

Liberating involvement is the locus of a spiritual experience in which we encounter once more that great prophetic theme of the Old Testament and of Jesus' preaching alike: God and the poor person. To know God is to do justice, is to be in solidarity with the poor person. And it is to be in solidarity with that poor person as he or she actually exists today—as someone who is oppressed, as a member of an exploited class, or ethnic group, or culture, or nation.

At the same time, a relationship with the God who has loved me—loved me first and loved me freely—despoils me, strips me. It universalizes my love for others and makes it gratuitous too. Each of the two movements demands the other, dialectically. Hence, for the Bible, there is no authentic worship of God without solidarity with the poor.

Living according to the Spirit. All this entails entering into a different world. A new Christian experience takes shape, an experience filled with possibilities and promises—but with detours and blind alleys, too. There is no easy, triumphal road for the life of faith. There are those who, when they become absorbed by the political demands of the liberation commitment and begin to live the tensions of solidarity with the exploited, then find themselves belonging to a church many of whose members are staunch advocates of the prevailing social order. They then lose their dynamic faith, and suffer the anguish of a dichotomy between being a Christian and being committed to political action.

More cruel still is the case of those who suffer the loss of the love of God in favor of the very thing that love arouses and sustains—love for their fellow human beings. A love like that, unable to maintain itself in the oneness demanded by the gospel, never comes to know the fulness it has locked up inside itself.

Such cases exist. The most elementary honesty forces this admission upon us. When you are out on the frontier of the Christian community where the revolutionary commitment is most intense, you are not in tranquil waters. A lucid, refined analysis is called for here, for many factors are at work. Christians involved in the liberation process are subject to many pressures. They are vulnerable to romanticism, emotional tensions, and even ambiguous doctrinal stances, which can lead them to attitudes of exasperation—or a facile breach with Christianity. But the responsibility of Christians who take refuge in their comfortable "orthodoxy," safe, secure, self-satisfied, and assiduously absent from any focal point where anything "new" is going on, content merely to point an accusing finger from time to time, is scarcely something to be congratulated either.

The difficulties, then, are real. But the paths to a solution can begin only from within the heart of the problem itself. Keeping oneself protected cloaks the reality and postpones a fruitful response. And it betokens a forgetfulness of the urgency and gravity of the reasons impelling us to involve ourselves with those exploited by a cruel, impersonal system. Ultimately, keeping aloof and "not wanting to get involved" is a failure to believe in the power of the gospel and the faith. The gospel proclamation may appear to sink away into the pure concrete historical *here*; but *here* is where theological reflection should spring up, together with the spirituality of a new preaching of the Christian message, in the here and now, incarnate, undiluted.

To evangelize, Chenu has written, is to enflesh, to incarnate, the gospel in time. This time of ours, today, is a confused and darksome one only for those who lack in hope, and hence do not know, or hesitate to believe, that the Lord is present within them.

And indeed for many Christians the liberation commitment is an authentic spiritual experience—in the original, biblical sense of the word: living in the Spirit, who leads us to see ourselves as free and creative children of the Father and sisters and brothers of all men and women. "God has sent the Spirit of his Son into our hearts; the Spirit that cries, 'Abba, Father' " (Gal. 4:6). It is only through concrete deeds of love and solidarity that our encounter with the poor person, with the exploited human being, will be effective—and in that person our encounter with Christ (for "you did it to me"—Matt. 25:40) will be valid as well. Our denial of love and solidarity will be a rejection of Christ ("You neglected to do it to me"—Matt. 25:45).

The poor person, the other, becomes the revealer of the Utterly Other. Life in this involvement is a life in the presence of the Lord at the heart of political activity, with all its conflict and with all its demand for scientific reasoning. It is the life of—to paraphrase a well-known expression—contemplatives in political action.

This is a notion to which we are little accustomed. A spiritual experience, we like to think, should be something out beyond the frontiers of human realities as profane and tainted as politics. And yet this is what we strive for here, this is our aim and goal: an encounter with the Lord, not in the poor person who is "isolated and good," but in the oppressed person, the member of a social class that burns with struggle for its most elemental rights and for the construction of a society in which persons can live as human beings.

History, concrete history, is the place where God reveals the mystery of God's personhood. God's word comes to us in proportion to our involvement in historical becoming. But this history is a conflictual one, a history of conflicts of interest, of struggles for greater justice, a history of the marginalization and exploitation of human beings, of aspirations for liberation. To make an option for the poor, for the exploited classes, to identify with their lot and share their fate, is to seek to make this history that of an authentic community of brothers and sisters. There is no other way to receive the free gift of filiation, of the status of children of God. It is an option for Christ's cross, in the hope of his resurrection. This is what we celebrate in the Eucharist: we express our wish and intent to make our own the meaning Jesus Christ gave to his life, and to receive the Spirit, the gift of loving as he loved.

It is in these concrete conditions that the process of evangelical conversion takes place, that central element of all spirituality. Conversion is an abandonment of oneself and an opening up to God and others. It implies breach, but most of all it implies new departure.[18] And this is precisely why it is not a purely "interior," private attitude, but a process occurring in the socio-economic, political, and cultural milieu in which we live, and which we ought to transform.

Encounter with Christ in the poor person constitutes an authentic spiritual experience. It is a life in the Spirit, the bond of love between Father and Son, between God and human being, and between human being and human being. It is in this profound communion that Christians involved in a concrete historical liberation praxis strive to live—in a love for Christ in solidarity with the poor, in faith in our status as children of the Father as we forge a society of sisters and brothers, and in the hope of Christ's salvation in a commitment to the liberation of the oppressed.

This is the life and attitude of a growing number of Latin American Christians—laity, bishops, priests, and religious. It is a unifying experience, one that frequently has difficulty expressing itself adequately, perhaps owing to the manipulated condition of theologies that tend to separate the two elements of this experience, and even to oppose them to each other, or perhaps owing to a defensive attitude on the part of Christians who see the liberation commitment as a threat to their privileges in the prevailing social order. This Christian experience is not exempt from the risk of oversimplified identifications and distortive reductions. But it is one that is striving, with daring and depth, to live in Christ by taking on the concrete experience of suffering and injustice of the poor of Latin America. This experiment has already partially succeeded in expressing itself authentically, succeeded in freeing itself from an indirect, mediated language, and to this extent its contribution has already begun to bear fruit for the whole ecclesial community.

The spirituality of liberation is admirably expressed in the Magnificat. The Magnificat is a song of thanksgiving for the gifts of the Lord, in the humble joy of being loved by him: "And my spirit exults in God my savior; because he has looked upon his lowly handmaid, . . . for the Almighty has done great things for me" (Luke 1:47–49).

But at the same time it is one of the most liberating and political passages in the New Testament. This thanksgiving and this joy are intimately bound up with the liberating activity of God in favor of the oppressed and his bringing low the mighty: "He has pulled down princes from their thrones and exalted the lowly. The hungry he has filled with good things, the rich sent empty away" (Luke 1:52–53).

The future of history lies with the poor and the exploited. Authentic liberation will be the deed of the oppressed themselves: in them, the Lord will save history. The spirituality of liberation will have its point of departure in the spirituality of the *anawim*.

Poverty and Solidarity. The praxis of liberation is coming of age. It is beginning to ask questions. Henceforward it will be the framework of politics, in the sense in which we have defined it above, where Christians committed to the poor and to the liberation of the exploited classes will live and think their faith. Christians will spontaneously orientate themselves toward poverty, a fundamental demand of the gospel. Identification with Christ, who came into the world to proclaim the gospel to the poor and to liberate the oppressed, demands poverty. Those who undertake this identification will be surprised at what they discover.[19]

Poverty in the Catholic Church, in theory as well as in practice, has been a prisoner of the "religious life." It has been limited to a particular way of living the *vow* of poverty. Viewed in itself, apart from the purity and nobility of the intentions of its practitioners, it was viewed as something privative—and as the private property of a particular type of Christians, who sometimes gave the impression of being rather wealthy in their poverty. Most Christians, it was said, are not called to poverty. In little doses, under the form of a certain sobriety of life, it was to be "counseled," but it was not a "precept," not anything that pertained to the essence of Christian life.

Basically it was not a bad division of labor, from the standpoint of the Christians who lived the vow of poverty. They were considered to be living in a "state of perfection," for they had renounced the goods and pleasures of this world. Those who continued to enjoy these goods and pleasures were not evil as such, but they paid a price for living in a lower state of the Christian life. Of course, by the very fact that they lived in the world they could gain something by supporting the practitioners of poverty with their alms. Thus almost everyone gained something. The gospel, however, gained nothing.

And the poor and exploited of this world gained nothing. For there was a graver—and more subtle—evil afoot here. Poverty was proclaimed as a Christian ideal. And its character as an ideal was maintained in a rather generalized way, so that the door was open to all sorts of abuses. In the Bible, material poverty is a subhuman situation, the fruit of injustice and sin. This poverty should not be a Christian ideal. This would mean aspiring to something considered demeaning for a human being. Further, it would place the gospel demands at cross-purposes with humanity's great desire and striving—to break free of subjection to nature, to eliminate human exploitation, and to create better conditions of life for everyone. It would likewise—and no less gravely—mean the justification, however unintentional, of the situation of injustice and exploitation that is the basic cause of poverty—real poverty, which the great majority suffer in Latin America. And yet, all this is exactly what became accepted, in theory and in practice.

But the witness of poverty, and theological reflection on it, has begun to undergo a change in recent years. The first cries for reform came from religious communities whose spirituality was centered on a life of poverty and contemplation. (The combination was no accident, and the natural link between poverty and contemplation continues to be verified today, however new the context.) Then the demand began to spread to other types of religious communities in the church. The vow of poverty began to reclaim its roots and grow richer in meaning. Finally the movement overflowed the confines of the religious life itself, and broad sectors of Christian laity began to make their own the demand for a more real and more radical witness to poverty. For they saw in poverty an essential trait of a life in conformity with the gospel. Now poverty was calling the whole church to account, and any counter-testimony in its regard met with critical and strong resistance.

But what we are dealing with here is not a simple extension of the demand for a poor life. Still less is it a mechanical transfer of "religious poverty" to new segments of Christian society. It is the manner of living and understanding poverty that has changed and is changing. Solidarity with the poor, involvement with the liberation of the exploited classes, and entry into the world of the political, has led a good many Christians to do a rereading of the gospel. For only a critique from within a liberation praxis enables one to denounce the ideological function performed by the various ways of mis-understanding poverty; this then leads to a reinterpretation of the gospel. Medellín, bolstered by the new experiences of numerous Christian groups, took its stand along the lines of this rereading.

Now evangelical poverty began to be lived as an act of love and liberation toward the poor of this world. It began to be lived as solidarity with them and protest against the poverty they live in, as identification with the interests of the oppressed classes, and as indictment of the exploitation of which they are the victims.

The ultimate cause of exploitation and alienation is selfishness. The deep reason for voluntary poverty is love of neighbor. Poverty—the fruit of social injustice, whose deepest roots are sin—is taken up not in order to erect it into an ideal of life, but in order to bear testimony to the evil it represents. Our sinful condition, and its consequences, were not assumed by Christ in order to idealize them, surely, but in order to redeem us from sinfulness, to battle human selfishness, to abolish all injustice and division among human beings, to suppress what divides us into rich and poor, exploiters and exploited.

The witness of poverty, lived as an authentic imitation of Christ, instead of alienating us from the world, places us at the very heart of a situation of spoliation and oppression. From there it proclaims liberation and full communion with the Lord. From there it proclaims, and lives, spiritual poverty: total availability to God.

Faith in Search of Understanding

All theology is rooted in the act of faith. But the act of faith is not a simple intellectual adherence to a message. It is vital acceptance of the gift of the word, heard in the community of the church as encounter with the Lord and love for one's fellow human beings. Faith pervades Christian existence in its entirety.

Accepting the word and making it life and concrete deed is the point of departure for an understanding of the faith. This is the meaning of St. Anselm's *Credo ut intelligam*, "I believe in order to understand," as he expressed it in this celebrated passage:

> I have no wish, my Lord, to plunge into your depth, for my intelligence
> could never exhaust it. I desire only to grasp in some measure that truth
> of yours that my heart believes and loves. I seek not to understand in
> order to believe. I believe in order to understand. For I am certain that if
> I did not believe, I should not understand [*Proslogion*, 1].

The primacy of God and the grace of faith are the raison d'être of all
theology. From this point of departure, one can properly appreciate that
Christians seek to understand their faith ultimately in function of "the imitation of Christ"—which means feeling, thinking, and acting as did he. An
authentic theology is always a "spiritual theology," as the fathers of the
church understood spiritual theology.

The life of faith, then, is not just a point of departure for theology. It is also
its point of arrival. Belief and understanding have an annular relationship.

Theology and Reasoning. Theology always involves a reasoning process,
though it is not necessarily identified with it. This reasoning process corresponds to the cultural universe of the believer. Every theology asks itself the
meaning of the word of God for its contemporaries, at a certain moment of
history. Any attempts we make to answer this question will be made in function of our culture, in function of the problems faced by the men and women
of our time. From within this cultural universe, we reformulate the message
of the gospel and the church, for our contemporaries and for ourselves.

The Rationality Crisis. This is what Thomistic theology attempted to do.
Daringly it took up an Aristotelian philosophy, with the whole worldview
that philosophy implied, and took a step of capital importance for the understanding of the faith. But today we have a crisis on our hands in the area of
classic theological rationality. This crisis has been thoroughly investigated,
and its causes laid out, so that there is no need for us to go into detail here. Let
it be noted only that the crisis has given rise to a philosophical eclecticism that
has become one of the traits of some of our contemporary theology. It has
also occasioned attempts, not to recover some impossible monolithic theological system, but to search out new ways of reformulating the word.[20] More
radically, doubtless, it has provoked questions in the area of the theory of
knowledge—an area of which theological thought perhaps takes insufficient
account, and one that calls for urgent examination.[21]

What are the presuppositions of theology in its approach to historical reality? What is the influence on our theological reflection of the position of the
institutional church in today's society? In other words, to use a current collo-
quialism, where is the theologian "coming from"? To what end, and for
whom, does the theologian speak? These are the questions that now give rise
to the one great question, the one that always comes up at moments in history
when one era is coming to a close and another is about to begin: What is it to
"do theology," to theologize? What is theology?

This set of questions cannot be addressed without also taking into consideration the role of the positive sciences, the role of modern scientific knowl-

edge. This is especially important when theology impinges upon history or upon psychology. The sciences are expressions of human reason. They reveal aspects of nature and aspects of the human being that escape other approaches. Hence theology cannot afford to ignore them.

Theological reflection—even as it breaks new ground—retains all its validity and grows rich in its ongoing dialogue with the sciences. It answers questions that are beyond the purview of the sciences. It makes its own contribution to an understanding of history, and to the role of free and creative human activity.

Two Approaches. This complexity, this multidimensionality of human knowledge, is at work in the concrete, historical praxis of liberation, and is contributing to its effectiveness. It is likewise present in the discourse on faith from within solidarity with the poor and oppressed.

A good part of contemporary theology seems to have arisen from the challenge of the nonbeliever. The nonbeliever questions our religious world, and demands a purification and profound renewal. Dietrich Bonhoeffer took up that challenge and formulated the incisive question we find at the origin of so many of the theological efforts of our day: How can one proclaim God in a world become adult, a world grown up, a world come of age?

In Latin America, however, the challenge does not come first and foremost from the nonbeliever. It comes from the nonperson. It comes from the person whom the prevailing social order fails to recognize as a person—the poor, the exploited, the ones systematically and legally despoiled of their humanness, the ones who scarcely know they are persons at all.

Furthermore, the religious world is not what these nonpersons principally question. They question first of all our economic, social, political, and cultural world. This challenge, then, unlike that of the nonbeliever, is a call for a revolutionary transformation of the very bases of a dehumanizing society. Hence the question here will not be how to speak of God in a world come of age, but rather how to proclaim God as Father in a world that is inhuman. What can it mean to tell a nonperson that he or she is God's child? These were questions asked, after their own fashion, by a Bartolomé de Las Casas and so many others in their encounter with native Americans. The discovery of "the other," the exploited one, led them to reflect on the demands of faith in an altogether different way from the approach taken by those on the side of dominators.

Today the historical framework is different, and social analysis is different. And yet what we have is a rediscovery of the poor in Latin America. To enter into solidarity with them is to enter into concrete, conflictual history. It means engaging in international and interclass confrontations. It means entering by the door of the dominated and oppressed. In addition, the social system that creates and justifies this situation cannot really be called into question by someone not actually participating in efforts radically to transform it, efforts to build a new order. Involvement in a praxis of liberation means being willing to take on what we referred to above as the complexity and multidimensionality of human knowledge. It means entering into a different cultural world.

It is from within this cultural world, into which we have entered by our voluntary involvement in the concrete historical process in Latin America, that we strive to reformulate today's message of the gospel. In this perspective, reflection on the faith will necessarily take a different tack from that of the theologian who attempts to respond to the challenges of the nonbeliever.

Praxis of Liberation and Comprehension of Faith

Involvement in the liberation process introduces Christians to an altogether unfamiliar world. They must make a quantum leap. They must now subject the social order and its familiar ideology to a new, radical questioning. In a word, they must break with the old ways of knowing.

As a consequence, any theological reflection undertaken from within a cultural context other than that of the liberation process will not afford much enlightenment. It may transmit the awareness that previous Christian generations had of their faith, and thus provide believers with certain points of reference, but it will not preserve them from theological orphanhood in this new cultural context. It will not provide them with the theological tools for doing theology in Latin America today, for it will not speak the strong, clear, and incisive language of the human and Christian experience actually being lived out today in Latin America.

Theory and Praxis. The tools for a new way of understanding the faith are being crafted in Latin America, in our ongoing experience of life in Latin America. And this new way of appreciating our faith is already helping us link together, understand, and transform both theory and practice.

The scope of our radical challenge to the prevailing social order would escape us, were we unaware of the change that has taken place in human self-understanding—the change that has occurred in the approach to truth, and in the way that persons relate truth to their concrete, historical practice. Since the birth of the experimental sciences, men and women have been playing an ever more active role in the acquisition and application of knowledge. They are no longer content with merely admiring nature and classifying what they observe. They interrogate nature now, they provoke nature. They discover its laws, they master it with their technology.

The advent of the social and psychological sciences extended this type of knowledge, in a way, to areas hitherto reserved to considerations of a philosophical type. These are the sciences that, preserving their internal character as theoretical sciences, tend at the same time to become "humane sciences." The "humane sciences" are only just being born. They are only just beginning to feel their way along. But they are already opening up new dimensions of what it means to be a human being; hence they cannot be assimilated purely and simply to the natural sciences.

This new development in the field of human science has brought us to the discovery of something that is rapidly becoming a basic trait of the contemporary outlook: that knowledge is linked to change. History—that is, nature and society, indissolubly linked—can be known only by transforming it, and transforming oneself. Vico said it long ago: human beings know well only what they do. Truth, for the contemporary human being, is something *verified,* something "made true." Knowledge of reality that leads to no modification of that reality is not verified, does not become true.

Marx, in his penetrating *Theses on Feuerbach,* felt that here he had his hands on the epistemological foundations of his own contribution to the scientific understanding of history. Thus the reality of history ceases to be the object of the application of abstract truths and idealist interpretations and becomes rather the privileged locus, the point of departure and return, of the process of knowledge itself. The praxis that transforms history is not a moment in the feeble incarnation of a limpid, well-articulated theory, but the matrix of authentic knowledge and the acid test of the validity of that knowledge. It is the place where human beings re-create their world and shape themselves. It is the place where they know the reality in which they find themselves, and thereby know themselves as well.

Biblical Truth. What is needed at this point is a rereading of the gospel. We shall then find something very traditional there—something authentically traditional—and perhaps this is why it is forgotten by "traditions" of more recent vintage. We shall find that "gospel truth" is veri-fied: it happens, it becomes.

Truth is a matter of deeds, St. John tells us (1 John 3:18), because this truth is love itself. A living love is an affirmation of God. Belief in God does not mean simply maintaining that he exists. Belief in God means commitment of one's life to him and to all women and men. To have faith is to go outside oneself and give oneself to God and others. Faith works by effective love, St. Paul says (Gal. 5:6).

Reflection on the faith means rethinking a faith that acquires real consistency only through deeds, and hence that goes beyond mere verbal affirmation and profession.[22] This reflection takes place within the movement of a promise—a promise fulfilled in the course of the historical process, while yet speaking to us of something beyond history. Truth, in the Bible, includes fidelity, justice, and constancy of purpose. To believe is to have confidence, to entrust oneself to God. To believe is to be "faithful."

God is worthy of faith because he is veracious—that is, because, as the prophets of the Old Testament never tire of reminding us, his word is "firm," solid. He always fulfills what he promises. But this fulfillment takes place in history, and thus God's veracity, too, makes its appearance in the course of history.

Christ is the fulfillment of the promise of the Father. For it is in Christ, in the deeds and in the words of Jesus, that the Father has made us his children, and it is in the death and resurrection of Jesus that the Father fulfills his promise. To be a Christian is to accept the fact that the promise begins to be fulfilled and actualized in a historical context. To be a Christian is to toil for the verification, the becoming-true, of this promise of the Father, in history, by revealing the Father's love in our own love for our brothers and sisters: "We have passed out of death and into life, and of this we can be sure because we love our brothers" (1 John 3:14). To be a Christian is to hope in the total fulfillment of the promise.

In the Bible, the act of knowing is not relegated to a merely intellectual level. To know is to love. The prophetic "word" *(dabar)* is always an event, a happening. The word pronounced in the name of Yahweh becomes concrete history. True orthodoxy is orthopraxis.

Theology from and on Praxis. In insisting upon the truth as something lived, as something verified, we are not urging a merely mechanical conformity with the contemporary call for a link between knowledge and change. But the cultural world we live in does permit us to discover a point of departure, and new horizon, for theological reflection. This theology must now take a new route, and in order to do so it will have to appeal to its own fonts.

Theology in this context will be a critical reflection both from within, and upon, historical praxis, in confrontation with the word of the Lord as lived and accepted in faith. Ours is a faith that comes down to us through manifold and sometimes ambiguous historical mediations. But it is also a faith which we relive every day.

Hence theology in Latin America today will be a reflection in, and on, faith as liberation praxis. It will be an understanding of the faith from an option and a commitment.[23] It will be an understanding of the faith from a point of departure in real, effective solidarity with the exploited classes, oppressed ethnic groups, and despised cultures of Latin America, and from within their world. It will be a reflection that starts out from a commitment to create a just society, a community of sisters and brothers, and that ought to see that this commitment grows more radical and complete. It will be a theological reflection that becomes true, veri-fied, in real and fruitful involvement in the liberation process.

Theology will thus liberate itself from a socio-cultural context that prevents it from working from where the oppressed and despoiled of the world are battling to be accepted as human persons. Theology will be converted into a liberating and prophetic force, and be able to make a contribution to a global understanding of the word—an understanding that ultimately takes place amid the facts of real life. This, and not simple affirmations, or "analysis models," will deliver theology from all the forms of idealism that beset it.

Jesus Christ: Hermeneutical Principle of Faith

To be a Christian is to believe that a human being of this concrete history of ours, who loved us in loving the men and women of his time to the point of giving his life for them, who loved the poor by preference and revealed God to us as a Father, and who therefore came into confrontation with the great and powerful of his time and was finally executed as a subversive, is God.

The great hermeneutical principle of the faith, and hence the basis and foundation of all theological reasoning, is Jesus Christ. In Jesus we encounter God. In the human Word we read the word of the Lord. In the events of history we recognize the fulfillment of the promise. And all this because Jesus is the Christ of God, the one sent by the Father: the Son. "Yes, God loved the world so much that he gave his only Son" (John 3:16).

For Jesus is the irruption into history of the one by whom everything was made and everything was saved. This, then, is the fundamental hermeneutical circle: from humanity to God and from God to humanity, from history to faith and from faith to history, from the human word to the word of the Lord and from the word of the Lord to the human word, from the love of one's brothers and sisters to the love of the Father and from the love of the Father to love of one's brothers and sisters, from human justice to God's holiness and from God's holiness to human justice.

Theology—the understanding of the faith—is animated by the will to help others live according to the Spirit.

The Salvation of History

Christ's Liberation and Political Liberation. What we have seen about the way to do theology differentiates liberation theology from the theologies of development, revolution, and violence to which it is sometimes linked and even erroneously reduced.[24] Liberation theology not only makes different analyses of reality, owing to its more global and radical political opinions and positions, but, more importantly, it takes a different approach to the theological task itself.

The theology of liberation is not an attempt to justify positions already taken. It has no intention of being a revolutionary Christian ideology. It is a reflection from a point of departure in the concrete historical praxis of human beings. It seeks to understand the faith from within this historical praxis and from within the manner of living the faith in a revolutionary commitment. As a result, theology comes after involvement. Liberation theology is a second act.[25] Hence its themes are the great themes of all true theology, but its focus, its manner of approaching them, is different. It has a different relationship with historical praxis.

To say that liberation theology makes no claim to be a revolutionary Christian ideology is not to say that it stands aloof from the revolutionary process. On the contrary, it has its point of departure precisely in an involvement with that process and attempts to help make it more critical of itself and hence more radical and global. And the way it attempts to do this is to situate liberating political commitment within a perspective of the free gift of Christ's total liberation.

The word of the Lord, received in faith, will be lived and understood today by human persons who move in today's concrete cultural categories, just as in the past it was lived and understood by men and women formed in Greco-

Roman patterns of thinking. Today this is a task that demands recourse to many different specializations, in order to gain a serious understanding of the various facets of contemporary thinking. Living and understanding the faith today requires, above and beyond a philosophy in dialogue with the humane sciences, a grasp of the instruments furnished by these latter for understanding the social realities that deny justice and undermine the community of sisters and brothers that faith seeks. This is how the action of living the faith will be efficacious.

A theological project immersed in the elements of a new rationality, a rationality of a kind to which traditional theology is little accustomed, creates conflicts and conundrums. It has always been thus: recall the hostility, and the accusations of distortion (and "humanization") of the faith, aroused by the first attempts to use Aristotelian philosophy in theology.[26] But today's hostility, baseless accusations, and even occasional condemnations—like those of yesterday—have no future.

The future lies with a faith that, in communion with the church, has no fear of the progress of human thought and social practice. It is a faith that permits itself to be interrogated by human thought and practice, even while challenging them. And it is richer for the contact. It does not subject itself to their criticism uncritically. This faith knows its conditioning and its presuppositions, but it knows its exigencies as well. A complex task lies before it, and this is why our faith today calls upon such a multiplicity of specializations, why it calls for a serious, scientific understanding of all the facets of contemporary thought, both philosophical and scientific, without which it would be impossible to pursue theology today.

In the particular case under consideration here, the theological project underway is quite modest, like others in the past. But the virulence of some of the reactions to it is anything but modest. It may be that these reactions have their explanation in nontheological reasons, for they do form a part of the defense of a social order that has little liking for questions—and still less for the prospect of being wiped out by the human being it marginalizes and despoils.

Faith—acceptance of, and response to, the Father's love—strikes at the very root of social injustice: sin, the breach of friendship with God and with the human community. But it will not tear up that root without coming to grips with historical mediations and with a socio-political analysis of these concrete historical realities.

Sin is present in the denial that a human being is sister or brother to me. It is present in structures of oppression, created for the benefit of a few. It is present in the spoliation of peoples, cultures, and social classes. Sin is the basic alienation. For that very reason, sin cannot be touched in itself, in the abstract. It can be attacked only in concrete historical situations—in particular instances of alienation. Apart from particular, concrete alienation, sin is meaningless and incomprehensible.

Sin calls for a radical liberation, and this necessarily includes a political kind of liberation. Only in aggressive, efficacious participation in the concrete historical process of liberation shall we be able to put our finger on the basic alienation present in all partial alienation. This radical liberation is the gift Christ brings to us. By his death and resurrection he redeems the human being from sin and all its consequences. Medellín says:

> This is the same God who, in the fulness of time, sends his Son in the flesh, so that He might come to liberate all men from the slavery to which sin has subjected them: hunger, misery, oppression and ignorance, in a word, that injustice and hatred which have their origin in human selfishness.[27]

But, as we have said repeatedly, political activity has its own demands and its own laws. To recall the profound meaning that political activity has for a Christian is the diametrical opposite of taking a "great leap backward" to times and conditions in which human beings were in no position to understand the internal mechanisms of a society of oppression—times and conditions in which political action had not yet come of age.

The gift of filiation, the gift that makes brothers and sisters of all women and men, will never be more than just a manner of speaking—never more than a pretext for smugness about the nobility of one's ideals—until it is lived, daily and conflictually, in history. For it is a gift crying for conversion into genuine identification with the interests of human beings suffering the oppression of other human beings, identification with the struggles of exploited classes. It is a gift that strives to enrich—creatively, critically, and from within—political processes that otherwise tend to close in upon themselves and mutilate authentic dimensions of the human being. It is a gift that must use the instruments furnished by the humane sciences for becoming acquainted with the social realities that negate the justice and the community of sisters and brothers it seeks. It is a gift thrusting toward efficacious action.

Two Dimensions of Liberation in One History. Christ's liberation cannot be reduced to political liberation. But it is present in concrete historical and political liberating events. One cannot merely leap over these mediations. On the other hand, political liberation is not a religious messianism. It has its own autonomy and its own laws; it requires social analyses, and very specific political options. But seeing human history as a history in which the liberation of Christ is at work broadens our outlook and gives the political commitment its full depth and genuine meaning. It is anything but a set of facile and impoverishing equations, or of oversimplified, distortive reductions of one thing to another. It entails mutual enlightenment and reciprocal demands.

The theology of liberation is a theology of salvation in the concrete, historical, and political conditions of our day. These concrete, current, historical and political mediations possess their own validity, and they change our experience. Thereby also they change our reflection on "the message which was a mystery hidden for generations and centuries and has now been revealed'' (Col. 1:26; cf. Rom. 16:25): namely, the Father's love and a fellowship of brothers and sisters. This is a salvation that takes place in time and gives human history its profound unity. There are not two histories, one of filiation and another of human community, one in which we become children of God and another in which we become one another's sisters and brothers. There is only one history, and it has both aspects together. This is what we mean when we say ''liberation.''

Distortion and Perspective

Theological reflection within the liberation context begins when we first perceive that the very context obliges us radically to rethink our being Christian and our being church. This reflection—a reflection upon the word received in faith—will call upon the various expressions of contemporary human rationality, and not only philosophy, but the humane sciences as well. Most of all, however, it will call for concrete historical praxis, and in a new manner.

This is the difference between a theology of liberation and any attempt to apply the cosmetic vocabulary of ''social concern,'' or even ''liberation,'' to old pastoral and theological stances. Facile attitudes, coupled with a certain ''trendiness,'' or penchant for the newest vogue, have encouraged some persons simply to tack on the word ''liberation'' to whatever they have always been saying anyway and go on saying it, hoping to update a sluggish old inventory by slapping a new label on obsolete goods. Another approach is to interpret Christ's liberation in a spiritualistic sense (not a spiritual sense, which would be something else, something deep and genuine). Both of these approaches are simply ways of evacuating the liberation concept of all its human and historical content, so that now it can be accepted by the political and ecclesiastical system. For now it questions nothing. And now ''the other'' in the system is forever absent—things are all nicely in the family again.[28]

But as we have said, by ''theology of liberation'' we mean something with a direct and precise relationship with historical praxis. And this historical praxis is a liberating praxis. It is an identification with the men and women, cultures and social classes, that are suffering misery and spoliation. It is identification with their interests and their battles. It means becoming involved in the revolutionary political process, in order to live and to proclaim the free and liberating love of Christ from within that process.

The theology of liberation today is only just on the drawing board. Our insistence on the importance of a theory of knowledge, and a rationality, bound up with the work of constructing a society in function of the oppressed and marginalized poses serious questions of theological methodology. Progress made to date now demands more work in the problems of biblical hermeneutics, for we need a better and more precise understanding of our Old and New Testament roots.

What we have already achieved is to have introduced a different perspective within which to develop the interconnections between faith and political activity. We have opened up new routes for a christological reading of solidarity with the poor, and we have raised radical questions in the area of ecclesiology. But all this leaves a vast amount of work still to be done. Doing that work will strengthen our line of thinking and fine-tune the questions posed by that thinking.

Furthermore, closer communication is necessary among those working in the various areas of the liberation movement. There is still little attempt to interrelate the different theological focuses that have arisen in the committed Christian communities of Africa and Asia, among the racial minorities of the developed countries, and in Latin America. Our "rough draft" of the theology of liberation stands to gain a great deal from encounters still in the offing.[29]

Faith comes to us through concrete historical mediations. The theological endeavor presupposes a critical examination of the forms in which the faith experience has been handed down across the centuries, and is still being handed down today, in the political practice of Christians. Otherwise we shall stall at the level of the abstract and ahistorical. And thereby we shall betray the basic intuition of liberation theology. We shall quickly slide back into new ideological manipulations, and no label that says "liberation" will make any difference.

And yet, ultimately, neither will we have an authentic theology of liberation until the oppressed themselves are able freely and creatively to express themselves in society and among the people of God. For the whole point of departure for the theology of liberation is a critical reflection on the liberating praxis of more and more groups and strata. But the popular classes are not yet present decisively and massively within this praxis. Liberation theology itself is only just underway. It is still "in first gear," so to speak. There is so much room for improvement. We can pay attention to new biblical themes. We can sink deeper roots in the tradition of the church. We can come to grips with other aspects of contemporary thinking. We can enter into dialogue with new tendencies in theology. We can compare and combine our experiences with those of other Christians. And all these things will be most useful. They are even urgent. But they will not total up to the quantum leap we are looking for. They will only provide better insights than the ones we had before.

We shall not have our great leap forward, into a whole new theological perspective, until the marginalized and exploited have begun to become the artisans of their own liberation—until their voice makes itself heard directly, without mediations, without interpreters—until they themselves take account, in the light of their own values, of their own experience of the Lord in their efforts to liberate themselves. We shall not have our quantum theological leap until the oppressed themselves theologize, until "the others" themselves personally reflect on their hope of a total liberation in Christ. For they are the bearers of this hope for all humanity.

Our theology will have no proper, distinct focus of its own until it takes its point of departure in the social practice of the Latin American peoples—the lowly, repressed, and, today as yet, silent peoples of Latin America.[30] This is where the impulse will arise for a rereading of the gospel message, with a reinterpretation of the experiences that that message has occasioned, and that constitute what we call Christian tradition.

All this implies a historical process of vast proportions. If what we have at present by way of a theology of liberation, with all its limitations, can contribute to that process, and thereby open up the possibility of a new understanding of the faith, then it will have fulfilled its transitional assignment. Like any theology, this theology too is only the new consciousness, in communion with the church, that one Christian generation has of its faith in a given moment of history. And our own generation has only just begun to break with the prevailing system and discover "the other" of the world it still has to live in. We have just begun to discover the presence of the Lord at the very heart of the history of the Latin American peoples.

TOWARD A CHURCH OF THE PEOPLE

Involvement in the liberation process constitutes a profound and decisive spiritual experience. Deep within the concrete historical commitment, and deep within all the political implications this commitment must necessarily have for us, an authentic spiritual experience awaits. For, as I have been attempting to explain, the liberation process is the greenhouse, the warm, rich planter, of a theology that will open up altogether new perspectives.

We are not interested in finding new areas in which to apply old theological notions. We are confronted with having to find ways of living and reflecting on our faith in new socio-cultural categories. This will not have been the first time in the history of the Christian community that this has happened.

We are driven forward in our search by a special urgency—the urgency of speaking the word of the Lord in the word of our everyday life. For what we are concerned with here is a rereading of the gospel message from within the praxis of liberation. Here theological reflection functions as a medium between a new manner of living the faith and the communication of that faith. After all, if theology is a rereading of the gospel, then theology must be done in view of a proclamation of the gospel message.[31]

Ecclesial Experience of Filiation and Fellowship

To know that the Lord loves us, to accept the free gift of his love, is the deep source of the joy and gladness of a person who lives by the word of God. Evangelization is the communication of this joy. It is the communication of the good news of the love of God that has changed our life. It is a free, gratuitous proclamation, just as the love in which it originates is free and gratuitous. In the point of departure of the task of evangelization, then, there is always an experience of the Lord—a living experience of the Father's love, the love that makes us his daughters and sons, the love that transforms us, making us more fully human, more fully brothers and sisters to all.

To proclaim the gospel is to announce the mystery of filiation and fellowship—our status as children of God and brothers and sisters of one another, the "message which was a mystery hidden for generations and centuries and has now been revealed" in Christ (Col. 1:26).[32] Hence to proclaim the gospel is to summon persons together, summon them into *ek-klesia,* into church, the assembly of those called together by God.

Only in community can faith be lived in love. Only in community can faith be celebrated and deepened. Only in community can faith be lived in a life of fidelity to the Lord and solidarity with all men and women. To receive the word is to be converted to the Other in others. We live this word with them. Faith cannot be lived on the private plane of the "interior life." Faith is the very negation of retreat into oneself, of folding back upon oneself. Faith comes alive in the dynamism of the good news that reveals us as children of the Father and sisters and brothers of one another, and creates a community, a church, the visible sign to others of liberation in Christ.

This proclamation of the gospel, summoning us together into *ecclesia,* takes place from within an option of real and active solidarity with the interests and struggles of the poor, the exploited classes. The attempt to situate oneself in this locus means a profound breach with the manner of living, thinking, and communicating the faith in the church of today. It demands a conversion to another world, a new way of understanding the faith—and it leads to a reformulation of the gospel message.[33]

In this reformulation, what has come to be called the "political dimension of the gospel" presents itself in a new aspect. For now we perceive more clearly than before that this is not something tacked onto the gospel from without, under the questionable pressures of the times. It is an essential trait of that gospel itself. Now we frankly admit and accept the political dimension of the gospel, without subterfuge. Its precise scope remains to be seen—we must not run the risk of an oversimplified focus here. But a self-proclaimed apoliticism can now no longer mask evident reality, or becloud a viewpoint growing more and more into a burning conviction of our day: the gift of filiation is lived out in concrete history.

We accept this gift when we make ourselves brothers and sisters to others, for it is a gift not of word but of deed. "It is not those who say to me, 'Lord, Lord,' who will enter the kingdom of heaven, but the person who does the will of my Father in heaven" (Matt. 7:21). To battle injustice, spoliation, and exploitation, to commit oneself to the creation of a more humane society of sisters and brothers, is to live the Father's love and bear witness to it. The proclamation of a God who loves all men and women must take flesh in history, must become history. A proclamation of this love in a society scarred by profound inequality, injustice, and the exploitation of some by others and one social class by another will transform this emergent history into something challenging and conflictual. This is why we have said that the political dimension comes to light in the very dynamism of a word that seeks to be incarnate in history.

The exigencies of the gospel are incompatible with the social situation in which Latin America is living, with the ways in which human beings relate to one another, and with the structures in which these relationships occur. But it is not a matter of the denunciation and rejection of this or that individual instance of injustice. No, we are confronted with the need for a different social order. Only an appreciable degree of political maturity will enable us to get a real grasp of the political dimension of the gospel and keep us from reducing it to a system of social service, however sophisticated, or to a simple task of "human advocacy." Such maturity will likewise enable us to avoid reducing the task of evangelization to some form of political activity, which has laws and exigencies of its own.

The authentic proclamation of God's love, of a community of sisters and brothers, and of the radical equality of all human beings, to the exploited of Latin America will lead them to the perception that their situation is contrary to the gospel. It will help them become conscious of the profound injustice of this state of affairs.

The oppressed segments of our society will acquire a clear political awareness only in direct involvement in the popular struggles. But in the complex totality of the political process, which now must break with a social order of oppression and erect a classless society—a community of brothers and sisters—the ideological struggle has an important place. In Latin America, the traditional "Christian" factor is made to play a role within the dominant ideology, an ideology that cements and affirms a capitalistic society divided into classes at odds with each other. Conservative circles frequently appeal to "Christian" notions in order to justify a social order that serves only their interests and maintains only their privileges. This is one of the great lies of our Latin American society. It is for this reason that the communication of the gospel message, reread from within the world of the other, the world of the poor, the world of the oppressed, will help to unmask all attempts to ideologize the gospel and justify a situation contrary to its most elemental demands.

Liberative Evangelization

Are we confronted with a political reductionism of the gospel here? Yes, we are—in the case of those who utilize the gospel and place it at the service of the mighty. But no, we are not, in the case of those who start out from its gratuitous and liberating message in order precisely to denounce this utilization. Yes, this is evangelical reductionism for those who place the gospel and themselves in the hands of the great ones of this world, but not for those who identify with the poor Christ and go in search of solidarity with the dispossessed of Latin America.

Yes, this is reductionism, if we keep the gospel prisoner of an ideology in the service of the capitalist system; but not if we have been set free by the gospel ourselves and now strive in our turn to free it from that captivity. Yes, for those who seek to neutralize Christ's liberation by reducing it to a "religious" plane, where it has nothing directly to do with the concrete world of human beings, we are faced with reductionism; but not in the case of those who believe that Christ's salvation is so total and radical that nothing can escape it. For these latter, the gospel is liberating because it is the proclamation of total liberation in Christ, a liberation that includes a transformation of the concrete historical and political conditions that men and women live in. But this is grasped in all its depth only when one knows that this liberation leads this same history out beyond itself, to a fulness that transcends the scope of all human doing or telling.

A rereading of the gospel from a position of solidarity with the poor and the oppressed will enable us to denounce the use made of the gospel by the mighty in order to place it at the service of their own interests. But this, too, will be grasped in all its implications only if we are conscious of the ongoing creative and critical character of the gospel's liberating message. For the gospel message is a message that can never be identified with any concrete social formula, however just that formula may seem to us at the moment. The word of the Lord is a challenge to its every historical incarnation and places that incarnation in the broad perspective of the radical and total liberation of Christ, the Lord of history.

A backsliding into ideology, to justify a determinate social situation, will be inevitable, unless we live the gospel as the word of a Father who loves us freely and gratuitously, loves us with a love that renews the face of the earth, and constantly calls us to a new life in his Son.

But the persons to whom the gospel is proclaimed are not abstract, apolitical beings: they are members of a society disfigured by injustice and by the exploitation of some human beings by others. Consequently the Christian community—to which these persons in one way or another largely belong—is not an ahistorical reality either. Its past and its present are intimately bound up with the history of the Latin American people. Apart from a historical approach, there is no way we can understand what it must be to proclaim the gospel today to a people to whom it has already been proclaimed, a people for whom it already forms part of life in one way or another.[34] At the same time, apart from a realistic appraisal of the situation of a church by and large bound up with the prevailing social order in Latin America, there is no way we can perceive the implications of the liberating character of this evangelization.

This historical and political conditioning must be analyzed in detail, in order to bring the proclamation of the message in the Latin American situation, and the experience of faith in political action, into sharper focus. We need a firmer grasp of the precise relationship between traditional theology and an attempt to understand the faith from within the praxis of liberation. This is surely the way for us to avoid idealistic and inappropriately theoretical positions of the question, which fail to really bite into reality.

The gospel is already incarnate in Latin American history, yesterday and today, and this incarnation sets up the parameters and possibilities of a new proclamation of the gospel. It permits us to foresee the conflicts that this new proclamation must necessarily arouse. The fate of Henrique Pereira Neto, Néstor Paz, and Héctor Gallego—to mention but three better known victims of these conflicts—is tangible proof of what we shall have to face. Others yet today are tortured and calumniated, in the name of "Western Christian civilization." They and many others like them only sought to witness to their faith along paths they themselves had to pioneer, paths the great ones of Latin America found unacceptable, the social order and paths that did not lead to a bolstering of the culture of oppression in which we in Latin America live today. All dissent is promptly punished by those in power, as likely as not to the accompaniment of fervent protestations of Christian piety.

Here we have put a finger on what we were speaking of at the beginning of this article: that involvement in the liberation process marks the dividing line between two experiences—two eras, two worlds, two languages.

Exploited Classes and the People of God

To proclaim the gospel from a situation of identification with the poor is to convene a church in solidarity with the popular masses of Latin America, in solidarity with their aspirations, with their struggles to have a place in their own history. It is a summons to the church to make a contribution, within the confines of its proper task—the proclamation of the gospel—to the abolition of a society built by and for the few, and to the construction of a different, more just, and more humane social order for all.

This leads us to profound breaches and reorientations in today's church. But these breaches and reorientations will bear no fruit if they express only one's own personal anxiety, identity crisis, emotional reactions, and impatience—however legitimate any of these personal reactions may be in themselves. This will only provoke defensive attitudes, blind authoritarian measures, and acts of fear and insecurity, and an escalating spiral of intraecclesial strife will be underway. These breaches and reorientations must be radical—that is, they must go to the root of the problem. In this case the root lies outside the strictly ecclesiastical domain. It lies in the way and manner of being a human being and a Christian in the present reality of Latin America. Today this way and manner will be found in identification with the oppressed classes.

Such breaches and reorientations presuppose new experiments in the task of evangelization, in the task of calling people together *in ecclesiam*.[35] We shall live new ways of being present in the world of the people, ways that will transcend all institutional rigidity. We shall be able to hear a voice different from the one we are accustomed to hearing in the church. We shall be able to make a critical appraisal of the social and cultural categories that imprison our manner of living and proclaiming the gospel, categories that make that gospel sound foreign in the world of the dominated peoples, marginalized ethnic groups, and exploited classes, and even contrary to their deep longings for liberation.[36] For these breaches and reorientations presuppose an authentic search for the Lord in an encounter with the poor, together with a lucid explanation of the meaning of this spiritual experience.

And so we shall have to create Christian communities in which the private proprietors of the goods of this world are no longer the owners of the gospel too. "Rebel communities," they were called, with anticipatory dismay, a few years ago.[37] And today we may add that they will be communities in which the dispossessed will be able to carry out a social appropriation of the gospel. They will be groups that prophetically proclaim a church entirely at the service—at the ever creative and critical service, because that service will be radicated in the gospel—of men and women battling to be human beings, and battling in a way difficult to understand for a world in which, nevertheless, the word of God has been, and continues to be, lived, reflected upon, and proclaimed.

Only by striking root in the marginalized and exploited segments of society —or rather, only by rising up out of these segments, out of their yearnings, interests, struggles, and cultural categories—will a people of God be forged that will be a church of the people, a church that will make the gospel message heard by *all* human beings, a church that will be a sign of the liberation wrought by the Lord of history.

But none of this would mean anything to us, and we should not have the faintest notion of what the future Christian community will be like, were it not for the fact that a rough draft—unpretentious and tentative—of this Christian community of tomorrow is already spread out before our eyes, all over Latin America. Here and there we already have a blueprint for the future.

These Christian communities spring up from ever growing involvement with the Latin American liberation process. Workers, professional persons, farmhands, bishops, students, priests have all begun to "get involved." It is only a beginning, and it calls for many a clarification and skimming off of excesses, for it is a call to take a free, critical position vis-à-vis any political process that oversimplifies reality, any political outlook that fails to take into account all the dimensions of a human being. It is a challenge to allow the voice of the popular Christian sectors to grow in volume, too, and express itself in its own terms. It will be a difficult commitment. It will have to traverse deserts. It will have to face the attacks of Christians and non-Christians attached to the old order of things. But it will be real, genuine commitment, and it is one that is already beginning to make its contribution to the revolutionary option, to an understanding of the faith, and to a proclamation of the gospel.

This is no time for euphoria. The system has proved its tenacity, and its capacity for either suppressing or commandeering attempts at renewal. Christian circles themselves have already thrown up a wall of resistance, which will have to be surmounted before the unsettling message of evangelical liberation can reach those inside.

In Latin America today, the spirituality of the exile is every bit as important as the Easter experience of the exodus. The joy of resurrection calls for many a death on a cross. But the experience amassed by the popular movements, in their struggles, in their determination to go out and build a new, different society, already constitute full authorization to proceed with the watch and the action. And there is more: involvement in this movement is blazing a trail for renewed fidelity to the Lord of history.

There is a multiplying apace of the number of Christians who understand that the free gift of filiation is received only as we make sisters and brothers of other human beings, only as we build a community of brothers and sisters in the concrete historical and political conditions of Latin America, only as we work from within the world of the other, the poor person, the exploited class.

Christian hope springs eternal. The situation we are living in Latin America today is perhaps enabling us to experience and to understand in a new way what St. Paul meant when he spoke of "hoping against hope" (Rom. 4:18, NAB).

NOTES

1. A good case in point would be that of the Christian Democrats in Chile.
2. The most typical example is in Chile, where the Christian Democrats unified scattered Christian political forces and held them together until 1969 or 1970. But the same thing occurred in certain other Latin American countries as well.
3. See the document of the bishops of the Northeast of Brazil, "He escuchado los clamores de mi pueblo," in *Brasil, ¿milagro o engaño?* (Lima: CEP, 1973).
4. See Johannes B. Metz, *Theology of the World* (New York: Herder, 1969); idem, "Politische Theologie in der Diskussion," in *Diskussion zur Politische Theologie* (Mainz and Munich: Kaiser-Grünnewald, 1970). See also M. Xhaufflaire, *La "Théologie politique"* (Paris: Cerf, 1972).
5. See Metz, *Theology of the World,* chap. 5, "The Church and the World in the Light of a 'Political Theology.' "
6. Ibid., p. 110.
7. Ibid., p. 112.
8. See G. Bauer, *Toward a Theology of Development: An Annotated Bibliography* (Geneva: SODEPAX, 1970).
9. See my critique of this approach in *A Theology of Liberation* (Maryknoll, N.Y.: Orbis, 1973), pp. 25–27.
10. See René Laurentin, *Développement et salut* (Paris: du Seuil, 1969). In English see *Liberation, Development and Salvation* (Maryknoll, N.Y.: Orbis Books, 1972). Laurentin recognizes the historical conditioning of the theology of development as it evolved.
11. See the collection of studies by E. Feil and R. Weth, eds., *Diskussion zur Theologie der Revolution* (Mainz and Munich: Kaiser-Grünnewald, 1969).
12. Richard Shaull, "Point de vue théologique sur la révolution," in *L'éthique sociale chrétienne dans un monde en transformation,* vol. 1 (Geneva, 1969); in English see *The Church amid Revolution,* ed. Harvey Cox (New York: Association Press, 1967). Shaull is the originator, and really the best representative, of the theology of revolution; his intuitions certainly surpass what has since been done under this heading. See also José Comblin's broad approach in his *Théologie de la révolution* (Paris: Presses Universitaires, 1970).
13. See the documents by Latin American Christian communities in *Signos de liberación* (Lima: CEP, 1973). For a treatment of this whole matter, see Ronaldo Muñoz, *Nueva conciencia de la Iglesia en América Latina* (Santiago de Chile: Nueva Universidad, 1973; Salamanca: Sígueme, 1974).

14. See Eric J. Hobsbawm's classic work *The Age of Revolution, 1789–1848* (Cleveland: World, 1962).

15. The industrial revolution received its original thrust from the creativity of artisans. Then, very shortly, the rise of the sciences provided additional dynamism.

16. See Kant on the Enlightenment in his "Ideen zur Philosophie der Geschichte," *Jenaische Literaturzeitung,* 1785, and Hegel's in his *The Philosophy of History* (New York: Dover, 1956). See also the classic work of Ernst Cassirer, *The Philosophy of Enlightenment* (Princeton University Press, 1951), as well as the study by W. Oelmüller, *Die unbefriedigte Aufklärung* (Frankfurt, 1969). For a theological treatment see J. B. Metz, Jürgen Moltmann, and W. Oelmüller, *Kirche im Prozess der Aufklärung* (Mainz and Munich: Kaiser-Grünnewald, 1970).

17. On the current concrete political options available to the liberation process in Latin America, see my *Theology of Liberation,* chaps. 6, 7.

18. See R. Schnackenburg, *L'existence chrétienne selon le Nouveau Testament,* vol. 1 (Paris, 1971), p. 35.

19. Evangelical poverty is treated more extensively in my *Theology of Liberation,* chap. 13, "Poverty: Solidarity and Protest."

20. For a survey of these questions and the responses offered by contemporary theology, see the study by Claude Geffré, *The New Age in Theology* (New York: Paulist, 1974). See also H. Bouillard, "Exégèse, herméneutique et théologie: Problèmes de méthode," in *Exégèse et herméneutique* (Paris, 1971); J. P. Jossua, "Ensemblement du discours chrétien," *Christus,* June 1973, pp. 345–54; and Edward Schillebeeckx, *The Understanding of Faith: Interpretation and Criticism* (New York: Seabury, 1974).

21. See J. Guichard's effort to place these questions in relief in "Foi chrétienne et théorie de la connaissance," *Lumière et Vie,* June–Aug. 1973, pp. 61–84.

22. Here we should perhaps reexamine Duns Scotus's work on praxis, and on theology as a practical science. See also the work of Frans van den Oudenrijn, *Kritische Theologie als Kritik der Theologie* (Mainz and Munich: Kaiser-Grünnewald, 1972).

23. Hence the theologian must be personally involved in the liberation process. Such involvement is necessary not only for concrete results, but for genuinely scientific work as well.

24. See my *Hacia una teologia de la liberación* (Montevideo: Ed. Centro de Documentación MIEC-JECI, 1969), and "Notes on Theology of Liberation," *In Search of a Theology of Development* (Lausanne: SODEPAX, 1970). See also E. Pironio, *La Iglesia, pueblo de Dios* (Bogotá, 1970); idem, *La Iglesia que nace entre nosotros* (Bogotá, 1970); Hugo Assmann, *Opresión-Liberación: Desafío a los cristianos* (Montevideo: Tierra Nueva, 1971); J. C. Scannone, "La teología de la liberación," *Revista del Centro de Investigaciones y Acción Social,* no. 221 (Buenos Aires, April 1973); L. Gera, "Teología de la liberación," *Perspectivas para el Diálogo,* no. 72 (Montevideo, May 1973); Julio de Santa Ana, "Introduction to Theological Reflection on Domination and Dependence" (Geneva: World Council of Churches, 1974); Pablo Richard, *Reflexión teológica desde la lucha del pueblo* (Santiago de Chile: ISAL, 1973); Ronaldo Muñoz, *Nueva conciencia de la Iglesia en América Latina* (Santiago de Chile, 1973); and Raúl Vidales, "Sacramentos y liberación," *Servir* 10/49, pp. 67–76.

25. See my *La pastoral de la Iglesia en América Latina: Análisis teológico* (Montevideo: Ed. Centro de Documentación MIEC-JECI, 1968), and *Notes on a Theology of Liberation* (Lausanne: SODEPAX, 1970). That this is the proper way to do theology was one of the earliest insights of liberation theology.

26. See Juan Luis Segundo, "Desarrollo y subdesarrollo: polos teológicos, *Perspectivas de Diálogo,* 43 (May 1970) 76–80.

27. Second General Conference of Latin American Bishops (Medellín), "Justice," 3 (CELAM-LAB translation, p. 58).

28. There is currently a great deal of effort being exerted to domesticate—tame, commandeer —the theology of liberation, for example by using its terminology but drained of any meaning, or by speaking of "pluralism" in such a way as simply to imply refusal to commit oneself.

29. See, for instance, James H. Cone, *A Black Theology of Liberation* (Philadelphia: Lippincott, 1970); and the promising work by Virgil Elizondo in a particularly interesting area for the Latin American theology of liberation, *Christianity and Culture* (Huntington, Ind. Sunday Visitor, 1975), and *Galilean Journey: The Mexican-American Promise* (Maryknoll, N.Y.: Orbis Books, 1983).

30. It is clear, for example, that the native peoples and cultures of Latin America are not yet adequately represented in our efforts of theological reflection.

31. Yves M.-J. Congar is a theologian with a deep sense of the ecclesial and the pastoral. He

has often stressed this link between theology and proclamation—e.g., in his *Situations et tâches de la théologie* (Paris: du Cerf, 1967).

32. "If God is the Father, the disciples are his children. Being a child is *the* characteristic of the kingly rule" (Joachim Jeremias, *New Testament Theology* [New York: Scribner's, 1971], pp. 180–81).

33. A biblical hermeneutics will be different depending on whether one considers the God of the Bible as the Utterly Other, having nothing in common with the universe in which the human being is so profoundly integrated, or simply as the Other "whose ways are not our ways" (cf. Isa. 55:8), nor whose thoughts are our thoughts, but whose children we are, "of whose lineage we are (cf. Acts 17:28)," Cazelles, *Ecriture, Parole, et Esprit* (Paris, 1970), p. 76.

34. See, for example, Enrique Dussel's *Historia de la Iglesia en América Latina* (Barcelona: Nova Terra, 1972).

35. See the perceptive and courageous observations of Karl Rahner on how we might conceive of the church of the future, in his *The Shape of the Church to Come* (New York: Seabury, 1974). See also the incisive, provocative report of an experiment, by Jorge Alvarez Calderón, *Así comenzamos: Una experiencia de evangelización liberadora* (Lima: CEP, 1973).

36. Unless the basic Christian communities manage to maintain this course, they will run the risk of becoming just one more form of escape from concrete historical conflict.

37. See Gonzalo Arroyo, "Rebeldía cristiana y compromiso comunitario," *Mensaje* 167 (1968): 78–83. This article provided the initial thrust to many experiments and reflections in Latin America.

4

The Historical Power
of the Poor

There is nothing less exact, or more laden with meaning, than a date on a calendar. And this is well, for meaning is motivating, whereas precision is not.

The year 1978, then, invites us to draw up a balance sheet. The ledger of the last ten years is closed, awaiting an audit.

Years of hope these surely were. Not euphoria, but hope. Hard, painful hope. Hope amid hardship. Hope amid struggles and failures.

It has been nearly ten years since the first *Signos* ("signs") appeared: *Signos de renovación* ("signs of renewal"), a collection of documents dated between 1966 and 1968. Here are "signs" indeed, signs of life, signs of a Christian life on the way to renewal, for it was then we started down the rocky road of the "defense of the rights of the poor."[1]

Then, in 1973, we published a second *Signos*, a volume of ardent testimonial to the will for liberation. Here was determination charged with hope—a "hope against all hope,"[2] as St. Paul described the hope of Abraham when he believed God's promise and left the land of Ur for an unknown "land of promise." Here again were "signs"—signposts along the way we had now begun to take, which we knew would be hard. They were not signs of a shallow optimism, which some persons today, whether out of ignorance or out of levity, reproach us for in those years.

The Latin American people—this poor, exploited, believing people—has taken a great stride forward in these past ten years. The price has been error, impasse, and martyrdom. But this is ever the case when history moves forward. And the trophy has been triumph, and the apprenticeship of the popular masses in the craft of their own liberation. It has been a decade of precious experience, during which the masses have promoted their own

The original Spanish text was first published as the Introduction to *Signos de lucha y esperanza: Testimonios de la Iglesia en América Latina 1973–1978* (Lima: CEP, 1978).

march forward themselves, their own historical alternative. Here "signs of struggle and hope" spring up indeed, challenging the pessimism and depressing prognoses of those whose description of the situation and its future has its point of departure (and, alas, of arrival) in analyses churned out in political and ecclesiastical ivory towers. But the true pulse of history can be taken only by listening to the heart of the lowly, so often anonymous, Latin Americans. Here is where we can seize both the old and the new—both what lingers on in the panicky spasms of the oppressor, and what is fresh and irreversible: the forward momentum of the oppressed of Latin America.

Yes, here are "signs of struggle and hope," testifying in word and work to the mighty deed of all who fight and die for liberation, for love of their brother and sister, the mighty deed of all who rediscover the Lord alive in the poor and the oppressed. Here is the witness of those who proclaim Christ risen and alive in the very midst of the death that seems dominator. Here are testimonials of living subversively the gladness of Easter right at the heart of a people's movement crushed and repressed. For that groundswell refuses annihilation. It continuously regenerates its leadership and uncannily lands on its feet. An intellectual elite may sway in the wind. But we have documentary evidence that it is and ever shall be the poor who are the makers of history, and we have it right in these pages.

The deeper meaning of what is presently occurring in Latin America is that, in spite of all vicissitudes, and however dramatic their setbacks, the ones hitherto "absent from history" are beginning to be present to it. The poor now come front and center in Latin American church and society. The result is fear and hostility for oppressors, but high hopes for the disinherited of the earth. This is the true essence of the Latin American process. This, and not the resurgence, or refinement, of oppression in some of the countries of our part of the world, is the irreversible axis of that process.

What we see here is a process of popular commitment, which calls forth the best the Latin American church has to offer in the way of imagination, creativity, and prophecy. The life and task of that church are undergoing redefinition, in our day, from a point of departure in the midst of the poor and in function of the poor—the poor with all their burden of misery and exploitation, but with their spirit of combat and faith, too. The road will be long, and we have only just started down it. Persecution, torture, and death have clarified its trajectory, as have also our struggles, experiences, and hopes. We see our way now. And when you can see your way, you have already taken the first step toward your goal.

Rarely has anything like the energy, life, and creativity of these years been seen before in Latin America, whether we consider praxis, or our reflection on that praxis. After all, rarely have we faced up to the merchants of fear and death so boldly, or so determinately cast sterile prudence to the winds.

The cowardly Cassandras of revisionism and historical impasse will have to hold their tongues now. They are being given the lie today—not in wordy debate, but in the massive and mighty deeds of the people. Let them, then, now retire to their ivory towers—the battlefield of their choice—once more to wrestle with their old, worn, compromise "solutions," and relabel them "viable projects for Latin America." And let them ready themselves to give the account that will be demanded of them for their lack of hope and prophecy.

Again, we know the road will be a long one, and doubtless beset with new barricades and blind alleys. But the pavement is solid and our step confident. There is nothing euphoric about that step. It is cautious. But it is bold and daring, too.

Then let us proceed to the balance sheet. What have these ten years been for us?

We make no attempt at an aseptic—and elusive!—"objectivity." We shall not be filling the columns of our ledger with cold analysis. What we enter there will be facts, yes, but facts with which we are passionately involved. For we shall be reflecting all the while—seeking the face of Christ in the poor and oppressed along the highways and byways of Latin America.

DYING BEFORE THEIR TIME

Bartolomé de Las Casas and a number of other remarkable figures of the sixteenth century in Latin America constitute an exception to the bloody beginnings of the path of murder and death that is the saga of colonial domination in Latin America. Their descriptions of the encounter of the poor one, the Amerindian, with the dominator, the conquistador, are anything but a portrait of the idyllic embrace that we are often pressured to accept today. Those noble persons were of the culture, nationality, and ethnic makeup of the oppressors; but their faith experience was different. Prophetically they denounced the brutal exploitation of the hapless Indian masses and their "death before their time."

From the very beginning, then, it was "death too soon" for the Indians. Their right to life was always cut off in midcourse. And, be it noted, this was an essential component in the social order then being built at their expense. Today that same basic element of Latin American colonialism continues its ravages, assaulting what Pedro de Córdoba, another noble spirit of those times, called "the life and temporal increase" of the poor. With great difficulty, the Indians were converted to Christ. But down across the centuries, out of the mouths of only a few protesting Christians resounded a protest to their murder, to the denial of their elemental right to life. Oppression ever ancient and ever new! It wears new guises today. But still it persecutes to the dust the ones who dare to raise their hand against it.

Wanted: A Therapy for Historical Amnesia

This story of captivity and deliverance—which must be retold, now, from the viewpoint of the oppressed—is the constant undercurrent of our contemporary praxis in Latin America. These years have given us many occasions to speak of the rise of a new political consciousness among Latin American peoples. But this new awareness is nothing other than our new perception of the concrete situation in which we live—the world of death created by the conquistadors. Of course, we gained our perception all the more rapidly as the prevailing system became the more oppressive and repressive—until this new popular awareness could burst forth as a social force in the popular liberation struggles of the 1960s. Latin American social situations differ from land to land, however, and the people's struggle reflects their variety. The dominant sectors take the occasion of this variety to allege that liberation struggles are the work of minority factions—little groups of radicals, students, and a few priests out of touch with the people—thus altogether ignoring the historical significance of these struggles. They are abetted in certain ecclesiastical circles by individuals and groups who repeat the rightist "party line."

But reality is complex. This simplification is either contrived or extremely naive. The dominators are clearly seeking to divest these events of their meaning and importance. Perhaps too they hope to be able to shore up some of the crumbling credibility of their favorite description of popular liberation struggles as "radical movements." But they distort the facts, and this distortion blinds them to what is occurring in the deep undercurrents of history's flowing waters. They are unable to identify the precise points of breach and continuity that shape that history. And the upshot is that they fail to grasp what is really at stake here today.

When all our failures and disillusionment are placed in one scale and our advances and victories in the other , what finally weighs in the balance is what we might call a certain realism of judgment. But it is a realism that eludes the privileged members of the present social order, for it disturbs them.

Another expression of our Latin American people's new political awareness is their better grasp of the socio-economic realities of their continent. A great help here has been what is called the "theory of dependency" in economics and sociology, by which relationships of domination are basically reduced to class confrontation. Despite its shortcomings and gaps, this analysis has by and large been a boon. It is an attempt to rethink our distinctive historical process in categories peculiar to that process. It received its impetus from the liberation movements of the 1960s and contributed to the crystalization of those movements. It helped the popular class to reject the politics of compromise and conformism during that decade.

However, the new condition of the popular movement, writhing now under a redoubled oppression in the presence of the current quantum leap in the internationalization of capitalism, requires new approaches. Now both our praxis and our theory will take a new turn. I shall say something about this in the subsection entitled "A New Form of Domination," below.

The new popular movement is better orientated, and better organized, than it ever was before. It has new instruments of analysis at its disposal, and its intent is now clearly and specifically anticapitalist, albeit in varying degrees of precision of design. As is evident to the eyes of all, the birth of this movement, in its radical and moderate expressions alike, was most savagely repressed. What a heavy blow we were dealt in the 1960s in Brazil, Guatemala, Colombia, Peru, and Bolivia. In the 1970s, with unheard-of refinements of cruelty and violence, it assaulted Chile—where a socialist program was finally underway—Uruguay, and Argentina.

With the armed forces, all political resources, and the public media firmly in their grasp, dominators have sought to dismantle all organized protest against the economic exploitation that lies at the base of the system from which they reap their profit of lordship. They have tried to "take the wind out of the sails" of any and all movements daring to represent the interests of the oppressed. And they have tried to isolate these efforts, together with the groups of persons engaged in them, from contact with the masses of the poor, among whom these movements had been begun with such enormous difficulty. But they had been begun, and the masses were awakening to a new political awareness. As far as the dominant groups were concerned, this development had to be crushed, nipped in the bud. Of course at the same time they were very much concerned to demonstrate that "nothing had happened" in Latin America; that these occurrences were the deed of some lunatic fringe, unaccountably at odds with "our Western Christian civilization."

Those who today uncritically accept and repeat on cue—particularly in ecclesiastical circles—the interpretation given out by the dominant classes might do well simply to ask themselves whether the huge military, political, and ideological apparatus mounted in those years to eliminate "little groups of crazies" was not after all somewhat out of proportion to the alleged threat. "You don't get a freakish hop on a smooth infield."

Of course, there was nothing smooth about the infield at all. We had begun to perceive the "social disparity," as the specialists like to say, in our social structure—the life disparity, if they will permit us—and never again would the poor hesitate to defend their rights. Nor would blows and repression any longer deter them from their quest for a socialist way, their search for a genuine democracy.

All these experiences in the life of the popular masses, in the 1960s as today, have been the hotbed of intense life, in Christian communities of a popular makeup and involvement. The attempt to reflect on these experiences in the light of faith is what we call the theology of liberation. For it is life experience that both affords this theology its strength and assigns it its limits. The theology of liberation is radicated in this historical, popular process. It has its roots in the faith as lived in this social experience—the experience of following Jesus in the defense of the rights of the poor, in the proclamation of the gospel in the midst of the struggle for liberation. This is this theology's turf and terrain, and so of course it will attend much more to what is transpiring on this terrain than to the analyses and critiques of the world of academic theology, however worthy these analyses and critiques may be in themselves.

The adversaries of a theology that so doggedly stresses the outlook of the poor, and the liberation of the poor, will naturally be most concerned to draw attention away from that which nurtures the substratum that gives life to this theology. Its adversaries, falsifying reality, say that its seedbed is a desert. They deny that it draws its sustenance from the radicalism of a faith lived deep in the effort of the masses to extricate themselves from the throes of a system that so marginalizes and despoils them. Our adversaries think that by thus ignoring the spring and source of this theology in a living faith—a faith rooted in popular experience—they can disqualify it as theology. They cannot admit that what the poor of Latin America have begun to do can be theology. Then too, of course, the dominant ideology feels less threatened by theological alternatives that do *not* have their roots sunk in the challenges of social conflict.

The defenders of the existing social system seek to disqualify our effort of reflection by claiming that its protagonists are not a people awakening to a new awareness, but a little group of partisans isolated from that people. This is what they are saying, really, when they attempt to deny a connection between the struggles of today and yesterday—when they try to cut off a people's memories, as they have succeeded in doing in some countries, and so keep them from perceiving what the battles they are waging owe to the battles of a few years back.

Defenders of the present social order are even enjoying a certain success in some Christian circles—circles that for one reason or another have not kept terribly close to the popular struggles of more than a decade now, and who only today are rediscovering the role of the poor and lowly of Latin America in their self-liberation. Surely this rediscovery is under way, and it is daring and creative. But it runs the risk of falling into the trap of the dominator and contributing in some way to the "historical amnesia" with which the latter seeks to infest the people. For this memory of past battles is not a matter of reassuring nostalgia and pleasant reveries. It is a subversive memory, and it lends force and sustenance to our positions, refuses to compromise or equivocate, learns from failures, and knows (by experience) that it has the capability of overcoming every obstacle, even repression itself.

The Optimism of Action

The euphoria that is supposed to have held sway in Latin America in the years around 1968 is but another facet of this same effort to disqualify everything new that came to light at that time. It is normal for hopes to rise when something exciting happens. Illusions are possible. And the new breadth, and radical depth, of the popular struggles of the late 1960s were certainly a new happening. But to assert that anyone entertained the illusion that revolution and the new society were just around the corner is to make a gratuitous travesty of historical reality.

What was happening during those years—in Brazil, Bolivia, Peru, Argentina, Mexico, and even Chile, along with the continuing tragedy of Paraguay, Nicaragua, and other countries—was scarcely calculated to encourage any light-minded illusions. Hope, yes—an uneasy one but still hope. It is not difficult to see why certain political events of the early 1970s, and of course the current initiated by the Latin American bishops' meeting in Medellín, provoked a certain optimism in Latin America. But I want to make it clear that this attitude was not present in the 1960s.

What the conservative elements are attempting to do here, by harping on the euphoria in the late 1960s, is retrospectively and retroactively to pull the rug out from under all the new undertakings initiated then. They are trying to render the involvement of Christians in the liberation process, and the power and prophecy of Medellín, devoid of meaning and importance. But we remember the power and the propheticism. And we long for it again.

Some, today, owing to a faulty grasp of what was at stake in those years, or understandably shaken by the new, refined forms of repression under which we agonize in Latin America today, unreflectingly repeat, without any attempt to sort out the reasons one might have for making such assertions, certain blithe comments being bruited abroad by groups with a special concern to falsify and distort a set of facts that disturbs their complacency.

Romantic illusions? No, rather a clear awareness that something new was afoot, something no repression could ever again quell or crush: a people's will to self-affirmation and to life. José Carlos Mariátegui, assailing the "idealistic optimism" of José Vasconcelos, said: "Pessimism comes from reality" (because reality can be tragic); "optimism comes from action" (because action can change reality). For indeed what is so sorely needed here is not a condemnation of reality, but a conviction that that reality can and must be transformed by the action of the people.

We affirm a utopia on the way to becoming a historical reality—through difficulties and hard struggles, to be sure, and with an open-eyed awareness of the present situation. Only in a concern to transform the present situation shall we ever be able to acquire an authentically realistic view of that situation. This "utopianism" clashes with the "realism" of the oppressor, who is incapable of appreciating the kind of historical rationality that springs from the power of the poor. In the final analysis, there is nothing more revolutionary, nothing more charged with liberative utopianism, than the ancient, deep-seated oppression suffered by the poor of Latin American.

Curiously—or perhaps very logically—the same persons who savored characterizing the mood of ten years ago as illusion-filled and euphoric are the ones giving us a pessimistic and plaintive description of the Latin American situation today. Repression, national security, and fascism, they assure us, have an unbreakable stranglehold on the popular movement. A whole continent, we hear, has suddenly been taken captive. We are told that we are faced with a new situation, one radically different from any we in Latin America have ever known. But our interlocuters and their "realism" are doubly in error. Actually, neither were things ever that good, nor are they that bad now! And both errors converge in a single result: mass confusion.

Such misconceptions only hinder the development of the revolutionary energies of the popular classes. In particular, they constitute an obstacle to the exercise of a liberating faith on the part of the Christian communities based in those popular classes. It is for this reason—because we have a concern for the development of popular revolutionary energies, and not out of an aseptic interest in historical accuracy—that it is incumbent upon us to rip off the mask of these pseudo-realistic interpretations and see what lurks behind them.

Contrary to what one so often hears, especially outside Latin America, the popular movement is currently enjoying a period of strength, not of weakness. Silent strength, if you will. But real strength. Yes, this is a moment of great difficulty and hardship. But it is a moment of unprecedented vitality and vigor, as well; a period of repression, but also of creativity, for the masses. We are living through a vital moment of self-criticism regarding our light-minded errors of the past. But even more, we are living through a vital moment of unreserved criticism of the system that exploits, marginalizes, and strangles the poor.

The masses of the people have suffered cruel blows, but they have also learned important lessons. The popular movement is aware of its retreats, of the ambiguity of some of the paths it has taken, and of the vagueness of some of its social stances. In these vagaries it is no different from any other historical process. But it is also firmly determined and full of hope. It knows when to be silent. It has a sense of political realism. The exploited masses have demonstrated their capacity for resistance, and that capacity is most disconcerting to dominators. It even surprises revolutionary groups, which until recently were carrying forward certain liberation projects and today are undergoing such brutal repression.

Recent social and political occurrences—doubtless still less than clear as to their nature and import—in countries whose population, mostly Indian and *mestizo,* living in dire poverty and harsh social captivity, and anything but vulnerable to facile illusions, have demonstrated that, beneath a surface overgrown with repression and setbacks, the popular movement has continued to press forward. Nicaragua, Peru, Bolivia, and Ecuador are the most obvious examples.

Those who had begun to convince themselves that the fires of popular protest against social repression had been extinguished are beginning to grow uneasy. What looked like a defeat will be shown to have been but one episode in a long struggle. In this struggle there will be other setbacks; but there will be new, more decisive advances, as well. For this process of popular self-liberation is deeply, securely irreversible. Historical processes can be seen in proper perspective, Gramsci insisted, only if we study sufficiently long segments of time. Only thus shall we avoid the pitfall of overestimating the importance of phenomena that are almost purely situational and thereby be able to project the true axis of the movements in question. The die of history has not yet been thrown, but the cup is surely rattling.

It is in this complex and stimulating setting that we witness the rise of the grassroots Christian communities. Here the word of the Lord is nurtured in a soil that is rich and creative, for here that word enters present history. And by the very fact of entering present history it defies it—prevents it from closing in upon itself. For the word charges it with futurity. It invests the present with a future fulness of love, a fulness prefigured and anticipated today in our love for our sister and brother in the here and now, in circumstances that are difficult and sometimes ambiguous. In these circumstances it is not easy to make decisions and then move ahead with the options we have made. But something deeply evangelical is in the making, something new, as the love of Christ is always new.

A New Form of Domination

As I have been insisting so strongly, the situation of captivity in which the peoples of Latin America find themselves today has its roots in history long gone by. This situation of ours is an ongoing one. I likewise emphasize the maturation, despite appearances, of the popular movement. But I am by no means denying that new forms of oppression exist in our region of the world today. I appreciate that our polemical tack may have given a wrong impression.

My purpose in taking this approach has been to recall the deep-rooted character of this exploitive situation and to point out that this is the reason why the popular classes raised the banner of liberation some years ago, not because they thought their deliverance was at hand. They called for liberation because they had become conscious of oppression. This may seem evident, but it apparently bears repeating today.

However, important and significant changes have taken place in the interim. To ignore them would be to become mired in the past. We would be condemning ourselves to historical sterility and ineffectiveness. In the light of what has been said before, we are now in a position to make a more correct evaluation of the new forms of oppression in Latin America. Now what is new in them will disconcert us no longer. Our experience will come to our aid, and we shall be able to confront "new" forms of oppression without committing the errors of the past.

The qualitative difference in this new state of affairs will be better perceived if we view these changes as the response made by the prevailing system not only to its own internal contradictions but to the popular movements of years past as well. Indeed, these movements flooded the dominant classes with the fear that they might lose their privileges, perhaps for the first time in the history of our nations. And fear never creates; it petrifies.

Internationalization of Capitalism. International capitalism has passed through various stages of development over the past several decades. Each stage has had a different meaning for the people of Latin America.

The aftermath of World War II witnessed a consistently high rate of growth in the capitalist economies. This expansive thrust even led a number of economists and politicians to envision the possibility of transcending the economic crises so characteristic of capitalism.

This period of continuous growth of capitalism produced the remarkable phenomenon of the transnational industrial conglomerates. In search of ever greater profit, companies in industrially developed countries now engineered a groundswell of productive capital to Europe and the Third World. First they transferred manufacturing facilities from the United States to the European Common Market. Then, on a more restricted scale, the United States, Europe, and Japan set up plants in underdeveloped countries that could offer suitable economic advantages—especially, as far as Latin America was concerned, in Mexico, Brazil, and Argentina. The majority of the countries of the Third World, however, representing the lowest step on the now complete international capitalist staircase, saw no substantial changes in the traditional form of their participation in the international order. The accelerating pace of industrialization took no root there, and these countries, making up the bulk of the Third World, were found useful only for high production at low wages through the exploitation of the labor force. The rare instances of "export platforms," such as Singapore and Hong Kong, do not alter the general situation in this respect.

During these years of the "big boom," of international capitalism, the proliferation of the transnationals gave rise to an ever more important trade network among them, but of such a nature that the term "trade" is used in a very attenuated sense: it should imply a minimum of autonomy on the part of the contractual parties. In fact, however, the assigned cost and market value of a product floated free of its real cost and value, and world capital became extremely liquid. Now the methods of "decapitalizing" the poor countries became even more sophisticated, and their effectiveness in exploiting labor and producing hunger was greatly improved.

At the same time, as part and parcel of this same process, financial resources themselves came to be concentrated in ever fewer and fewer capitalist enterprises, to the accompaniment of a diversification of the areas serving as intermediaries in the decapitalization of poor countries.

Next, technological capabilities were concentrated in the United States, the emergence of economies such as those of Japan or Germany notwithstanding. This concentration of technological power, and its appropriation by a small group of countries, was owing in no small measure to the development of the arms industry to which these economies are devoted. Thus the power to master nature through technology was cruelly achieved by the development of the power to destroy humanity.

Finally, the control by the United States of a huge proportion of the world's food surplus completed the hexagon of concentration of economic, financial, military, technological, commercial, and alimentary power in a small clutch of countries, headed by the United States.

This process of growth and restructuring within the capitalist economic order has scarcely signaled progress for the nations of Latin America, especially where the masses of the people are concerned. The distance between the poor countries and the rich ones in our capitalist world is widening, as numerous studies by international agencies have shown. The upsurge of capitalism, and the situation of the poor, in recent decades has demonstrated once again that capitalist development is of its very nature detrimental to the masses, as the naked exploitation now endured by the poor nations of the world all too abundantly attests.

But around 1970, the unbroken capitalist advance and its seeming security began to teeter and sway. A number of different researchers are currently engaged in a study of the origins, depth, and foreseeable duration of the international capitalist crisis. Their studies concur in exonerating the oil-producing countries for the crisis in international capitalism, in spite of efforts to spread the impression that it was they who were responsible and thus discourage the formation of cartels by producers of other raw materials.

Instead, it would seem, the international capitalist crisis is a result of the industrial decline of economic leaders such as the United States (as, earlier, of the United Kingdom), with a consequent weakening of the dollar. These findings suggest that the current crisis may be a long one. It will very likely last until new industrial technology can increase profitability, and until stable political and economic relationships among the capitalist nations will allow for a reliable international monetary standard.

In the meantime, until all these problems can somehow be resolved, international capital copes with the problem of profitably applying substantive technological improvements, and thus achieving a fiscal stability that will encourage long-term investment, by brutally devaluing the contribution of the world labor force. Only thus, it is thought, can profit be increased in the short run. Thus wage earners in the underdeveloped countries, in addition to their traditional prostration, now bear the burden of the sacrifices and deprivation demanded by this "interim" approach to stemming the tide of the new crisis.

The outlook for the poor is dismal, then, whether the capitalist system prospers or languishes. In either case the function of underdeveloped economies is to provide more capital, either to enhance an already flourishing foreign economy or to collaborate in the solution of its problems.

Changes in the international economic order, begun in decades past and seemingly immune from crisis thus far, entail no diminution whatever of the level of dependency of our Latin American countries. On the contrary, they diversify and deepen it. Accordingly, the apostles of compromise have abandoned their half-hearted longings for viable nationalisms, and now unashamedly throw themselves into the arms of transnational capital. The hypocritical mask of "negotiation" fails to disguise the capitulation. Thus any hopes for national liberation slip from the hands of the other social strata into the laps of the exploited classes alone.

Exploitation and Democracy. Reorganization of the world economic system can be carried out only to the accompaniment of social and political contradictions. Efforts to resolve these in the manner most favorable to powerful economic interests have led to certain lines of action, differing from region to region. But naturally many other factors, especially political ones, then come into play.

For example, if you subordinate everything to the purposes of the transnationals, without taking into account the relationship of their interests to those of a particular nation (which may be quite different), then you facilitate your task of interpretation. And you render the task of the popular masses more difficult, for resistance to new forms of domination always runs the risk of oversimplification. Here we shall attempt to point out only a few aspects of the Latin American political situation under this new form of domination.

We hear a great deal these days about the ideology of "national security," and the regimes this ideology inspires. And here we have our finger squarely on a sore spot. This is a key aspect indeed of the current state of affairs in Latin America. But we must avoid getting bogged down in doctrinal analysis —that is, in an attempt to treat the problem outside the framework of the class struggle now under way in Latin America. Ideologies cannot be understood apart from the social classes that constitute their historical subject.

The national security regimes are but an expression of the measures capitalist imperialism and local dominant classes have deemed necessary for the imposition of their new conditions on the masses of the people, and for the containment of the efforts of change that these classes initiated in the 1960s. This response, and this coercion, may or may not appeal to the national security doctrine, depending on the national situation in each case. But in all situations it is a response and a coercion that has created a repressive condition of refined cruelty in many Latin American countries—superimposed on the ancient oppression already being suffered by the poorest of the poor.

These necessities of reorganization in the capitalist system and popular resistance to repression are inspiring efforts to mask the ugly face of domination. We have for example the much heralded project of the Trilateral Commission, seeking to reestablish cohesiveness in the international policies of capitalism, in which the U.S.A. has ceased to exercise exclusive leadership, having taken Western Europe and Japan into partnership. The need for more democratic forms of government—"restricted democracy," to be sure—now comes into play as an element of the new politics, its purpose again being to ensure the best conditions for the smooth running of the economic order that international capitalism is beginning to implement in the Third World.

These projects—national security and restricted democracy—are present and incarnate in Latin America today. But Latin American reality is multifaceted and does not always conform to theoretical models. And many other elements come into play—some of them of ancient stamp and with a long, unbroken history—all conspiring to one basic end: the exploitation of the masses. In some countries—Brazil and Chile, for example—repression has reached an incredible pitch of savagery. This is all the more shocking in view of the democratic forms of coexistence that had begun to form part of the tradition of those lands. In other countries the violation of the most elementary human rights has reached social strata that until now had been relatively immune from the oppression that constitutes the masses' daily fare. Now some persons are persecuted who had, from time to time, actually enjoyed some of the liberties the popular classes in these same countries have always been denied. Today, in some countries, we are beginning to see the first new glimmer of a "restricted democracy," which the system grants to the people because it serves its purposes to do so. The new dawn is a murky one, but at least we see that things can be changed, even today, in certain circumstances.

The Rights of the Poor. All this makes for a complicated and explosive setting for the presence and voice of the church in Latin America. The coming of age of the popular masses' political awareness over the last decade, the growing involvement of Christian groups in the liberation process, and the fact that repression has begun to strike the official church to a degree hitherto unknown, coupled with the brutality shown by repressive regimes during these same years, have moved bishops' conferences and other church groups to undertake a vigorous defense of human rights. At times, the church's voice has been the only one to be raised against the crushing of human liberties. Thus the church has helped bring this nefarious situation to the attention of the world, with the effect that its scope has been reduced.[3]

At the same time, a structural analysis better suited to Latin American reality has led certain Christians to speak of the "rights of the poor" and to interpret the defense of human rights under this new formality.[4] The adjustment is not merely a matter of words. This alternative language represents a critical approach to the laissez-faire, liberal doctrine to the effect that our society enjoys an equality that in fact does not exist. This new formulation likewise seeks constantly to remind us of what is really at stake in the defense of human rights: the misery and spoliation of the poorest of the poor, the conflictive character of Latin American life and society, and the biblical roots of the defense of the poor.

One of the traps that may yet ensnare the church in Latin America will be a facile, naive acquiescence in the "restricted democracy" mentioned above. Certain liberties and individual rights could be formally restored, but the profound social and economic inequality that undermines them would be left intact. The church's denunciation of violations of human rights will quickly become a hollow cry if church officials rest content with the beginnings of a "democracy" that is only for the middle class and actually only enhances the flexibility with which the prevailing system exercises its domination over the popular masses.

Only from within the poor classes of Latin American society will it be possible to grasp the true meaning of the biblical cry for the defense of human rights. Only thus will it be clear that, for the church, this task is an expression of the proclamation of the gospel in Latin America today. The church may not, then, content itself with alleviating the most blatant forms of repression, as long as the cause of this brutality—institutionalized violence—remains in place. A full and forthright protest of all abuses of power, in their very roots, will also shield the church from the subtle temptation to self-promotion through respectful complaint, which might incline the church to present itself as a political alternative in Latin America.

Persecuted in the Cause of Right

The hand of the dominator reaches out ruthlessly to castigate any protest on the part of the oppressed, any attempt at altering a social order that routinely manufactures a poor class. One of the significant facts of Latin American life in recent years is the open, brutal repression that has struck down groups and persons explicitly calling themselves Christian, including many who exercise official responsibilities in the institutional church.

These realities, already in the making ten years ago, today are commonplace. They are painful but unmistakable evidence, full of promise, that our Christian community is moving ever closer to the poor of Latin America, that we have actually begun to experience the lot of the poor. These Christians—these farmhands, laborers, priests, bishops, university students, nuns—are not jailed, tortured, and murdered for their "religious ideas" but for their social praxis—their evangelization. They are persecuted because, believing as they do in a God of liberation, they denounce injustice done to the poor, and become involved in the lives and the struggles of the poor. They are struck down because they try to rethink their faith from a viewpoint of solidarity with the liberation of the oppressed. Frequently they are persecuted by governments themselves claiming to be Christians, regimes that loudly announce that their efforts "in defense of Western Christian civilization" certify them as champions of the faith and protectors of the church. This monstrous lie has been denounced by many representatives of the church. But many others embrace it, and this is a scandal. Some even support and justify it, with what has been called a "theology of massacre." Still others prefer to keep silent in the face of this taking of the name of the Lord in vain, be it out of cowardice, or out of a secret, unconfessed complicity.

I cite the persecution of Christian groups. But I am by no means suggesting that Christians constitute the most persecuted sector of the Latin American population. I only wish to underscore the fact that being a Christian, or even a priest or bishop, no longer (thank God!) automatically confers immunity from the assaults of the oppressor's might. On the contrary, Christianity has become subversive in the eyes of the powerful and dangerous for those who have dedicated their lives to the poor. The entire phenomenon also sets in relief the pitch of exasperation to which the dominant classes have come in defense of their interests.

Brazil, that land of the pioneers of so many Christian movements, has unhappily become the initiator of an undulating wave of imprisonment, torture, and murder of Christians involved in the popular movement. This began fifteen years ago, but the terrible, somber years of 1968 and 1969 are still

fresh in the memory of those who lived the church's incarnation among the Latin American people then. What was being avenged was solidarity with efforts of liberation by a people beginning to be dangerously aware of the structural causes of their misery and spoliation. Lest this gradually become a collective memory, an enterprise of repression was set in motion, with the intent of eradicating the precise locus of a rereading of the faith in poverty, collectivity, and conflict.

From Brazil, just in the past decade, this new type of persecution of the church (for "Christian" motives!) has spread to Argentina, Chile, Honduras, El Salvador, Mexico, and the whole length and breadth of Latin America. Its ferocity has become notorious, and its lists of martyrs is one of the great riches of the Latin American church.

Here a poor, exploited, and believing people waxes rich. The dominators view it with no little surprise when someone actually lays down their life for a faith that, to them, means no more than freedom from botherment and religious justification for secular social injustice. Hence their attempt to explain the deaths of these martyrs in a way that will deprive them of any connection with faith or hope in a Christ of liberation. After all, what does such faith and hope have in common with their own experience of Christianity? And so, they are surprised.

But even more, they are alarmed. For these martyrs are testifying that there is poverty in Latin America and that the poor are calling the status quo to account.[5] This is reality, and it is a reality that the dominators would like to forget; so they either ignore it or attribute it to nonstructural causes. But the most outrageous reaction occurs in the form of a "spiritualization" of poverty, in which the poor, instead of posing problems with their disquieting material poverty, are understood to offer solutions instead, in the form of a badly misinterpreted, inoffensive (and hence unbiblical) "spiritual poverty." The latter-day martyrs of Latin America attest to the fact that the poor "die before their time," from hunger or the bullet. As someone pointed out in one of our discussions, their very corpses are subversive, and this is why the powerful refuse to surrender them, *or* to release data that would make public the true cause of death, as happened in the case of Bishop Enrique Angelelli, in Argentina, for example. The dominator fails to appreciate that it is through the critical experience of the empty tomb that the followers of Jesus today, like his friends of yesterday, come to grasp the fulness of the life of the risen Christ who conquers all death.

The names of the bishops and priests, and some of the nuns and lay persons, who have been kidnapped, tortured, or murdered, are fairly well known. Their number, and the ecclesiastical functions they performed, are evidence of the polarization underway in the Latin American church. Less well known, but by no means less important, are the *campesinos,* laborers, and students who have suffered the same fate. These are "history's anonymous witnesses"—protagonists of hope in the midst of repression, faceless as the poor from whom they spring and for whom they die.[6] The blood of those "persecuted in the cause of right" is prompt to plead the new claim of the ones the Bible calls the "poor of the earth" to have their land now as their own, and be able to work and live as human beings. Faith in the power of a God who delivers, and who conquers fear and death, lives once again.

Rarely have so many deaths enriched a people and a church with such life. As the prophet Ezekiel learned, there are no dry bones of death where hope abounds. For the living God is with his people. His Spirit lives in our dead and fills them with life. And he now raises up a whole people, "a great, an immense army" (Ezek. 37:10), and makes his people a promise:

> I shall put my spirit in you, and you will live, and I shall resettle you on your own soil; and you will know that I, Yahweh, have said and done this—it is the Lord Yahweh who speaks [Ezek. 37:14].

THE RIGHT TO EXIST AND TO THINK

All genuine theology has its point of departure in the life of faith. Faith, after all, is what leads us to become disciples of Christ, and theology is about discipleship. Discipleship is not simply listening to a teaching. Before all else, discipleship is the following of Christ. Discipleship means making his practice our practice.

In the first part of this chapter we considered the deeply human and Christian meaning of the "temporal life and increase of the poor." That is, we considered the meaning of the physical life of the poor, the area in which, precisely, the poor are despoiled and have their most elemental rights violated. For there is a dialectic between the life of faith and the life of the body, between faith in the resurrection and our temporal death. In this dialectic the theology of liberation represents *the right of the poor to think*.

What do we mean by the right of the poor to think? We mean the right to express—to plumb, comprehend, come to appreciate, and then insist upon— that other right that an oppressive system denies them: the right to a human life.

Hence it will be appropriate to consider the points of breach and continuity between the theology of liberation and other theologies past and present. What will be the same, and what will be different, about a theology whose point of departure is the life of faith on the "underside of history"?

At the same time, we shall be coming to an appreciation of the meaning and potentialities of theological reflection as the right of an exploited and believing people that struggles to throw off the shackles of oppression that drag it to the dust to speak up and tell us about its faith and its hope.

Theology and Social Processes

Theology is done by persons who, whether they know it or not, are caught up in particular social processes. Consequently, all theology is in part a reflection of this or that concrete social process. Theology is not something disembodied or atemporal. On the contrary, theology is the attempt to express the word of the Lord in the language of today—in the categories of a particular time and place. Of course, I am speaking of authentic, relevant, theology. No meaningful theology can be elucubrated in disconnection from concrete history, by stringing together a set of abstract ideas enjoying some manner of interior logical connection. No meaningful theology springs forth fully arrayed from dusty tomes of yesterday. No, a meaningful theological reflection consists in an expression, and a calling into question, of broad historical processes. Only as such will theology fulfill its role as a reading of the faith from within a specific social practice.

Reflection on the faith is an effort on the part of particular believers, or groups of believers, who reflect on their belief in determinate social conditions, in order to work out interpretations and courses of actions that will affect those conditions—that will play a role in the events and struggles of a given society. The theologian is not adrift in some historical limbo. His or her reflection has a precise locus, a precise point of departure. It springs up out of the material foundations of society. Like Archimedes of old, the theologian, too, needs a "place to stand."

The theology of liberation began to be articulated in systematic form in 1968. Contrary to the misapprehensions of some observers of good will, doubtless occasioned by the emphasis of liberation theology on the political dimension of the gospel and on social analysis, it did not have any intentions of being a "leftist political theology." Neither was it a spin-off from certain secular theologies, as was alleged by persons of less good will and perceptivity, perhaps owing to its emphasis on the autonomy of historical praxis. In retrospect, these criticisms are easy to understand. Who would have thought that there could be theology outside the classic centers of theology, other than one merely parroting the theology of the dominators?

Today it is easier to isolate the first insights of liberation theology. We are not jealous or presumptuous. We have no stake in a reputation for intellectual originality. Our concern is only for a deep, fruitful fidelity to a way of living the faith in a world of oppression, a way of living the faith in the midst of the struggle of the poor for their liberation. What we care about is not a matter of having "our own theology," the way the petit bourgeois used to dream of having "their own house some day." Such a dream does haunt the intellectual world. No, our concern is to establish the fact that theologies arise out of concrete historical ambiences, and then to go ahead and produce a theology out of our own ambience. Having our very own theology is thus of no importance.

What we have said from the very beginning—and it is being more and more accepted today—is that the theology of liberation has a different "interlocutor" from other contemporary theologies, be they Catholic or Protestant, "postconciliar" or "progressive." The best thing about these latter theologies is their attempt to deal seriously with the challenges of the modern spirit and liberal ideology.

Western civilization, proclaimed the Enlightenment triumphantly, has "come of age." The bourgeois revolutions of eighteenth-century Europe promulgated a code of "modern freedoms." Theology today in Europe and North America has come to grips with this modern mentality. Its historical agent is the bourgeois middle class. For, from an exclusively economic turf in the beginning, this class moved out to the realm of the political, assumed complete power, and endeavored to create a complex of new social relationships.

Thus it is the point of departure of "progressive" theology—which it explicitly and perceptively recognizes to be its conversation with the "modern human being"—that distinguishes it from "traditional" theology. "Traditional" theology is theology still bearing the mark of the feudal world. It has stuck fast in the ancien regime and the world of classical philosophy.

The same point of departure also distinguishes "progressive" theology from the theology of liberation. The theology of liberation begins not with the problematic of the "modern (bourgeois) human being," but with that of the poor and dispossessed—those whom the bourgeois dominators seek to maintain "without a history," while they present their own, middle-class society, which they have only just molded, as pertaining to the natural and constant order of things.

But the oppressed and marginalized are oppressed and marginalized precisely by the interlocutor of "progressive" theology—by the bourgeois class. Oppression is oppression, and we should not allow ourselves to be deceived by either streamlined or camouflaged exteriors. Instead, these should help us isolate the precise point of breach between the perspective of modern (bourgeois) theology and that of liberation theology (the theology of the oppressed). And we may seek this breach at the levels of history, politics, and social class.

"Progressive" theology seeks to answer the questions of the *nonbeliever;* liberation theology confronts the challenge of the *nonperson.* The spirit of modernity, typically skeptical, or even frankly nonbelieving, where religion is concerned, calls the faith into question by challenging the meaning of religion for human life. Its critique originates in an individualistic, and indeed critical, mentality. It takes its point of departure in its own proclamation of the modern freedoms. It prefers to situate the debate on religious terrain, attacking the philosophical presuppositions and historical truth of religion, along with the role of the church in traditional society.

To be sure, when we say "nonperson" or "nonhuman being," we are not using these terms in an ontological sense. We do not mean that the interlocutor of liberation theology is actually a nonentity. We are using this term to denote those human beings who are considered less than human by society, because that society is based on privileges arrogated by a minority.

We seek to call attention to the historical and concrete conditions of the situation of the poor and the exploited. We refuse to attempt to conceal the conflictive nature of society under the cloak of generic, innocent-looking terminology. For it is from their place in society that these nonpersons call us to account, and this is why their questioning goes to the economic, social, political, and ideological root of the society that marginalizes them. The yawning chasm that divides these two theological perspectives, that of progressivist theology and that of liberation theology, mirrors a rift in the real world, where persons live and die—not in the world of ideas.

Progressivist theology, in its efforts to come to grips with the challenge of the bourgeois, middle-class unbeliever, necessarily comes in contact with the problematic of the modern mind. The historical bloc, the concrete matrix and context, in which this theology has been shaped, is the key to an understanding and an explanation of the contributions it is making to theological thought. I do not imply that its reflection on the faith is limited to the mechanical transposition of the themes of modernity into the field of theology. On the contrary, the great power and meaning of the best part of the progressivist theological endeavor is precisely its own critical sense and its independent thought. And yet this theology is a situated theology. What structure of thought is not? Thus, to divorce it from the historical process of its social and cultural world would be to render it incomprehensible. But that social and cultural world is modern society, and middle-class, or bourgeois, ideology.

The point of departure of liberation theology is not only different from that of progressivist theology, it is in historical contradiction with it. The contradiction has its roots deep in social reality itself. Liberation theology is an expression of a dialectical opposition to bourgeois ideology and the dominant culture that comes up out of the popular classes. It is the exploited segments of society, the despised ethnic groups, the marginalized cultures, the persons we may know in their energy and vitality only by looking at them from the underside of history—in a word, those whom the Bible calls "the poor"—who are the historical agent and repository of this new understanding of the faith.

The breach of liberation theology with other theological perspectives is not simply theological. It transcends the world of theology strictly so called—the realm of ideas—and enters real history, where persons and social groups live in confrontation. In modern society—or more precisely, within the social class that incarnates the mentality of modernity—a difference in religious convictions creates a division among persons who share the same basic social world, and a similar lifestyle, a similar quality of life. This is the sphere in which the modern spirit launches its critique of religion, and this is the sphere in which progressivist theology elaborates its answer.

With the theology of liberation, and the society of the nonperson, however, the case is the other way around. Here, right from the start, the rift that separates persons is not a "religious" one at all. Here the rift is between oppressed and oppressors—sharing the same faith, at least superficially. Here the breach is not religious, but economic, social, and political. And this breach is sharp and clean to the point of being a situation of oppression of some by others. It leaps out at you. It is impossible not to see it.

To tolerate such a total lack of correlation between faith and the historical reality in which that faith is to be lived does not come off very well when confronted with the word of God. And there, at the widest extremity of the breach, where the social tension is sharpest, and where the inviability of this separation between faith and life is most perceptible—if that faith is a biblical faith—there the theology of liberation rises to speak.

Taking the Road the Poor Must Tread

Here is a theology expressing the faith of the poor. Here is a theology that breaks with the theology of the dominator, in order to keep continuity with the history of the poor—a history all but unknown, but a history rich and full of promise. Here is truly a "theology oppressed," a theology rejected by the powers that be, in complicity with powerful elements in the church.

Our record of the interpretation of the faith that rises up from among the poor is generally fragmentary and oral, as manifested in customs, rites, and the like. Only rarely, until now, has their interpretation reached the surface of intellectual consciousness, as for instance in Bartolomé de Las Casas, or, to a lesser extent, in certain other missioners of the same era, who openly took sides with the Indians. And the poor themselves have had to follow a road even more difficult in order to make themselves heard. And yet the memory of history, the memory of faith, is there, awaiting reconstruction. The task will be complex, and it is urgent. It is the task of reconstructing the memory of the poor, a memory that is always subversive of a social order that despoils and marginalizes.

Subterranean Currents. The theology of the dominated sprang ever from the life and struggles of the poor who believed in the living God. Consequently it suffered their fate: destruction and oblivion. To follow the road of the poor through history will be a most fruitful endeavor for the theology of liberation, for here that theology must grapple with the crucial question of its own historical continuity.

These reflections of the poor upon their faith, this theology of the poor, will be sought in vain in our histories of academic theology. But this does not mean that they are entirely absent from academic theology. There are oases in the desert. Underground springs do manage to break to the surface here and there. But the perspective of the poor never constitutes the central element of an academic expression of theology.

We usually find the theology of the poor emanating from spiritual movements of the poor, which are frequently social movements as well. A number of currents of medieval piety constitute a good example of this tendency. This is significant, for the life and reflection of the poor always have a contemplative and mystical dimension—and a dimension of protest and social transformation.

Perhaps the reason for all this will become clearer if we refer to the biblical sources that maintain the privileged position of the poor with respect to the gospel message. Jesus called the poor "happy," "lucky." In spite of stubborn resistance, spiritualistic interpretations of this basic point of departure for an understanding of the meaning of the kingdom of God have been losing ground. One of the reasons for their decline is the faith experience of the poor themselves. Another is a series of exegetical studies that make the point clearly: the gospel of Jesus proclaims that God loves the poor just because they are poor, and not necessarily, or even primarily, because they are better believers than others, or morally firmer than others.[7] God loves them simply because they are poor, because they are hungry, because they are persecuted. Only from this standpoint is it possible to appreciate any enriching considerations upon "spiritual poverty." The latter are derivative. What is primary, when it comes to God's special love for the poor, is literal, physical poverty.

This position may seem insensitive. For example, it may seem that we entertain precious little interest in persons' spiritual attitudes. It could even seem that we disdain qualities of faith or of morality in the poor. But such is not the case. We are only seeking to avoid beginning with secondary, derivative considerations in such a way as would confuse them with what is primary and basic, creating an interminable labyrinth of hair-splitting distinctions and logical contradictions that in the end only yield ideas devoid of interest or historical impact. The history of the theology of the Beatitudes is ample proof that the danger is there!

But the gravest danger is the danger of infidelity to the gospel. The Beatitudes are less a revelation about the poor than they are a revelation about God. They tell us who God is. They tell us what his kingdom is like. They tell us of God as defender of the poor, as the protector, the liberator, of the poor. Then, secondarily and derivatively, they tell us something as well about the privileged role of the poor—the physically, concretely poor, the dispossessed and oppressed—in God's kingdom.

And here we are confronted with a paradox. If we "spiritualize" this gospel message about the poor too soon, as it were—out of proper order and sequence—and maintain that the "poor" in the gospel are *first and primarily* the "spiritually" poor rather than plainly and simply the materially poor (if we may so call them, in contradistinction to the classic concept of the "spiritually poor"), then we have an easy time with God. We "humanize" God. We make him more accessible to human understanding. Now God will love, first and foremost, the good, the "meritorious"—just as we do ourselves.

But if, instead, we take the gospel statements at their face value, unflinchingly and courageously, then what we have is God's love for the poor first and foremost simply because they are poor, simply because they are literally and materially poor. Now we have no easy God at all. Now we are faced with the mystery of God's revelation, and the gift of his kingdom of love and justice.

Now we stand before a God who is a challenge, a God who overturns our human categories, a God who will not be reduced to our mode of thinking, and who judges us on the basis of our concrete, historical actions toward the poor ("In so far as you did this to one of the least of these brothers of mine . . ."—Matt. 25:40). Now we face a God who cuts straight through the love of a liar—the love that forgets sisters and brothers and pretends to direct itself toward God instead, pretends to direct itself "spiritually" (more to domesticate God than to feel itself called into question by God's word). For "anyone who says, 'I love God,' and hates his brother, is a liar, since a man who does not love the brother that he can see cannot love God, whom he has never seen" (1 John 4:20). Thus, in order to know and to love God, one must come to grips with the concrete life situation of the poor today, and undertake the radical transformation of a society that makes them poor.

This is the kingdom of God that Jesus reveals to us in his de facto practice—a messianic practice, a practice that turns topsy-turvy not only our values, but historical realities and social status as well. Here the mighty fall weak, and the feeble "gird themselves with strength." Here the sated hunger, and the hungry are satisfied. Here the humble are lifted on high, and the exalted are cast to the earth. Here the poor wax rich, for "he raises the poor from the dust, he lifts the needy from the dunghill" (cf. 1 Sam. 2:4–8; Luke 1:51–53, 6:20–21).

Of course, his practice took him to a violent death. He died in solidarity with the violent death of the oppressed in this world. But what is said to have happened to another personage in history (was it written with irony or ingenuously?) did not happen to Jesus—that "at the end of his days, he died." No, Jesus did not die "at the end of his days." He died before his time, by execution. Nor were his days thereby ended, for his resurrection is an affirmation of life, confirming him as the Christ, the messiah, and setting the seal of God's approval on his message of justice and life, the message that defied a homicidal society.

To be a disciple of Jesus is to make his messianic practice our own. Our discipleship is our appropriation of his message of life, his love for the poor, his denunciation of injustice, his sharing of bread, his hope for resurrection. The Christian community, the *ecclesia,* is made up of those who take up that messianic practice of Jesus and use it to create social relationships of a community of brothers and sisters, and thereby accept the gift of being children of the Father. Messianic practice is the proclamation of the kingdom of God and the transformation of the historical conditions of the poor. It is the word of life, backed up by the deed of deliverance.

A People Exploited and Believing. "Poor," as we have said above, is a term that always implies collectivity and social conflict. The "poor" in the Bible are a social group, a whole people, "the poor of the land." They are a people poor and tormented, despoiled of the fruits of their labor, writhing under the oppressor's injustice. This is what we mean when we say that the peoples of Latin America, too, are "poor": we mean it in this same complex and fertile sense. And in these peoples, at once poor and Christian, there is a concrete point of departure, charged with consequences, for church life and theological reflection. For this is the case with the poor of Latin America: they are both poor and believing. In them we have two dimensions and two potentialities, both residing in the same people.

The situation of oppression and exploitation under which these peoples labor is well known. But it is known in general terms. It should now be subjected to a close examination in its precise, current forms. Nothing can replace a serious, scientific knowledge of the nature of the exploitation that the popular masses are suffering. It is equally urgent that we be able to differentiate between various strata and groups within the popular masses—that we come to recognize which are more advanced and which are more backward, both in terms of their basic relationship to the productive process, and in terms of their potential for mobilization (in function of their experiences with social struggle, for instance).

It must be granted that one of the things afflicting the popular classes, owing to the presence among them of the dominant ideology, is fear. It brings with it the urge to move up the social ladder in search of individual, selfish solutions to their problems. But this is not these classes' fundamental thrust. These are just unfortunate byways, along the high road that comes up out of the same situation of exploitation: the road to radical change, the potential for revolution. This is the people's real will.

It is not enough, then, to call attention to the spoliation and state of oppression in which the popular classes live. One must also see to it that these classes create the objective conditions in which they may begin the struggle for their rights, begin actually to take power in a society that has refused to recognize them as human beings at all. In the struggle, the masses will come to an awareness that they are a social class, that they may be the agents of a revolution, that they may go forth and build a different society. Their revolutionary potential is something to be cultivated and organized, with a view to concrete efficaciousness in history. Such is the latent, but emerging, power of the oppressed.

But as we have said, there is another vector, impinging upon the first. These persons are not only poor and exploited, they are also believing. And this is evident not only in their explicitly religious expressions, but in certain aspects of their life in its entirety. We have to take into consideration what Mariátegui called the "religious factor" in the life and history of the people of Peru. What we call popular piety is one of its expressions, but it is not the only one. The "religious factor," unfortunately, has frequently been, and still is today, a stumbling block to the people's advance in the perception of its situation of oppression. Much popular piety still reflects the dominant ideology, and any "religious populism" that ignores this is to be avoided. We are faced with a complex reality here, and our approach must take the complexity into account.

The believing dimension of the people also implies, as is demonstrated in practice, the immense potentiality of a liberating faith. This faith has come to expression in different forms throughout history, inspiring dogged resistance to oppression, and even open rebellion against it. Those who have this faith—who believe in the God of the Bible—are oppressed. But their faith is also oppressed and imprisoned, in a very real way, in a capitalistic, dehumanizing society. Faith has a liberating potential, but it must be developed. If we fail to

develop it, the rich and varied life of the Latin American people will be muti-
lated, and we will be deprived of the message God wishes to reveal to us
through a poor and simple people's understanding of him.

In the service of this development, and out of the very dynamism of this
faith, the basic Christian communities, the grassroots Christian communities, are springing up. A popular church is being born, under the impulse of
the Spirit of truth and freedom. This is a faith that makes dominators uneasy,
for it is a faith that liberates. Dominators prefer not to believe it exists, prefer
not to believe in its capacity to reveal God in our concrete history. But in
denying this faith, dominators reveal themselves for what they really are—
the "fool" of the Bible, the atheist, who refuses to believe in the God of
deliverance.

We are dealing with two inseparable correlations here, and it is important
to emphasize this. The potential of a liberating faith, and the capacity for
revolution, are intimately bound up together in the concrete life of this poor
and oppressed people. Hence it is impossible to cultivate the one without
cultivating the other as well, and this is what many find so unsettling. The
development of the people's political awareness and its Christian awareness
go hand in hand. The life and work of many of Latin America's new basic
Christian communities have been strongly marked by the experience of this
intimate link between faith and revolution.

In real life, then, it is altogether possible to overcome the neat dichotomy
certain theologies would like to impose. A dichotomy between faith and revolution is unknown to the practice of the basic communities. Its absence has
long been criticized in their theological reflection, as well. And yet, be it
noted, the convergence of these two vectors is the result of a process. Inevitably, the development of the political dimension and of the faith dimension
will not always be in step. At times one element will grow faster than the
other. The urgency of the link between them is profound, and stems from the
biblical message and the people's situation alike. But it is an urgency that
demands reflection and systematic elaboration. Reality is complex here, and
this complexity creates our task and challenge.

But if we take this route, we must be prepared to accept the consequences.
Let us be very clear about this. We must reject completely all reductionism
where evangelization is concerned, both the reductionism of a disincarnate
spiritualism masquerading as "religion," and the reductionism of a political-
action approach that ignores the reality of the people's faith (for this, too, is
idealism). Both reductions are one-sided, and thereby unreal, and betray an
ignorance of the real situation, an ignorance of the real potential of the popular masses. History has shown what dangers lie that way.

I continue to be convinced—and the praxis of the poor confirms me in this
conviction—that a fertile, imaginative challenge lies in the particular form of
"contemplation in action" by which persons may transform history. For this
is where we encounter God in the poor: in solidarity with the struggle of the
oppressed and in a faith full of hope and gladness. For this glad and hopeful

faith will be lived in the midst of a liberation process whose agents are the popular masses themselves.

But our rejection of political reductionism in no way implies a failure to recognize the role of revolutionary political action. Still less does it indicate a failure on our part to appreciate the character of this action as part and parcel of integral evangelization. The global nature of evangelization reflects the dialectic of faith: faith is in word, and faith is in deed. Reductionisms allow the dialectic to fall by the wayside. They fail to perceive the relationship, in the concrete life of an oppressed and believing people, between the will to transform society and a liberating faith.

Reductionisms, then, mutilate a rich historical reality. Idealistically, they turn their backs on life. They go against the grain of practice. They refuse to penetrate to the heart of the matter, where political radicalism and gospel radicalism converge in a mighty embrace of mutual strength and support.

Should We Continue Doing Theology?

Does it make any sense to continue to do theology in today's world of agony and oppression?

Is the task before us not rather a social and political one? Is this not where our study and our action should be directed? Can we justify spending time and energy in the laborious upbuilding of an understanding of the faith in view of the urgent conditions prevalent in Latin American life today? Are we not allowing ourselves to be led more by the momentum of our theological training than by the exigencies of the faith of a people battling for its liberation?

There are many among us who are asking these questions, and they are right to do so. No task is self-evident. We must continually review our endeavors and reexamine our priorities.

The question may be uncomfortable, because it is demanding. But it is legitimate. We have to recognize, honestly, that when we began the work of liberation theology this question did not seem as urgent or demanding as it does today. Our thrust was more spontaneous in those days. Our theological reflection simply sprang up out of the praxis of the basic Christian communities. More or less intuitively, we felt a need to systematize the insights of our faith.

But new problems are arising today. Besides, this theology of ours, welcome or not, has attracted some publicity. It has found a place on the theological map. Hence now we have to ask ourselves, in today's terms, the why and wherefore of what we are about.

But there is another reason as well, an intrinsic one. By asking ourselves, autocritically, what we are about, we may hope to avoid the purely intellectualistic (or worse, "editorial") thrust of abstract discussions among the theologians. They carry us far afield from the historical matrix of a theological interpretation of the faith: the life and struggles of the poor on the road to their liberation.

There is another difference, too, between our autocriticism today and that of yesterday. Today, we ask our questions with greater realism. True, these are methodological questions, questions therefore that logically precede the theological task, but which in actuality are only seriously asked after the theological task is already underway. This is what happens with all questions of methodology, if they are not to remain purely formal and sterile.

For my part, I believe that our theological work has meaning not in spite of, but precisely because of, the situation in which we in Latin America are living today. When persons "die before their time," the question of the kingdom of the living God becomes all the more meaningful.

Of course, the answer is not going to be as facile as that. Our questions—the ones with which we opened this section—challenge us very radically, and we must keep them constantly in mind as we seek the appropriate reorientations of our theological task. Some theologians are already moving in this direction, and their results are most fruitful.

Pseudo Responses. Before we address ourselves to our proper task—that of determining the relationships between theologizing upon the faith and struggling for economic, social, and political liberation—it behooves us to clear the ground by removing some of the pseudo responses to these same questions. For there are pseudo responses in the air, both in Latin America and elsewhere, arising from particular theological interests, and situated against other theological horizons, that are not in the least germane to these methodological questions as we must pose them here in Latin America.

I refer, first, to those theologians in Latin America and elsewhere, who quickly answer, "No, you may not keep doing theology, for what you are doing is not theology." To conservative theologians, our theological efforts seem a strange and bastard mixture of theology and sociology, with a generous sprinkling of politics.

Be it noted, these persons do not undertake to disagree with the content of our reflection—something that they would have every right to do. No, they simply deny that our reflection is theology. Arrogating to themselves the authority of final arbiter in such matters, they simply deny that our reflection enjoys a level of scientific seriousness that would permit them to consider it authentically theological.

Then, along the same lines, although from the opposite end of the political spectrum, other observers admit that what we are doing is "spiritual," hence perhaps a kind of rhetorical theology—but surely not a scientific effort to respond to modern questions of faith.

Thus theology would be our critics' private property. And here we must take our leave of them, with their opinions and their disqualifications. They and we are divided by the most fundamental methodological question of all—that of the very nature of the work of theology. To put it another way, the real questions are: Who are the elaborators of the various modes of reflection upon the faith? Within what concrete historical channels do these streams of reflection situate themselves? What are the criteria for the verification of their findings?

We must also take our leave of those who prefer that when we in Latin America dare to speak, we speak only of our deprivations and our problems, taking a purely descriptive approach, without presuming to reflect on our faith from a point of departure in our concrete situation. After all, our faith, they feel, is their faith as well, and they resent our disturbing incursions into the sphere of reflection on that faith.

Elements of an Authentic Response. And so we return to our questions. I shall not pretend to exhaust their depth and scope, but shall only make certain observations, along the lines alluded to above.

Even the poor have the right to think. The right to think is a corollary of the human right to be, and to assert the right to think is only to assert the right to exist. "Blacks assert that they exist," begins a famous text of black theology published by black church leaders in the United States.

This kind of language could be somewhat shocking. But it is altogether justified. The right to be, to exist, is the first demand of those whom James H. Cone, the principal representative of black liberation theology, calls the victims of history. Of course, recognition of blacks' existence is sure to be subversive, hence disquieting for the dominating classes.

The right to engage in theological reflection is part of the right of an exploited Christian people to think. The faith of the poor in the God of their deliverance seeks, from its own exigencies, to understand itself. This is the classic Anselmian *fides quaerens intellectum.* Christians have the right to think through their faith in the Lord, to think out the experience of their own liberation. They have the right to reclaim their faith—a faith that is continually diverted away from their experience of being poor—in order to turn it into an ideological exposé of the situation of domination that makes and keeps them poor. They have the right to repossess the Bible, and thus prevent the private proprietors of this world's goods from being the private proprietors of the word of the Lord as well.

This is what I meant when, some years ago, I spoke about a social appropriation of the gospel. The social appropriation of the gospel is a reading of the gospel in solidarity with the struggles of the poor. It is a militant reading of the Bible. The interpretation that the poor give their life situation opens a rich vein for the understanding of the gift of God's kingdom. A point of departure in that life situation will enable the theologian to take into account the data of modern scientific exegesis and give it a new, radical dimension.

In this perspective, the theological endeavor, from a point of departure in (and through the actual agency of) the exploited, pertains to their right to liberation. We dare not forget that all reflection is a way of exercising power in history. It is only one way, of course, but it is a real way. It makes a real contribution to the transformation of history—to the destruction of the system of oppression and the construction of a just and humane society. Reflection on the faith as lived in this struggle is a necessary condition for the proclamation of the living God from a pulpit in the midst of the poor.

This is the reason why certain Christian communities committed to the liberation process have, for some time now, been attempting to develop an elaboration of the faith out of their own experience—an elaboration of which they themselves are the primary historical subject. Similar theological undertakings have arisen among the black descendants of slaves in the United States, in the cruel context of racial discrimination in South Africa, and in the midst of the oppression suffered in certain Asian countries (the Philippines and Korea, for instance). The same thing is occurring among women in today's society—especially women who, as members of the popular classes, are doubly exploited, marginalized, and degraded.

We are seeing only the beginnings. But these beginnings already show a way of taking account of the hope of the Lord that is present at the very heart of the historical praxis of liberation. For the first time in many centuries, the confluence of these various currents is producing an effort of reflection on the faith outside the classic centers of theological production. The international conferences of the Ecumenical Association of Third World Theologians are a case in point.[8] They are examples of reflection springing up from the "underside of history."

To renounce thinking, as some persons seem to advise us, is to give ground. To give up thinking would be to betray the vitality of the faith of a people struggling for its liberation. It would mean creating a vacuum that would promptly be filled by reflection representing other categories, other concerns and interests.

In view of all these considerations, I hold that theology should be looked upon as an expression of the right to think on the part of the "wretched of the earth."

Along these same lines, I wish to make another point as well. Much is being said in some circles about the "death of theology." We are not directly concerned with this point here. I shall not, therefore, engage in subtle distinctions between the death of a certain type of theology and the death of theology as such. Nor shall I have recourse to paradoxical language and proclaim that "the only way to make a thing come alive is to pronounce it dead." No, whatever the meaning of the "death of theology" may be, a much more important and striking phenomenon has been the death of the theologian.

I am not playing with words here. I am not speaking figuratively. I mean real deaths. The prophets, then John, Paul, and so many others who attempted to interpret and proclaim the word of God, were theologians—and as theologians they were put to death. History records many other examples, as well, but we need think only of the present time in Latin America, where living and thinking the faith in solidarity with the struggle of the exploited classes has led so many Christians to prison, exile, or death.

As we have said, the proclamation of the gospel in a situation such as ours entails a risk. Reflecting on the consequences of God's love for the poor is no tranquil, peaceful task. Denouncing mystifications of the Christian message means challenging the mighty, for the mighty love to use the gospel to justify and defend their special privileges. This means danger for Christians who cultivate a theology from within grassroots Christian communities.

But there is another meaning of the "death of the theologian." It is the one implied in the celebrated text of Paul:

> The language of the cross may be illogical to those who are not on the way to salvation, but those of us who are on the way see it as God's power to save. As scripture says: *I shall destroy the wisdom of the wise and bring to nothing all the learning of the learned* [1 Cor. 1:18-19].

What is to be done away with is the intellectualizing of the intellectual who has no ties with the life and struggle of the poor—the theology of the theologian who reflects upon the faith precisely from the point of view of those from whom the Father has hidden his revelation: the "learned and clever" (Matt. 11:25). Paul announces the annihilation of thought, but it is not the thought of the "little ones," the poor. For it is only to the poor that the grace of receiving and understanding the kingdom has been granted. To the lowly—to those who cannot or are not allowed to speak—the word of God is given, so that they can go and proclaim the kingdom.

The illogical language of the cross is death for the wisdom of the wise—for those who do not understand the word. Reflection on the faith that does not accept that illogicality, that folly, reflection that does not accept death, that does not accept the revelation granted to the poor, mistakes its way. If we are serious about the divine message to the poor, if we refuse unduly to spiritualize the direct meaning of the texts that are the bearers of this message, an immense harvest of meaning awaits us.

In the perspective of liberation theology, theology "comes second." We call theology "second act." "First act" is involvement in historical liberation praxis, and the simple proclamation of the word in relation to that praxis. This does not mean, however, that theologians should situate themselves in the second moment alone. Their presence in what we call the "first act" is a necessary precondition for their reflection in the second. What comes second is theology, not the theologian.

In other words, the theologian is to be an "organic intellectual," a thinker with organic links to the popular liberation undertaking, and with the Christian communities that live their faith by taking this historical task upon themselves as their own. Sometimes this commitment entails the risk of physical death. And it always means the death of the intelligence of the intelligent, the "wisdom of the wise."

Consequently, when we speak of "first act" and "second act" we are not just talking methodology. We are talking lifestyle—a way of living the faith. In the last analysis, we are talking spirituality in the best and most authentic sense of the word. It can be put this way: in liberation theology, our methodology is our spirituality—a life process on the way to realization.

And this brings us to a third consideration. A theology that insists so much on the concrete grounds of the faith experience at the heart of a liberation process ought to be prepared, one would think, to face questions concerning its impact and influence on the historical process of the Latin American peoples. If praxis is so important for this theology, then its theologians ought to go to the heart of the matter and ask what influence their theology has on praxis. But in order to go to the heart of the matter, they are not to begin by asking directly what the "impact" of liberation theology is on praxis. They are to begin by asking what the concrete situation is in Latin America, what it is that constitutes the matrix of that theology, and hence is all-important for that theology: the liberation process, and the proclamation of the gospel within that process, in Latin America today.

We have been treating these two elements all through these pages. Here we may simply reposition the question, because the first statement seems to assign an importance to liberation theology that in point of fact we do not accord it, and in the final analysis falsifies its perspective by displacing the legitimate field of verification. Intellectual discussion tends to exaggerate the scope of theological reflection. Theology has a meaning and function of its own, but it cannot substitute for what is of ultimate importance: the proclamation of the gospel and involvement with the liberation of the popular masses.

Strictly speaking, this proclamation and this involvement are not theological at all. Hence the first treatment of them will not be theological either. This proclamation and this involvement are not theological: they transcend an exclusively theological field. Many nontheological factors enter their makeup. But if we respect these priorities and face up to the complexity of our task, we may indeed hope to have a serious and realistic answer to the question of the meaning of liberation theology for Latin America today.

Theology seeks to be an utterance that is coherent with praxis. This is what makes theology dangerous. It seeks to express what is being done and, in so expressing it, expresses as well the hope that lies in the doing. Thus theology is an interpretation of hope in the Lord, the hope lived by the poor at the heart of their historical struggle.

Theology is not a wisdom closed in upon itself. Its cohesiveness is not in its reasonings. It is not a finished discussion. Rather, it keeps open to the practice that it must interpret. And from there it opens up to history, and all the new and surprising practices of "a faith that makes its power felt through love" (Gal. 5:6). These new practices will reiterate the hope that a new and different world is really possible, and that the kingdom of God, the kingdom of love and justice, is in the making.

The key to every theological interpretation is Christ, and it was precisely the coherence of Christ's word with his practice that led him to his death. A christological approach makes it possible to subsume the experiences of, and reflections on, the faith that the poor have realized throughout the course of history, and incorporate these experiences and reflections into a valid and authentic theology. At the same time a christological perspective will open up for us the future of the resurrection—the life that conquers death, and that we know we have within us "because we love our brothers and sisters" (cf. 1 John 3:14).

These, in brief, are some of the reasons and conditions for doing theology from within the experience of an exploited Christian people. But we must always remember—in order to keep the meaning and potential of this reflection on the faith alive and demanding—to keep our feet solidly planted on the earth that gives theology its life.

Joy Is Subversive

Only "from the ground up," only from a point of departure in popular movements, and in the Christian base communities, will it be possible to isolate what is permanent, deep, and irreversible in the Latin American historical process, as well as what is alive and creative within the church. "Signs of struggle and hope" are multiplying all over Latin America. The maturity, the outreach, the life commitment, and the depth of spiritual experience of our Christian communities, rooted as they are in popular movements, are charged with promise, holiness, and prophecy.

The praxis of evangelization of the masses led to what we began a few years ago to call "two-way evangelization." The expression is a faltering one, but it expresses a profound reality: in seeking to bring the good news to the poor, one has a real experience of being evangelized by the poor themselves. This experience brought us to an understanding that it is the poor themselves who evangelize. And it gave a brand-new meaning to the maxim that God reveals himself in history through the poor.

God's love is revealed to the poor. They are the ones who receive, understand, and proclaim this love. From this viewpoint, the task of evangelization consists in involvement with the proclamation process of the poor themselves. The ones the Bible calls the poor are not only the gospel's privileged recipients, but—by that very fact—its messengers as well. Indeed "the kingdom of heaven belongs to the wretched of the earth."

But we also know that the poor, the masses of the people, are history's transforming power, the agents of a liberating praxis. This is not a matter of "parallel affirmations"—sheer coincidence. The relationship between evangelization and subversion is a profound one, for these two praxes are bound up together at the very heart of history. No, it is no accident that the poor evangelize and subvert at the same time.

This affirmation, this conception, far from allowing us to take our ease in triumphalistic illusions, far from allowing us to rely on superficial historical techniques, places us before redoubtable challenges and tasks.

Evangelization, which is the proclamation of the good news of the Father's love, takes place within the same liberation process in which we express our love for our sisters and brothers. Thus we have learned from praxis itself that not only are the poor evangelized on the road to their liberation, but they themselves evangelize while liberating themselves. This profound and reciprocal relationship between evangelization and liberation is established, in the first place and primarily, on the concrete terrain, in the real life, of the exploited Christian people of whom we have been speaking. We know the God of the Bible as *Go'el,* the rescuer of the oppressed, through the evangelizing witness of the poor who battle for their liberation.

The poor person is a member of a people, and hence, as poor, the product of a social structure. As such, he or she is the product and result of a historical process—a conflictual historical process. In that situation of conflict, God reveals himself as a God who takes the part of "the poor of the land." His love is universal, yes, but it is from a point of departure in his preference for the poor that he manifests his universal love, his love for all humanity.

Our own love for all men and women, too, if it is to be concrete, must pass by way of this particularity. It must take a stand for those who suffer injustice. Thus the proclamation of the gospel leads us to an encounter with the living God, right in the life and death of the people in their struggles and hopes.

This same encounter also comes to expression in one of the richest and deepest phenomenon to be observed today in Christian sectors involved with the popular struggles: the birth of a new spirituality. This new spirituality is disquieting and disturbing to those who prefer to cut themselves off from the reality of the poor. To them it seems to lack an essential element of Christian life: prayer and celebration.

In the world of the people, it is doubtless difficult to understand the fertile, creative spiritual reality that, eschewing the escapism of purely formal, superficial "prayer and celebration," surges up from the struggles of the poor. Nowhere is the living God sung with more faith, hope, and joy than in the world of the masses. It is not easy, of course. "How could we sing one of Yahweh's hymns in a pagan country?" asked the people of Israel, overwhelmed by the weight of the Babylonian captivity (Ps. 137:4). The people of God in Latin America ask themselves the same question today. They too are in exile—in their own land. But at the same time they know they are on the road to their exodus. They are on the road to freedom.

"How can we sing to the Lord in a strange land," a land not ours? A searing question indeed for faith in a liberating God. Here is a question that arises from real life. As such, it rejects all facile answers. It is a question that changes our perspective. It places us before a new face of the Lord, before the gratuity, and demands, of his love. It ushers us into his presence at the very heart of the effort to establish what the Bible calls "justice and righteousness." There is, perhaps, nothing more impressive and creative than the prayerful praxis of Christians among the poor and oppressed. Theirs is not a prayer divorced from the liberating praxis of the people. On the contrary, the Christian prayer of the poor springs up from roots in that very practice.

Here, on the terrain of real life, among the very poorest, is where the eucharistic celebration takes on its full meaning of a sharing in the death and resurrection of Christ. In "the breaking of the bread"—that staple lacking to the disinherited of the earth—the life of the resurrected Christ becomes present reality. This life of his assures us that death is not to triumph, and that sin and injustice will be abolished.

In the fullness of life brought to us by liberation in Jesus Christ, and in the historical power of the poor, we discover the source of the remarkable joy that the poor manifest in their struggle, in their prayerful praxis. No superficial glee, this; no empty "joy" born of unawareness of the reality of oppression and suffering. This is Easter gladness—joy that passes through death and pain, in intense, profound hope.

The poor know that history is theirs. They know that if they must cry today, tomorrow they shall laugh (cf. Luke 6:21). And they are discovering that that "laughter" is an expression of deep confidence in the Lord, the confidence we find in the songs of Hannah (1 Sam. 2:1–10) and Mary (Luke 1), the confidence of the poor who live in the midst of a history they seek to transform. It is a subversive gladness—subversive of the world of oppression, and this is why it disquiets dominators. For it denounces the fear of waverers and reveals the love of the God of hope.

NOTES

1. *Signos de renovación* (Lima: Comisión Episcopal de Acción Social, 1969).
2. Ibid., p. 36; cf. Rom. 4:18.
3. See, for example, the documents by the bishops' conferences of Brazil, Bolivia, El Salvador, Chile, Uruguay, and Peru, to point out but a few representative sources.
4. In so doing, they are only repeating the clear and unambiguous language of Medellín, which had already declared: "Following the gospel mandate, we should defend the rights of the poor and the oppressed" (Medellín Document on Peace, 22 in *Between Honesty and Hope* [Maryknoll, N.Y.: Orbis, 1970], p. 208). This concept is historically more perceptive, and richer in biblical overtones, than many formulations more in vogue today.
5. Someone, not altogether remarkable for his interest in liberation and poverty, was complaining one day about the document in which a Latin American episcopate criticized the preparatory document drawn up for Puebla by a group of *periti*. "Wearisome," he said, "it's irritating. All you find here is 'the poor, the poor, the poor'!" To which someone else replied, "Yes, indeed. And the worst of it is, that's all you find in the streets too!"
6. See Martin Lange and Reinhold Iblacker, ed., *Witnesses of Hope: The Persecution of Christians in Latin America* (Maryknoll, N.Y.: Orbis, 1981).
7. See especially Jacques Dupont's exhaustive studies *Les Béatitudes* (Paris: Gabalda): vol. 1, *Les Béatitudes: le problème littéraire* (1969); vol. 2, *Les Béatitudes: la bonne nouvelle* (1969); and vol. 3, *Les Béatitudes: les Evangélistes* (1973).
8. Conference papers published by Orbis Books, Maryknoll, N.Y.: Sergio Torres and Virginia Fabella, eds., *The Emergent Gospel: Theology from the Underside of History* (1978); Kofi Appiah-Kubi and Sergio Torres, eds., *African Theology en Route* (1979); Virginia Fabella, ed., *Asia's Struggle for Full Humanity: Towards a Relevant Theology* (1980); Sergio Torres and John Eagleson, eds., *The Challenge of Basic Christian Communities* (1981); Sergio Torres and Virginia Fabella, eds., *Irruption of the Third World* (1983).

PART III
PUEBLA

5

The Preparatory Document for Puebla: A Retreat from Commitment

The Preparatory Document (PD) proposes to deal with the task of evangelization in the Latin American church, on the threshold of the third millennium of the Christian era. This orientation to the future characterizes the entire text. The task of evangelizing, as seen in the PD, will consist of forming a new civilization, a Christian civilization, because "if the evangelization of a people does not produce an authentic Christian culture, then it has been superficial." The creation of this new civilization means generating a "new type of urban-industrial society."

This is the great challenge that faces the church in these last decades of the twentieth century, the PD insists, and this must be the theme of Puebla. Let us explore this central idea, placing it in context and relating its key notions: urban-industrial society, culture, and the people.

FROM SOCIAL INJUSTICE TO SECULARISM

The PD affirms repeatedly that we are in transition from an agricultural-urban to an urban-industrial society. Because in Europe this process was related to secularism, "separation from God," and because the church had

---

The Preparatory Document for the October 1978 meeting of the Latin American Episcopal Conference to be held in Puebla, Mexico, was drawn up under supervision of the conference secretariat and offered for study and response for the bishops' deliberations. It could be radically amended at the outset of the meeting or rejected altogether. Much of the response to the document was strongly critical. Gustavo Gutiérrez's article printed here was generally regarded as one of the most significant critiques of it. The present text first appeared in *Christianity and Crisis*, Sept. 18, 1978, translated by Diana Houston and Robert McAfee Brown. It is a condensation of the author's "Sobre el Documento de Consulta para Puebla," written in April 1978 and published in *Páginas*, 3/16–17 (Lima, June 1978): 1–24. The text has been edited for inclusion in the present volume.

its roots in the "ancient agricultural-urban world," the transformation to an industrialized society brought about a disorientation of the church. But secularism, the PD declares, "is not an inherent part of industrialization"; its dominance is contextual, not structural, even though "many Marxists and modern sociologies" would like to pretend otherwise.

This fact gives the Third World, and Latin America in particular, an opportunity. Today we are under the impact of the "third industrial revolution." The problem and historical possibility for the church, then, is knowing how "to evangelize urban-industrial society so as to transfigure it without negating it"—that is, how to "generate a new type of urban-industrial society," because this new civilization must also overcome poverty and guarantee justice and participation. The church is called to assist in "the overcoming of modernism, integrating the values it has provided, but in the context of a new civilization." These values can be redeemed if we can separate industrialization from secularism.

The difficulty with this approach is that while the PD skips along the mountaintops with broad generalizations, problems multiply on the mountainsides and in the valleys, problems directly affecting the pastoral task of the church. Note that little or nothing is said in the analysis above about the social costs imposed upon the Third World—particularly in Latin America—as a result of the industrialization process that is de facto taking place, centered as it is in the affluent countries.

Further: the PD manages to speak of industrial society without mentioning the working class, without entering the world of the underemployed and unemployed who provide the supply of cheap labor for an industrial system that benefits multinational corporations and their local allies. Actually, the industrialization process of the past decade has been and is carried out under conditions that are specifically designed to keep us in a subordinate and limited place in the international division of labor within the capitalist system. Yet little or nothing is said in the PD about the "dependent capitalism" that creates the exploitation of the poor in Latin America. The PD, in other words, skirts around all conflictual aspects of social reality.

The fundamental reason for this is that the PD has adopted a basic position that informs its entire world outlook. Because its authors believe there has been excessive attention to the issues of oppression and social injustice, the PD simply bypasses the crucial problem of the Latin American church, focusing instead on what it feels is a more radical challenge to the faith: "secularization" and its consequences. The major issues with which the PD deals are influenced by this perspective, which differs basically from the line of thought adopted by the church at Medellín. The PD's analysis betrays a strong European influence, as though European rather than Latin American problems were being confronted. This puts it at a great distance from what is distinctive about our own reality.

In contrast, the approach taken at Medellín began with the questionings of the poor and oppressed, those whom the system strips and casts aside, and who are not really considered as human beings with a right to live. *This* is where the great challenge for the proclamation of the gospel is to be found, for a faith in a loving God and, therefore, for theological reflection. Only from such a perspective can the challenges of the nonbeliever in the Latin American context be fully understood.

This is the place, I believe, for a criticism of "modernism"—the great preoccupation of the PD—a criticism that can lead to the root of the problem rather than remaining on a purely ideological level. To proclaim a "postmodern era" while the pillars of the economy are still standing and the representatives of the social class—the bourgeoisie—who sustain the modern ideology are still in charge, is to entertain illusions. It is to deceive ourselves and unfortunately to deceive others as well.

LATIN AMERICA AND THE WEST

It is impossible to understand a historical process and, what is more, bring about radical change in society without taking account of the cultural aspects of the Latin American people. The PD's mechanical and schematic analysis makes this mistake, failing to take account of those oppressed cultures where the poor nonetheless resist domination and express their most fervent sorrows and joys, fears and hopes.

For the PD there is a homogeneous Latin American culture. Although it acknowledges national differences and even the presence of "cultural subsystems," this acknowledgment carries no weight in the development of the subject matter. What is stressed is the origin of this culture rather than its specific characteristics: "If Latin America is a culture, it is because its people have decisive convergences in their roots as well as in the challenges that confront them." And these roots are in Europe: the "present cultural ambients are interrelated by their participation, to different degrees and in different ways, in so-called Western culture, the nucleus of which is to be found in Western Europe." The history, culture, race, philosophy, science, and techniques of the West are central for the PD, because according to it the "world is unified by 'westernization' and it is with it or within it that the greater cultural diversities are found."

Our initial interest in knowing that our peoples' cultures will be discussed is dashed as we discover how the issue is actually developed. The presence of ancient indigenous cultures is courteously acknowledged, but their voices go unheard as the resounding marching notes of westernization drown out the sound of their primitive instruments. The music of the poor, however, is a basic way of expressing their longing for freedom and their singing from Latin America to the God of the Bible—to say nothing of the culture of poverty, of painful alienation, of ruptures of ways of life, of unfeeling exploitation, and of basic insecurity in which the poor of Latin America live. All this is part of the cost and waste of the industrialization developed by the capitalist system (the only system that really exists in Latin America, save for Cuba).

The peoples of Latin America have been increasingly active in making their presence felt in ongoing history, seeking to take control of their own destiny and leaving behind their passivity or susceptibility to mass manipulation. This is true also in the church, not only through the increasingly active participation of the laity but above all through the role that the poor of Latin American countries have begun to play in recent years.

But once again the perspective of the PD on this important matter disappoints and worries us. A people, we are told, "is not simply a number, a mass of persons who inhabit the same land, but a unity joined together by a common development and participation in a similar culture"—that is, "in a lifestyle," and in the "close sharing of a people." As a result, it is not very clear who would *not* be included in this broad definition, and this is serious indeed because here we confront a key notion in the document as a whole.

Turning to the definition of "culture" is not much help. Stating that Latin American culture is the offspring of the West only adds to our confusion, and we begin to fear that the indigenous population who did not participate in developing this culture will therefore be excluded from this notion of the people. So whereas we might have expected that dominant groups and the oppressors of the majority—those who are at the other end of the social scale—would be excluded from being part of the Latin American people, we find that the definition tends rather to exclude the members of the oppressed cultures whose presence in Latin America is overlooked by the PD.

THE MEANINGS OF POVERTY

The PD refers to poverty at various times, and although it does not make poverty central to its concern, it does dedicate a significant section to it in the promising context of a discussion of evangelization. Even though—at the risk of being interpreted as a latent opposition—the title of the section juxtaposes "Evangelizing Everyone" with "Evangelizing the Poor," the PD does state correctly that evangelization is for everyone (though we presume that the monotonous insistence on this point has a polemical motivation). It acknowledges the need to question "painful and illegitimate inequalities." Never, however, does it indicate with precision *what kind* of inequalities are meant. This is a pity, because the preceding section states that the "church starts in its mission of evangelizing from the assumption of the legitimate existence of anthropological, social, and economic differences. In offering the gospel to all and incorporating persons from different social groupings in its fold, the church also takes on those differences."

These statements need clarification to avoid misunderstandings, of which this section unfortunately is full. The PD begins by stating that "there are many poor persons in Latin America." The brevity of this statement, which is the sum total of §650, does not predispose us too positively toward the text. But the heart of the difficulty lies in the "broader definition" of poverty that the PD seeks to formulate. In the first place, the poor are "the weak and powerless," and this is true at all levels—"economic, social, political, or human." The last term, rarely used when talking about the poor, is an attempt to include the "new poor": the alienated, the uncared-for, the elderly. In the second place, the meaning of the term "poor" is rather abruptly defined in a "more profound, religious, and specifically Christian" way, as a spiritual attitude of those who open themselves to God. This gives us a "rich and complex concept of the poor."

What we actually have here is the classic distinction between material and spiritual poverty. But the PD, fearing the "reductionism" to which the notion of the poor is susceptible, is so cautious that many of its statements are ambiguous. They reflect a great preoccupation that the notion of poverty will be reduced to a "mere objective, economic, and social condition of deprivation." There is less concern that it might be reduced to a "new subjective attitude." And the text forgets to state clearly that the powerlessness mentioned in the first definition is rejected by the Bible, which, moreover, does not speak about poverty only as a spiritual attitude.

It is particularly unfortunate that the PD does not say, as was said in simple, clear, and biblical terms at Medellín, that material poverty is *evil*. The omission becomes more serious when the passage on poverty as a spiritual attitude is concluded with a statement that "the concept of poverty *has its meaning synthesized therefore* in the following aspects: faith, hope, and trust in the Lord" (italics added). Why speak of "synthesizing" the significance of the term poverty? The incorporation of the first meaning into the second seems to make it evaporate into the concept of something "specifically Christian." But the distinction and dialectic between these two meanings is what gave strength to the concept, as Medellín showed so well. Because the PD expresses itself so equivocally, the notion of poverty is so diluted that few persons or none are excluded from it.

Entering confidently into a terrain full of ambiguities, the PD next deals with the way in which the materially poor receive the word of God. Unfortunately it does so in a fashion that indicates a lack of sensitivity to the scandal of the miserable poverty suffered by the great majority of the people. By seeking to avoid one "reductionism," it falls more deeply into the other one that the same text had pointed out earlier. There is praise for "the image of the poor that is a symbol in itself of an objective social condition of deprivation with a high level of spiritual richness," but there is no inclination to reject as inhuman and un-Christian that "objective condition of deprivation." Because it fails to do this, the text gives the impression that poverty is inevitable, caused by the human shortcomings of the poor, rather than something against which we should protest and struggle. The detached language takes no account of *the concrete situation of the poor* of Latin America, and opens the door to misunderstandings that Medellín had taken the trouble to clear up.

This impression increases as we read §657:

As they are evangelized and received into the fold of the church, the poor are given a supreme hope by the church based on the promises of God. Even when deprived of everything else, the church tries to provide them with the richness of having a God who, being rich, made himself poor (2 Cor. 8:9), and with faith, as the word that gives strength that will allow them to live with fortitude and with that happiness given by the coming of the kingdom—which no human pain can take away.

Whatever the intention of the writers, given the pain and want, the oppression and repression that the poor in Latin America suffer, this text appears to preach a counsel of resignation. The contrast is cruel, particularly in the context to which it is meant to speak. Even though the tone of the next paragraph is better, the detached language continues, and the text as a whole is simply devoid of an awareness of the pain and the hope of the women and men who live and die in poverty today in Latin America.

Is it surprising that the Medellín text on poverty is never quoted here? If "reductionism" was to be avoided, the clear-cut statements of Medellín would have provided the best antidote.

God loves the poor with special love because they are poor and not necessarily because they are good. The Beatitudes tell us more about the goodness of God than about the goodness of the poor. They reveal a *Go'el* God, defender and protector of the real-life poor, those deprived of what is necessary to live as human beings. It is this condition that makes them the preferred people of God. Medellín gave a great boost to commitment with the poor, and that commitment is the most authentic way of proclaiming the God of the Bible. This was the great strength of Medellín and the reason its pronouncements do not become dated.

Such commitment and proclamation of God has sent many Christians to prison, torture, and death—whether they were peasants, bishops, priests, workers, religious, or students. It is shocking that the PD makes not the slightest mention of the persecution suffered by the church in these years. The blood of our brothers and sisters, who have died giving an account of their faith in God and having loved to the full those loved by God, is what gives the contemporary Latin American church its greatest richness. The blood of these martyrs proves that the word of Medellín was not in vain and proves also that it will not be easy to erase its memory from the hearts of the poor of Latin America.

This lamentable omission is but another expression of the PD's reluctance to deal face-to-face—beyond small verbal concessions—with the vast dimensions of social conflict in Latin America. What is even more painful and offensive in this silence is that those who persecute often act in the name of "Christian principles" and in defense of our "Western and Christian civilization."

I shall make only a few observations on the section called "Elements for a Diagnosis," the very title of which indicates the modesty of its intention.

We are dealing here with a cold, descriptive text, lacking any sense of commitment. This is why it has little relevance for a pastoral perspective. The PD is guilty here of what it criticizes elsewhere—namely, confining itself to "sociological background.'' Mere data are accumulated, and, what is worse, the causes of poverty are presented without any sense of which ones are most important. This is unfortunate, because a good analysis of the causes of ''extreme poverty,'' for example, could well elicit concrete pastoral engagement. Simply enumerating the causes, without internal clarification, is insufficient.

The special place given to demographic problems attracts our attention. But bewilderment changes to concern when the key to the diagnosis—and the foremost concern—becomes demographic growth. After praising in various ways the benefits of Latin American economic development, the PD points out that the problem does not arise from the ''unquestionable accelerated rhythm of economic development,'' but from the fact ''that the economically active population has been GROWING MORE RAPIDLY than the capacity of the various countries to provide employment'' (capitalization in original text). This diagnosis recalls those given by the World Bank, along with its recommendations of massive population control.

INJUSTICE IS NOT AN ACCIDENT

Praise for the increased production rate observed in Latin America is followed by the affirmation that *''unfortunately''* we have not yet arrived at a more equitable distribution of income; emphasis has been placed on the increase of production, *''neglecting''* its adequate distribution. In reality, we all know that this does not happen ''unfortunately,'' but that it is the fault of the system itself, due not to ''neglect'' but to the very logic of the system. Inevitably we get the impression that the capitalist system is being justified, because, seemingly, all that needs to be done is to change the emphasis and stop ''neglecting'' the distribution of income. In no way is poverty linked to the kind of society that generated this economic growth.

Furthermore, the possibility of significantly improving the distribution of income by correcting some aspects of the system's functioning, without altering the system itself, is no longer believable after the experience of many attempts at ''reform'' in Latin America. These experiences clearly demonstrate that those with capital are not willing to accept redistribution of income, and that the most trifling attempts to better the situation of the majority of the people will be met without fail, in most countries, by the removal of capital, business boycotts, disinvestment, promotion of black markets, and political sabotage. It is clear that international capital seeks countries that offer submissiveness and cheap labor, and that when it does not find those conditions in one country it goes elsewhere in search of better conditions for exploitation, thereby destabilizing the regimes that tried the reforms.

In this section the PD offers a dangerous explanation of the regimes motivated by the doctrine of national security:

These regimes have emerged in many places as a reaction to the socioeconomic chaos that threatened the daily existence of the people in those places where the social network was seriously damaged. No society can resist a vacuum of power. Confronted by tension and disorder, resorting to force is considered inevitable.

Statements such as "vacuum of power" and "resorting to force as inevitable" are weighty—weighty indeed when it is proposed that they be endorsed by the bishops of a church that is seeking to plant its roots among the poor.

A little further on, with more insight, it is acknowledged that these regimes have provoked "a wave of human rights violations," but the misunderstanding as to causes persists. The more extensive paragraph in the PD dedicated to the same theme in a section on "social doctrine" is a little better. It introduces other aspects and makes the outlook more complex. But its detached tone keeps it from providing a corrective to what is said about national security in "Elements for a Diagnosis." Now, whether inspired by this doctrine or not, we have today many repressive regimes, violators of the most elemental human rights (as the text acknowledges) that have emerged to resist every move for social reform. The Latin American episcopate has carried out a firm and energetic battle against them, but this is not even mentioned in the PD.

Finally, let me underline an interesting point that should have been further developed; the point that calls attention to the scandalous reality that "extreme poverty" is suffered by nearly a hundred million persons in Latin America, in what is called a "Christian population." Day by day we live alongside these brothers and sisters who lack the most basic necessities to enable them to live as human beings. All this constitutes a demand for the future, at the same time that it is a harsh criticism of the evangelizing accomplishments of a church that has been massively present on the continent for nearly five centuries. That is why I lament that this point, so on target, should have been mentioned only in passing and in a single phrase.

A PURPOSEFUL READING OF HISTORY

In the historical portion of the PD there is an important section that presents an interpretive outline to which the document returns many times. It deals with "the two stages" the PD thinks it can discern in the postconciliar period, by means of which it tries to understand different aspects of this complex moment in the life of the church. The best thing at this point is to reproduce the text:

(a) From the social point of view Vatican Council II first takes a section of clergy and laity active in apostolic movements. It treats the nucleus of the elites most committed to the church initially within the framework of the urban middle class. Logically, then, they are the sectors that have access to more information, and are most attentive and sensitive to new happenings. The problems, conflicts, opposition, and inventiveness are localized especially within the dynamic of small

groups. Renewal then passes through the apologetics of the small committed communities, which break off from the Christian people and
return to it as a ferment for bringing about change. Dynamic groups
become strongly aware of the great structural injustices of our society
and feel a liberating solidarity with the poor. Medellín incarnated the
best expression of that moment.

(b) In a second stage, after Medellín and as a result of its motivation,
the circle of the people is penetrated. But they return to the past and
totally rethink it. To reach the Latin American Christian people it is
necessary to hear them. In this endeavor the elites take a new turn and
change the axis of their action. They are no longer the center; the pastoral action of the people moves to center stage. Thus the former stage
is not eliminated but transfigured; it begins to acquire a new logic. Popular religiosity is reevaluated. The problems of Latin American culture
are stated. From sociological attention in the present, the center of interest moves to historical consciousness.

The distinction centers on the transition from small groups and elites to the
people. This is an arbitrary analysis—and not an innocent one. On the contrary, it is loaded with implications. The first thing to be said is that it is very
difficult to fit the complexity of what has happened in the Latin American
church in recent years into the Caudine Forks of this narrow analysis. It
would be tiresome to enumerate all the events, so well remembered by all,
that challenge it, so let me mention only two: (1) Where do we fit the repression of the freedom of action of the church and Christian groups, their defense of the rights of the poor, and the persecution they have suffered?
(2) Where do we place the *comunidades de base*, the small grassroots communities, that have been multiplying all over Latin America?

What this distinction allows the PD to do is to discount the action of what it
considers small groups of clergy and students, many of them linked to apostolic groups, that entered into the fray after Vatican II, escaping from theologies of secularization. At the same time the distinction allows the PD to calm
down all disquiet. The spoilsports have left; everything has become orderly
once more; the people who supposedly went unappreciated in the first stage
are now strengthened, and authentic Christian values (or "Catholic values,"
as we would have to say at this point) are reaffirmed.

The PD repeatedly opposes elitist groups and the people. But it is not referring to the minority groups who hold the economic and political power and
who are benefited by an unjust social order. Here the distinction is intraecclesial, and this changes the perspective.

References to Medellín—the bishops' conference in 1968—cannot be
avoided in the PD, and even though there are not too many of them, those
included are important, decisive, and controversial.

In my comments above, references to Medellín have been frequent and
spontaneous. So let me note that the intention here is not to make a fetish of

Medellín or to defend its documents feverishly (as though I were the exclusive bearer of a correct interpretation). I strongly believe, furthermore, that the greatest faithfulness to Medellín is demonstrated not by quoting passages but by being caught up in its spirit. It is in this way that we can go "beyond Medellín," developing its concerns as clearly as possible.

In the historical section of the PD, a long section is devoted to what has been going on between Medellín and Puebla. The distinction given there also serves to locate Medellín historically. I must confess that reading those pages was a bitter blow. I believe that they represent a real and serious misunderstanding. For according to the PD, Medellín should be placed in the first stage, the time of the elites, the small groups, rather than as an expression of the people. The conference, "the early fruit of conciliar renewal," embodied "the best expression" of the first stage. What is said of this stage, then, and of its major participants, applies also to Medellín. Saying only this, with no further commentary, indicates a judgment about the meaning of Medellín that I find unacceptable.

RESPONSE TO THE POOR

It is rather the case that Medellín heard the voices of the poor in Latin America; it was in response to those voices that its choices were derived, along with its subject matter and the prophetic tone that has so deeply marked the history of our people. It is paradoxical to think that Medellín, if it had been the product only of small groups of elites, could have found the incisive language to speak of the pain and hopes of our people, stressed the dependency in which the Latin American countries find themselves, opted for the liberation of the poor, and given a testimony to evangelical poverty. On the other hand, it is ironic that the PD, presumably responding to the "second stage," which is that "of the people," adopts a distant, academic language, speaks of the industrial process without mentioning the working class, focuses its historical vision about the people of God on the history of the episcopate and forgets all about the men and women of that people of God (perhaps members of the elite?) who have forfeited their lives for listening to the cry of the poor.

The whole "two-stage" analysis is narrow and unfortunate; instead of helping us locate Medellín's limitations, it reinforces, by contrast, a reaction that does not allow us to analyze them with honesty and calmness. The whole criticism of Medellín is gratuitous and unproductive, as well as unjust. It is legitimate and important for the church that we go "beyond Medellín," but to do so we must embrace its spirit, adopt its sensitivity, possess its prophetic audacity, and share its willingness to listen to the people, understanding by the latter the poor and dispossessed of Latin America.

From the very beginning of the PD, evangelization is related correctly to God's revelation and to the human proclamation of the message: "Evangelization is the public proclamation from person to person of what God has

revealed." The perspective taken here by the PD in speaking of a self-reveal-
ing God will generate controversy. God is "the providential God." To believe in this God is to have faith that "the Lord is not a passive but active God,
supernaturally present in the world, and that the world is not unaffected by
this divine action." Given the abundance of negatives, this passage really
serves to *minimize* the action of God in history for Christians in Latin
America who have a vigorous awareness of the action and presence of the
Lord in history. To say that the world "is not unaffected" by God's action
seems to respond more to the modern mentality that so preoccupies the PD
than to the poor of Latin America. A similar minimizing results from speaking of God as "supernaturally present."

What is being underlined is that God is "a real person, definitely different
from the world he transcends." What this is seeking to express is obvious, but
the way of doing it seems cold and distant, using theological terms that lack
both vitality and biblical content. The PD repeatedly does this; its polemical
preoccupation with orthodox language removes it from the concrete experience of the Christian communities of Latin America, who have a more than
verbal instinct for orthodoxy.

The notion of the providential God, which no doubt expresses some of the
aspects of popular faith in God's love, is rigidly limited in the PD to the
concerns of Western civilization. This both hardens and devalues the notion
for Latin Americans, placing it within a discussion of the crisis of the West.
The document, with its marked preference for discussing ideologies, says of
this crisis:

> [It] takes hold at the roots, on the ideological level. At the basis of many
> Western ways of thought—be they called rationalism, liberalism,
> agnosticism, or a variety of one of their forms—we find secularism as a
> common denominator and as the spirit that impregnates modern cul-
> ture. This is an important point that, in the process of industrialization
> and urban growth described above, deserves our attention.

Such secularism, the PD goes on, "is equivalent to the project of organizing human life and history on the basis of the principle of pure immanence."
Faith in the providential God is excluded from such an outlook. But in doing
this the West is negating itself as a culture:

> Faith in the revelation of the providential God is the basis on which
> Western culture has built itself. It should not be surprising that
> throughout history we have gone over, again and again, arguments that
> endeavored to make a closer intellectual synthesis concerning the prob-
> lems of the relationship between reason and faith, theology and philos-
> ophy, providence and human freedom, grace and free will. These prob-
> lems touch the very heart of a Christian civilization.

Western civilization should be a Christian civilization; breaking the umbilical cord of faith in the providential God is therefore choosing death.

THE WORLD OR THE IVORY TOWER?

In full consistency with the rest of the PD, I find that when we look at what it feels are the great problems that "touch the very heart of Christian civilization," poverty is not among them, nor are exploitation and social injustice, nor even the fact that these things are actually happening within countries "that call themselves Christian," to use the words of Bartolomé de Las Casas. The issues discussed, although certainly real issues, have a distinctly "academic" flavor.

The consequences of this outlook become serious when applied to Latin America. "The same faith in God who reveals himself providentially, the Lord of life and history, has been transmitted by the evangelization of the people of Latin America, who have put their own stamp upon it." But then we would find the same crisis as in Europe, which, as we already know, has been produced by modern culture. But why not refer here, if not to social injustice, to the exploitation of the majority by dominant minorities, at least to the consequences of that exploitation?

The text does this, but lacking any strong positions at the appropriate moments, when speaking of the situation of poverty and misery experienced by the poor in rural and urban areas, it again expresses itself in terms that—quite apart from any judgment about intention—remain ambiguous:

> Faith in the loving and paternal presence of God in the daily events of human life is profoundly imbedded in the heart of our people. In times of hardship and sorrow, comfort and strength are found in the certainty that their suffering will also have a place in the designs of Providence.

In the strict meaning of the words, such a sentiment can be sustaining from an individual perspective, provided one recognizes the danger of its being reduced to something private. But if we take into account the social causes (such as "institutional violence") that lead to the suffering of our people, the text sounds like another example of preaching a counsel of resignation.

Actually, however, popular faith in a loving God is much more than this. And in the Latin American experience, that providence, that love, has been much more active as the expression of a God who liberates, who is a God of the poor. This perspective is lacking in the document—no doubt because of the confusion produced by secularism—but this, nevertheless, corresponds to the richest experience of the poor of Latin America.

As we know, the prophetic voice of Medellín, proclaiming the God of the Bible, has played a principal role in this. The PD tells us lucidly that from its point of view "the basis for any proposal the church can make lies in the conviction that there cannot be a really human civilization that is alienated from God.'' The problem is knowing *what* that alienation consists of, and *when* we can say that the Lord is not present. For this reason Medellín, making the harsh experience of the Latin American people its starting point, states clearly: ''Wherever unjust social, political, economic, and cultural inequalities are found, there is a refusal of the gift of peace; moreover, a refusal of the Lord himself'' (Medellín Document on Peace). From within this perspective a very different analysis emerges, along with a different concept of ''Christian civilization'' and a different task for the church.

''Popular religiosity'' occupies the place in the PD that ''the poor'' had in Medellín. Inasmuch as Latin Americans are religious, the fact that they are oppressed is less relevant and does not figure in the main theses of the PD. At Medellín the condition of poverty and exploitation of the Latin American people was the great challenge for a continent that called itself Christian; it was the source of an unpleasant task for the church; and, finally, it was a place for living out the faith based on the God of liberation.

RELIGION AS TRANQUILIZER

But the treatment of all this in the PD is not a disquieting challenge; it is presented in tranquilizing fashion. The condition under which the poor live does not trouble those in the church. Quite the contrary, it calms their concerns. After all, the interior life of these persons is Christian and, happily, has not been touched by secularist ideology. That they live and die in want and poverty is not deemed important. Free of secularism, although victims of shameful exploitation, they are the bearers of a faith in the God who is the basis of Western civilization.

So the peoples of Latin America do not present problems; rather they offer solutions to the questioning of a secularist elite. They cease being the agents of their own liberation or the breaking down of an oppressive system and become instead its solid support, ''a fountain of energies'' for the construction of the ''new civilization,'' which the authors of the PD are interested in seeing within a ''Christendom'' perspective—a Christendom that seems less ''new'' than when we began these pages. In fact, the popular religiosity that is presented to us here is a bulwark of the traditional values betrayed by the secularist crisis.

Popular religiosity is a complex and rich theme. It is being studied, and no doubt this will lead us to a closer understanding. It is something around which the intuitions of Medellín could be further developed. But to do this it would be necessary to adopt the liberation perspective given by Medellín. *The Latin American people is a Christian people, but it is also an exploited people*. Within this duality we find the ambivalence of popular religiosity, but also its liberating potential. We cannot forget that the dominant classes who oppress this people use Christianity to justify their privileges, but neither can we forget that the suffering of an oppressed people is revealed in popular expressions of the faith. In them we find a resistance and a protest against domination, as well as a vigorous witness of hope in the God of the Bible. The PD sees popular religiosity in quite another way, fulfilling a role of spiritual rescue from the urban-industrial process.

If the great challenge to faith in Latin America is a secularist ideology rather than the brutal exploitation of the poor, then the providential God will replace the God who liberates, the God of the poor of Medellín. Popular religiosity (as understood by the PD) will have the role poverty had; the notion of culture will take the place of liberation; the people, formed by all those who establish one identifiable culture, will replace the poor exploited classes; the people, considered in its material poverty, will be replaced by a people spiritually rich. In such a situation the task of evangelizing will be to discern the values of the modern world in order to build a new civilization, rather than to *denounce* the scandalous conditions of social injustice in Latin America, or to *announce* the love of the Father who raises his arm against the oppressor and frees the oppressed.

These shifts explain the absence of prophecy and pastoral perspective in the PD. It would be absurd to deny the problems that arise from what the text calls "secularism." But in Latin America they must be seen from another viewpoint—the viewpoint of social injustice produced by an oppressive system that crushes the poor. That is why the poor of Latin America feel so distant from this text. What bewilders and hurts in the document is the lack of acknowledgment of what constitutes the most living and creative part of the experience of the Latin American church during these recent years, of all that emerges from the poor and oppressed majorities. This is the reason for its lack of joy, its difficulty in communicating, the squalid nature of its hope.

Because this is only a *"preliminary* document," some may think that it does not merit too much attention. It has been very fruitful that the PD has been widely discussed throughout Latin America. The document takes clear positions on matters that have been present in the polemics of the Latin American church during this time. Studying it, then, can be more than situating ourselves in the context of the preparatory stage for Puebla; it can also help to provide clearer long-range positions.

The conference at Puebla will be an important moment in the pilgrimage of the people of God in Latin America. The PD is not necessarily, nor does it pretend to be, the document that will emerge from Puebla. But the positions taken in it invite us to state our own positions with equal clarity. Let us hope that these confrontations will somehow help us to get situated on the road to faithfulness to the poor and oppressed of Latin America, who struggle for liberation, for the right to live. May it also help us to see the demands that the Spirit makes on a church that seeks to be born from the people and be in solidarity with the poor of Latin America, in whom it recognizes with anguish and hope the presence of God.

6

Liberation and the Poor:
The Puebla Perspective

The reality of poverty, misery, and exploitation in the life of the vast majority of Latin Americans doubtless constitutes the most radical challenge to the proclamation of the gospel. After all, as Puebla repeatedly stressed, this is a society that is supposed to be Christian. But the gospel reveals to us a God who—as Karl Barth put it, echoing the message of Scripture—takes sides with the poor.[1]

It should be scant cause for astonishment that the matter of poverty came up as a key one in the preparation for Puebla. It was a matter the bishops would very possibly themselves wish to raise, it was thought, in witness to the authenticity of a church that ought to be laying itself open to questioning by the word of God, as well as by the concrete situation of the poor and oppressed in whom it ought to be recognizing the countenance of its Lord. The general theme selected by the bishops for Puebla made the subject of poverty even more pressing: "Evangelization in Latin America's Present and Future."

But there was another factor at work here as well. Over and above any empty words of compliance and conformity that might be pronounced—apart from all the courtesy nods—what about real continuity with Medellín? After all, Medellín had made a clear option of solidarity with the poor and their liberation. Nor was anyone ignorant of the fact that the perspective of the poor had been a central theme in Latin American theological reflection on liberation for at least ten years, and this was another bone of contention.

All this occasioned heated discussions during Puebla's preparatory stage.

Spanish original, "Pobres y liberación en Puebla," published in *Páginas,* 4/21-22 (Lima, April 1979), pp. 1-32.

In the judgment of many, the subject was being slanted away from its raw, massive reality and radical evangelical demand. Basic Christian communities, the *comunidades de base,* were crying out against what they considered to be efforts to skirt the question by giving it a spiritualistic focus, foreign both to the Christian message and to the concrete circumstances of Latin America's poor.[2] These pressures, admittedly, had been brought to bear by a minority, but that minority played an important role in Puebla's preparatory stage.

Then there was the opposite fear: that if the grassroots protests won out, everything would be so simplified that the rich, complex gospel theme of poverty would be reduced to merely one of its many dimensions. Hence the bishops were rightly asked to take a clear stand in the matter at Puebla. And indeed Puebla did hotly debate the subject, and it is no secret that the document "A Preferential Option for the Poor" encountered heavy weather.[3] Nevertheless, the life of a poor people, and the experiences of the church in Latin America over the preceding years, finally worked their way into this capital question.

Some points were settled, others were left as a task to be undertaken. But the subject of poverty is very much to the fore in the documents of Puebla, and not only in the one especially devoted to it (which without a doubt constitutes one of the better and more homogeneous of the Puebla texts) but in others as well. This must be kept in mind when attempting to analyze the treatment of poverty in that episcopal conference.

The pages that follow make no pretense of an exhaustive analysis of all the Puebla documents. Indeed, a chapter-length piece could scarcely hope to accomplish a like task. Let me make this clear at the outset, lest there be any misunderstanding. We shall limit our considerations here to the question of poverty itself, along with some points concerning liberation where it touches the question of the poor as such. These have been matters of harsh debate over the past years and are critical for the church's practice and reflection in Latin America. And of course they provide a point of departure for the examination of other themes, taken up in Puebla.[4]

IN THE FOOTSTEPS OF MEDELLÍN

Puebla explicitly asserts its continuity with Medellín, and it does so with a straightforwardness that we do not find in the preparatory texts. Nor is this continuity limited to express declarations; in fact it is found mainly in Puebla's manner of approach to certain central themes.

A Clear and Prophetic Option

In its exordium as in its conclusion, the document on the "preferential option" clearly states Puebla's intention of following in the footsteps of

Medellín. Such a frame for the presentation of the text is significant in itself. Chapter 1 opens:

> With renewed hope in the vivifying power of the Spirit, we are going to take up once again the position of the Second General Conference of the Latin American episcopate in Medellín, which adopted a clear and prophetic option expressing preference for, and solidarity with, the poor. We do this despite the distortions and interpretations of some, who vitiate the spirit of Medellín, and despite the disregard and even hostility of others [§1134].[5]

The intention, then, is to resume the position Medellín takes regarding the poor. This option is unhesitatingly qualified as *prophetic*. And this is indeed the impression left on the Latin American people by Medellín, in spite of all efforts since then to consider the whole thing to have been just a matter of euphoria and romanticism, and in spite of all the complicated distinctions brought to bear on this prophetic stance in an effort to divest it of its original meaning—which was the proclamation of the word of God from a point of departure in the reality of the poor person, a judgment rendered upon the offense committed against the Lord in the outrage and spoliation of the oppressed.[6]

Furthermore, Puebla here takes up a key term used by Medellín to concretize its option for the poor: *solidarity*. The document before us repeats the word several times—once quoting Pope John Paul II—thereby specifying what is meant by this "option," and precluding its investiture with the ambiguities and tenor of paternalistic condescension toward the poor, which some would have liked to attribute to it. In this wise the accent falls rather on a real involvement with the sufferings and the joys, the struggles against injustice and the longing for liberation, of the poor, as will be stated in texts we shall cite below.

In the same context, Puebla adopts, with certain precisions of its own, the "three meanings of poverty" as presented in Medellín, thereby stating its position with respect to it:

> The gospel demand for poverty, understood as solidarity with the poor and as a rejection of the situation in which most people on this continent live, frees the poor person from being individualistic in life, and from being attracted and seduced by the false ideals of a consumer society [§1156].

The option for the poor, as Puebla says more than once, is preferential and not exclusive. The pope had already emphasized this in various discourses he had pronounced on his visit to Mexico.[7] Let us be clear about this. Some have wished to see a criticism here of the practice and reflection that have been under way in Latin America over these last years. They are mistaken. There is nothing to be gained by beating about the bush here. There are distorted interpretations abroad, insistently repeated, and we may as well come right out and tell the truth of the matter.

This alleged exclusivity would be an evident mutilation of the gospel message. That message is directed to every human being, as someone loved by God and redeemed by his Son. The gospel is not anyone's private property, to do with as one might wish. *Preference* for the poor is written into the gospel message itself. But this alleged exclusivity, if it gained the upper hand, would—paradoxically—deprive that very preference of its historical "bite."

Precisely what so many find insupportable in the preferential option for the poor is its claim to announce the gospel within the dialectic of a universality that moves from and through the particular, from and through a preference. But it is precisely this preference that makes the gospel so hard and demanding for the privileged members of an unjust social order. An "exclusivity" would rather leave them on the sidelines, where this proclamation denouncing whatever despoils and oppresses the poor would go right on by them.

No, the gospel is addressed to every human being; only it has a predilection for the poor, and therefore makes its proclamation from a position of solidarity with the oppressed. This is what gives it such a precise tone in Latin America, where the majority are exploited and oppressed. No one is excluded from the proclamation of the good news, or from the concerns of the church, especially if it is to continue in solidarity with the life, sufferings, and aspirations of the ones the pope called "God's favorites."

For it is in just such terms that Medellín had couched its own preference for the poor. For example in the Medellín Document on Poverty, under "Solidarity and Preference for Poor," the episcopal conference says:

> The Lord's mandate is to preach the gospel to the poor. We must therefore distribute our apostolic personnel and efforts so as to give a preference to the poorest and neediest, and to those who are segregated for any reason. We must encourage and step up the studies and initiatives that are directed to this end [§9].[8]

Then this document adds:

> We wish to heighten our awareness of the obligation to have solidarity with the poor, an obligation that is prompted by charity. This means that we shall make their problems and struggles our own, that we shall find ways of talking to them.
>
> This must be fleshed out by our denunciation of injustice and oppression, by a Christian struggle against the intolerable situation of many

poor people, and by a process of dialogue with the groups responsible for this situation that will help them to appreciate their obligations [§10].

Puebla speaks in the same sense. Hence after reaffirming the meaning of gospel poverty as solidarity with the poor and protest against poverty (as in the text cited above), Puebla continues:

In like manner the witness of a poor Church can evangelize the rich whose hearts are attached to wealth, thus converting and freeing them from this bondage and their own egotism [§1156].

This is what the theology of liberation had attempted to do, both before Medellín and after. For the reasons noted, no exclusivity is ever affirmed. Instead, Puebla emphasizes a preference, stressing the special place the poor have in the message of the Bible and in the life and teaching of Jesus and the position they ought therefore to occupy among those who consider themselves his disciples.

From this point of departure it is possible to proclaim the gospel to *every* human being. Solidarity with the poor, with their struggles and their hopes, is the condition of an authentic solidarity with everyone—the condition of a universal love that makes no attempt to gloss over the social oppositions that obtain in the concrete history of peoples, but strides straight through the middle of them to a kingdom of justice and love.

Thus the assertions of John Paul II to the effect that it is a matter of preference, not exclusivity, far from being a criticism—as was claimed by international news agencies that seemed to have taken it upon themselves to dispel illusions about Puebla, and as was even thought with a great deal of good will by persons simply unfamiliar with the matter—actually corroborate precisely what is clearest and sanest in recent Latin American theological experience and reflection.

Of course another reason to rejoice in these assertions of the pope's is that they had the effect of promoting the option for the poor into one of the key themes of the Puebla conference. It was to enjoy an importance in the texts that perhaps it would not have had had it not been for the pope's insistence. And indeed the theme is missing from the preparatory documents.

There is one more matter deserving of our attention here with regard to Puebla's avowed effort to follow the lead of Medellín. The Puebla text recognizes and admits that, in spite of Medellín's clear option, that conference had afterward not been spared a number of "deviations and interpretations" that had been enjoying great currency in the years between Medellín and Puebla. But it also emphasizes the disregard and even hostility that Medellín's prophetic voice had encountered, as other texts will lament, in the dominant sectors of Latin American society. These circles had countered the teachings of Medellín with a studied neglect, on the pretext that its denunciations of social injustice suffered by the popular classes amounted to an abandonment of the true "spiritual" mission of the church.

We shall return to this point later on. For the moment let us simply observe that there could scarcely have been anything naive about Puebla's announcement that it was resuming the position of Medellín.

A Specifically Christian Concept of Poverty?

Puebla's continuity with Medellín is even more striking if we take into account the distance between Puebla and its own Preparatory Document on the subject of the poor. It would be superfluous to detail here the elements of this discrepancy.[9] Suffice it simply to note that the Preparatory Document does not even refer to Medellín, either explicitly or implicitly, and bypasses the subject of the preferential option for the poor in favor of an examination of what it calls the "deeper meaning" of poverty—a poverty it terms "specifically Christian." Such an approach, regardless of its framers' intentions, resulted in a de facto refinement and spiritualization of the notion of poverty to the point where it no longer had any direct reference to actual poverty.

This is another point to which we shall have to return. For the moment, however, let us merely observe that Puebla made a clean break with the approach taken in the preparatory texts and, as we have just seen, resumed the Medellín approach. The retrenchment attempt had been nipped in the bud.

A note that the Working Draft devoted to the topic ("The Poor and Poverty"), although timid and not altogether bereft of ambiguities, is a noticeable improvement over the Preparatory Document. The change had been provoked by the contributions of the national episcopates, many of which bore the mark of the experience and reflection of their basic Christian communities. Among these contributions the Peruvian document is outstanding on this point, as the note just referred to clearly shows. Peru's contribution had in turn been worked out on the basis of the contributions of regional bishops' assemblies, at which different sectors of the Peruvian church had had the opportunity to express themselves. Thus in the note we have a return to the three meanings of the notion of poverty that appear in Medellín, together with a sketch of certain points that Puebla would adopt and clarify, and of which we shall be speaking below.

Here we merely wish to point out that the note seeks to adjoin what it calls a "fourth type" of poverty, which Puebla did not adopt as such. (Medellín, by the way, does not speak of types of poverty but of different meanings of the *notion* of poverty.) The Working Draft reads, "He [also] is poor who remains open to the community." The reason for the exclusion, for that matter, is advanced in the Working Draft itself: the "fourth type" would be only one aspect of the second meaning delineated by Medellín. Hence the appendage would only have created confusion.

The "preferential option document" closed, as we have indicated, by ratifying its continuity with Medellín:

> With its preferential but not exclusive love for the poor, the Church present in Medellín was a summons to hope for more Christian and humane goals, as the Holy Father pointed out. . . . This Third Episcopal Conference in Puebla wishes to keep this summons alive and to open up new horizons of hope [§1165].

A clear conclusion can be drawn from this reaffirmation of fidelity to Medellín. It is a conclusion that is valid not just for the "preferential option" document, but for all the Puebla texts together. This episcopal conference had no intention of substituting itself for Medellín. Medellín retains all its validity. Its clear, prophetic option for the poor and for solidarity with them, in intimate nexus with Puebla, will continue to be demanded by "fidelity to the poor Christ"—to use the document's own expression.

THE POOR

The most significant fact in the political and church life of Latin America in recent years is the active presence that the poor are coming to assume in it. As can be imagined, this does not fail to provoke fear and hostility. Thus some actually went so far as to accuse Medellín (or interpretations of its texts characterized by them as capricious and irresponsible) of having itself created the problems and questions, and hence the aspirations and hopes.

What an incredible denial—from our point of view—of such a massive reality! Of course it stemmed from private interests. And so a polemic arose, eventually entrapping even the well intentioned. The point at issue was the true meaning of real poverty—"material" poverty, it came to be called—for Christian faith. It was feared that all the insistence on material poverty was going to cause the spiritual and genuinely evangelical sense of poverty to drop out of view.

On a terrain so long crisscrossed by blind alleys and wrong ways, where Medellín had sought to map out some clear paths, it was no great matter to kick up a few dust clouds that would send persons scurrying back to the old accustomed routes, especially persons having little understanding of biblical questions, or fearful of the radical conversion demanded by raw reality. On the other side, the need for immediate action led some persons to use expressions that oversimplified a complex situation. And so Puebla had some precisions to contribute on the matter.

The Reality of the Poor

In Puebla, a commission, the first, was given the assignment of presenting a survey of the real situation in Latin America from a pastoral point of view.

This did not prevent many other documents from framing their subjects in reference to the concrete situation in which they were to be found. But poverty, as a total question and the greatest challenge to the task of evangelization, naturally found its place in the text presented by this first commission. Examination of the reality of poverty thus occurs in the introductory text of the Puebla document, as part of the first commission's overview of Latin American reality as a whole. This can only underscore the importance of this analysis.

Right from the start, Puebla proclaims its continuity with Medellín:

> So we place ourselves within the dynamic thrust of the Medellín Conference . . . , adopting its vision of reality that served as the inspiration for so many pastoral documents of ours in the past decade [§25].

When one thinks of the attacks leveled at Medellín for its analysis of the social reality of Latin America, the full validity of this language can be appreciated. But the case was not closed with this verbal declaration of loyalty and continuity. Puebla now proceeded with content, in the form of a description of the situation, an examination of its causes, and the judgment in faith that all of this merits.

Institutionalized Injustice. Repeatedly, the Puebla bishops declare that we in Latin America live in a situation they call "institutionalized injustice." The expression is forcefully reminiscent of one of the boldest and most embattled assertions of Medellín—that our situation in Latin America is one of "institutionalized violence." (Puebla uses the latter expression as well—for example, in the document entitled "Church Activity on Behalf of the Person in National and International Society" [§1259].)[10] But there is a difference. Medellín mentions "institutionalized injustice" only once, and of course two long documents dealing with the same kinds of topics will inevitably employ similar terminology. (Medellín's use of these words is especially powerful, of course, because its immediate context is concretely topical.) But Puebla uses it on various occasions[11]—either in so many words, or in synonymous phraseology such as "in the position of permanently violating the dignity of the person" (§41).

The Puebla documents seek to define precisely what is meant. Thus the situation of poverty is identified as the result of a prevailing social order, of a structure, indeed of a "structural conflict." The document cites "two clear tendencies" in Latin America: "a thrust toward modernization, entailing strong economic growth," and "on the other hand the tendency . . . toward the pauperization and growing exclusion of the vast majority of Latin Americans from production" (§1207). Then it goes on:

> These contradictory tendencies favor the appropriation by a privileged minority of a large part of the wealth as well as the benefits created by science and culture. On the other hand they are responsible for the

poverty of a large majority of our people, who are aware of being left out and of having their growing aspirations for justice and participation blocked [§1208].

The passage concludes:

So there arises a grave structural conflict: "The growing affluence of a few people parallels the growing poverty of the masses" (Pope John Paul II, Opening Address, III, 4) [§1209].[12]

That is the only sort of statement a serious examination of the social situation in Latin America can lead to. Indeed, as the pope says:

Analyzing this situation more deeply, we discover that this poverty is not a passing phase. Instead it is the product of economic, social, and political situations and structures, though there are also other causes for the state of misery. In many instances this state of poverty within our countries finds its origin and support in mechanisms which, because they are impregnated with materialism rather than any authentic humanism, create a situation on the international level where the rich get richer at the expense of the poor, who get even poorer [Opening Address, III, 3].

For that matter, the pope had insisted on these structural factors in the mechanisms that generate poverty when he told the Amerindians of Oaxaca and Chiapas that they have "a right to have the barricades of exploitation removed." In turn, the "preferential option document" denounces "the grave injustices stemming from mechanisms of oppression" (§1136) and demands "the required change in unjust social, political, and economic structures" (§1155; cf. §1264). This is all groundwork for a denunciation of the capitalistic system prevailing in Latin America and of the presence of multinational corporations (e.g., §47, 312, 342, 1277).

Puebla offers us a vivid description of the poverty of the great majority of Latin Americans, in a sketch accompanied by a demanding pastoral and theological focus. (Let us not forget that Puebla proposed to offer "a pastoral view of the real Latin American situation." It achieved its aim admirably). This situation of poverty is said to "take on very concrete faces in real life. In these faces we ought to recognize the suffering features of Christ the Lord, who questions and challenges us" (§31). Then come the faces, group by group. In spite of the length of the description, we think it will be helpful to reproduce it in its entirety:

[They include]
—the faces of young children, struck down by poverty before they are born, their chance for self-development blocked by irreparable

mental and physical deficiencies; and of the vagrant children in our cities who are so often exploited, products of poverty and the moral disorganization of the family;

—the faces of young people, who are disoriented because they cannot find their place in society, and who are frustrated, particularly in marginal rural and urban areas, by the lack of opportunity to obtain training and work;

—the faces of the indigenous peoples, and frequently of the Afro-Americans as well; living marginalized lives in inhuman situations, they can be considered the poorest of the poor;

—the faces of the peasants; as a social group, they live in exile almost everywhere on our continent, deprived of land, caught in a situation of internal and external dependence, and subjected to systems of commercialization that exploit them;

—the faces of laborers, who frequently are ill-paid and who have difficulty in organizing themselves and defending their rights;

—the faces of the underemployed and the unemployed, who are dismissed because of the harsh exigencies of economic crises, and often because of development-models that subject workers and their families to cold economic calculations;

—the faces of marginalized and overcrowded urban dwellers, whose lack of material goods is matched by the ostentatious display of wealth by other segments of society;

—the faces of old people, who are growing more numerous every day, and who are frequently marginalized in a progress-oriented society that totally disregards people not engaged in production.

We share other anxieties of our people that stem from a lack of respect for their dignity as human beings, made in the image and likeness of God, and for their inalienable rights as children of God [§§31–40].

In speaking of institutionalized injustice, Puebla does not restrict itself to calling attention to the situation of *oppression* in which we live in Latin America. It also refers to the *repression* present here. And it is well aware of the connection between the two. Immediately following the long text just cited, Puebla denounces the "permanent violation of the dignity of the person," and then goes on:

To this there are added other anxieties that stem from abuses of power, which are typical of regimes based on force. There are the anxieties based on systematic or selective repression; it is accompanied by accusations, violations of privacy, improper pressures, tortures, and exiles. There are the anxieties produced in many families by the disappearance of their loved ones, about whom they cannot get any news. There is the total insecurity bound up with arrest and detention without judicial consent. There are the anxieties felt in the face of a system of justice that has been suborned or cowed. As the Supreme Pontiffs point out, the Church, by virtue of "an authentically evangelical commitment" (John Paul II, Opening Address at Puebla, III, 3), must raise its voice to denounce and condemn these situations, particularly when the responsible officials or rulers call themselves Christians [§42].

A "pastoral view" should make a deeper analysis of this situation, and that is what the document now proceeds to do, examining this poverty and this misery from the viewpoint of the faith.

A Situation of Sin. Many were those who, in the years following Medellín, rent their garments over another of that conference's bold expressions: that we in Latin America are in a "situation of sin."[13] Even at Puebla there were those who, though in full retreat before the use of the expression "structure of sin" by the Holy Father himself in his addresses, performed the same hypocritical ritual, decrying the "problems of conscience" aroused by such terms for the "children of good families" or for sisters who belonged to wealthy religious congregations.

But the only thing the protesters managed to achieve by their protests was that they themselves were left standing before the eyes of all in stark theological nakedness. For the expression "situation of sin," besides having such extensive biblical roots, unmasked a lacerating Latin American reality. But it is true that this expression is incompatible with a bourgeois, individualistic conception of friendship with God and with one another, and consequently of the breach of this friendship, which is what we call sin.

Echoing Medellín and the discourses of John Paul II, Puebla now pronounced its theological judgment, calling the institutionalized injustice in which we live in Latin America "social sinfulness"—and noting that the sin is all the more grave for the fact that this pernicious social order exists in countries calling themselves Catholic:

Viewing it in the light of faith, we see the growing gap between rich and poor as a scandal and a contradiction to Christian existence (cf. John Paul II, Opening Address, III, 2). The luxury of a few becomes an insult to the wretched poverty of the vast masses (cf. Paul VI, *Populorum Progressio*, 3). This is contrary to the plan of the Creator and to the honor that is due him. In this anxiety and sorrow the Church sees a situation of social sinfulness, all the more serious because it exists in countries that call themselves Catholic and are capable of changing the situation: "[The exploited] have a right to have the barriers of exploitation removed, . . . against which their best efforts at advancement are dashed" (John Paul II, Address to the Indians of Oaxaca and Chiapas) [§28].

The statement is a clear one. It places the responsibility for the misery at the door of a society that claims to be Christian. Nor are we dealing with an isolated text. The same phraseology is repeated in various places, with different nuances, as social dimensions of sin are cited and described as "very broad" (§73), or in a context of sin at once individual and social.[14]

The same idea, the same judgment, rings out in other expressions as well. In the "preferential option document," for example, the bishops declare: "Committed to the poor, we condemn as anti-evangelical the extreme poverty that affects an extremely large segment of the population on our continent" (§1159).[15] In "Church Activity on Behalf of the Person in National and International Society" the bishops resume a point on which Puebla is most sensitive—the scandal of social injustice in a society claiming to be Christian:

> The people of Latin America continue to live in a social situation that contradicts the fact that they inhabit a continent which is Christian for the most part. The contradictions existing between unjust social structures and the demands of the Gospel are quite evident [§1257].

The poverty—the "inhuman poverty" (§29)—in which Latin America is living represents an "anti-evangelical situation," a situation contrary to the gospel, and cries out against the guilty. The breach of friendship with God, and among persons—that is to say, sin—is the true root of the institutionalized injustice. Puebla says this with all the frankness one could wish for. There are the guilty, and there are victims. This must be denounced. The denunciation refuses to whitewash the facts, and turns into a challenge:

> Faced with the situation of sin, the Church has a duty to engage in denunciation. Such denunciation must be objective, courageous, and evangelical. Rather than condemning, it attempts to save both the guilty party and the victim. Such denunciation, made after prior agreement has been reached between pastors, appeals to the internal solidarity of the Church and the exercise of collegiality [§1269].[16]

As in Medellín, a structural analysis of a social order that oppresses and despoils the poor is accompanied by a judgment and a denunciation from the standpoint of faith that leave no loopholes. Both the analysis and the judgment have been objects of practice and theological reflection during recent years on the part of Christians committed to the process of liberation of the exploited masses of Latin America.

"Avenger of the Lowly"

Reinforcing the thinking of Medellín and the theology of liberation, Puebla understands the gospel demand for poverty in terms of solidarity with Latin America's poor, and protest against the situation of spoliation and oppression that prevents them from living as human beings. This solidarity and rejection are set forth as the indispensable condition for authentically living and proclaiming that central aspect of the gospel constituted by spiritual childlikeness—understood as availability in the sight of the Lord.

After all, to become as little children is a condition for entry into the kingdom of God, and, as Puebla reminds us, "the poorest sometimes seem to intuit this Kingdom in a privileged and forceful way" (§132). For "many of the poor incarnate in their lives the evangelical values of solidarity, service, simplicity, and openness to accepting the gift of God" (§1147). For some persons, as we have already noted, emphasis on the concrete situation of the poor and oppressed meant a neglect of the spiritual perspective they considered essential to the genuine notion of evangelical poverty. They were mistaken. Let us examine Puebla on this point.

The Reason for a Preference. To which "poor" do the documents refer when they speak of their "preferential option"? Clearly, the poor as they actually exist in Latin America and as rendered poor by the prevailing "mechanisms of oppression." Of this there cannot be the slightest doubt. In order to set the correct tone and preclude the possibility of any misunderstanding, the document on the "preferential option" tells us right at the start which poor are meant: "The vast majority of our fellow humans continue to live in a situation of poverty and even wretchedness that has grown more acute" (§1135).

A footnote, which in the document actually approved in Puebla had formed part of the main text, explains what is meant:

> [The] vast majority of our people lack the most elementary material goods. This is in contrast to the accumulation of wealth in the hands of a small minority, frequently the price being poverty for the majority. The poor do not lack simply material goods. They also miss, on the level of human dignity, full participation in sociopolitical life. Those found in this category are principally our indigenous peoples, peasants, manual laborers, marginalized urban dwellers, and, in particular, the women of these social groups. The women are doubly oppressed and marginalized [§1135, footnote].

The list is unequivocal. May we be allowed to call the reader's attention to the appearance in the list of the native peoples, the Indians—elsewhere described as "the poorest of the poor" (§34)—and the special concern of the conference for the women of each of these social sectors—"doubly oppressed and marginalized," because they are not only poor, but poor women.[17]

A little further on, after indicating that the gospel commitment of the church should be like that of Christ who took on full solidarity with humanity, and therefore should be a commitment to those most in need (§1141), the explanation appears: "When we draw near to the poor in order to accompany them and serve them, we are doing what Christ taught us to do when he became our brother, poor like us" (§1145).

Between these last two texts comes the forthright statement that "the poor merit preferential attention, whatever may be the moral or personal situation in which they find themselves" (§1142).[18] The preference for the poor is based on the fact that God, as Christ shows us, loves them for their concrete, real condition of poverty, "whatever may be" their moral or spiritual disposition. The text reveals its source admirably, and the latter helps us understand it better. The note "The Poor and Poverty" in the Working Document had said:

> It is our brothers' and sisters' indigence as such, without regard for their moral or personal situation, which creates the right they have to our attention . . . for, independently of their faith or goodness, Jesus Christ took all weaknesses upon himself in order to heal them [§187].

The source of the Working Document, in turn (and explicitly recognized as such), is the material contributed by the Peruvian episcopate, which expresses the same idea with all desirable clarity and with a solid basis in theology:

> The privilege of the poor, then, has its theological basis in God. The poor are "blessed" not because of the mere fact that they are poor, but because the kingdom of God is expressed in the manifestation of his justice and love in their favor.[19]

The conclusion is unmistakable. The preferential option is for the poor as such, the poor as poor. The value of their attitude of openness toward God is not neglected, and we shall return to this point below. But this does not constitute the primary motive of the privilege of the poor, as is clear from our Puebla document when it says:

> This central feature of evangelization was stressed by Pope John Paul II: "I have earnestly desired this meeting because I feel solidarity with you, and because you, being poor, have a right to my special concern and attention. I will tell you the reason: the pope loves you because you are God's favorites. In founding his family, the Church, God had in mind poor and needy humanity. To redeem it, he sent his Son specifically, who was born poor and lived among the poor to make us rich with his poverty (2 Cor. 8:9)" (Address in the Barrio of Santa Cecilia, Jan. 30, 1979) [§1143].

The barrio of Santa Cecilia is a poor neighborhood of the city of Guadalajara. The pope maintains that, in their quality as poor and marginalized persons, and independently of their spiritual dispositions, those who live in this neighborhood are "God's favorites." The quotation from the pope in the next paragraph, again from a homily delivered during his Latin American visit, reinforces this perspective. It is an important statement, and Puebla introduces it with another assertion charged with meaning:

> In her Magnificat (Luke 1:46–55), Mary proclaims that God's salvation has to do with justice for the poor. From her, too, "stems authentic commitment to other human beings, our brothers and sisters, especially to the poorest and neediest, and to the necessary transformation of society" (Homily in Zapopán, 4) [§1144].

This interpretation of the Magnificat has been a favorite element in the life and reflection of Christians committed to the process of liberation in Latin America.[20] It receives further papal encouragement later on in the Zapopán address:

> As my predecessor, Paul VI, states in his Apostolic Exhortation *Marialis Cultus* (37), Mary is also the model, as faithful handmaid of the will of God, of those who refuse passively to accept the adverse circumstances of their personal and social life, who refuse to be victims of "alienation," as you say today, but who proclaim with her that God is the "avenger of the lowly," and that if need be he "pulls down the mighty from their thrones"—to use the words of her Magnificat once more.

Then, too, there are innumerable occasions when the Puebla documents cite—and denounce—the situation of the poor, who lack "the most elementary material goods." The conference leaves no room for doubt as to the character of this poverty—so frequently modifying "poor" with expressions such as "oppressed," "most needy," "suffering," "forgotten," and so on.[21]

I have already cited passages where this concrete situation of the poor is referred to. Here let me simply call attention to the fact that Puebla considers it to be just this aspect of their poverty that occasions the "preferential option" constituting one of the central aspects of its message. The language is clear as day:

> This option, demanded by the scandalous reality of economic imbalances in Latin America, should lead us to establish a dignified, fraternal way of life together as human beings and to construct a just and free society [§1154].

The option is demanded by the scandalous reality of poverty. There is no way to think that the scandal may have been provoked by "poverty of spirit."

The Anti-evangelical Nature of Poverty in Latin America. There is something that has to be added to what we have said so far about the reason for Puebla's preference for the poor. We have emphasized the concrete, material nature of the poverty motivating Puebla to make a preferential option for the subject of that poverty. And we have based our stance on text and context, as Puebla luminously propounds its view. If one does not grasp this, then "Blessed are the poor" loses its meaning.

But Puebla puts us on the track of further implications when it characterizes poverty here and now in Latin America as "anti-evangelical." There is no abstraction going on here, there is no playing with the gospel and with human beings, after the fashion of those who make poverty a sweet and tender ideal (which they are at great pains to avoid striving for).

Puebla, like Medellín, not only does not use this ambiguous language about an "ideal," but explicitly rejects it, and continues to stress material poverty. The poverty in which the poor and oppressed of Latin America are living is contrary to the Christian message, and a denial of the God who reveals himself in the Bible. As a Bolivian *campesino,* Paz Jiménez, put it in a press conference on February 2, 1979, with an insight that is profoundly biblical: "an atheist is someone who fails to practice justice toward the poor."

It is knocking on the wrong door to wish to salvage the spiritual nature of the Christian message by trying to rid it of the clear and direct meaning of material poverty in the Bible as a determinate, concrete, human, social condition. On the contrary, a heightened consciousness of it is what most lucidly reveals the meaning of the proclamation of the kingdom of God.

The Beatitudes are a proclamation of Jesus' central message: "the kingdom of God is at hand." Hence they have in the first instance a *theological* character: they tell us who God is. Secondly, they are *anthropological.* That is, they emphasize the importance of spiritual dispositions in those who hear the word. These two aspects are not opposed; they are complementary. But the theological aspect—the emphasis on God and his goodness toward the poor—is the primary.

What does this mean? All exegetes agree that the message of the Beatitudes is a genuinely religious message. But those who have studied them in greater depth contradict those who think the way to maintain the religious nature of the Beatitudes is to assert that they refer exclusively, or at least primarily, to somebody "spiritually poor," lest they canonize any determinate social group.[22] This is not only faulty biblical interpretation, it is ignorance of the texts themselves.

To assert that the proper, original message of the Beatitudes refers first of all to the "material poor" is not a "humanization" or politicization of their meaning. It is a recognition that God is God and that God loves the poor with all freedom and gratuity—and that God does so not because the poor are good, or better than others, but just because they are poor. That is, they are afflicted, they are hungry, and this situation is a slap in the face of God's sovereignty, God's being the Go'el ("Savior, Redeemer"), the Defender of the poor, the "Avenger of the lowly."

The Beatitudes are, before all else, a revelation about God. Their theological perspective is primary. Only if we recognize and accept this fact will we be able to understand the Beatitudes as a declaration of the dispositions that human beings must have in order to hear the word—which is their secondary, anthropological, perspective.

Once the primary notion is appreciated, we can address the secondary. To be sure, the "blessedness" of the poor is constituted by the fact that the God of the Bible is a God of justice, and hence a God of the poor. There is a consequence to be drawn here—in complementarity, not in contradiction, with its theological antecedent. Spiritual poverty—that is, spiritual childlikeness—is the condition for being able to hear the revelation of the kingdom. At the same time it remains clear that if we forget that the Beatitudes are talking about the materially poor, and therefore are talking about God, we will not understand what they tell us about the spiritually poor, the "poor in spirit."

It must likewise be understood that the religious character, the authentically spiritual nature of the message, is not limited to discourse about spiritual poverty. The religious nature of the Beatitudes is apparent mainly in their first meaning: blessed are those who are caught in a position of social inferiority, for God is God. As the document from the Peruvian episcopate put it, "the privilege of the poor . . . has its theological basis in God."

Viewed in this light, our insistence that it is the materially poor who are blessed is not reductionist in the least. The kingdom is at hand, and the kingdom is contrary to all injustice. What we are dealing with is a *paradox:* if we "spiritualize" the poor too early, before the proper moment in the dialectic, we "humanize" God. We make him more accessible to human understanding by attempting to fit him into bourgeois categories and a middle-class mentality. But the theology of the Beatitudes must always come before their anthropology. God, one could think, would surely have a preferential love for the good. After all, the good have more merits. But if instead we maintain that God prefers the poor just because they are poor (again, materially poor)—then we may be flying in the face of logic, but we are standing point-blank before the mystery of God's revelation and the gratuitous gift of his kingdom of love and justice.

We are in the presence of something that defies our human categories. We are before the mystery of a God who is irreducible to our mode of thinking. But does this not deprive spiritual poverty (spiritual childlikeness) of its meaning and thereby contradict the gospel and the Christian tradition. On the contrary, it affords us a better understanding of it. Spiritual "childhood," or childlikeness, as Medellín said repeatedly, is one of the central elements of the gospel message. Hence Puebla sáys:

For the Christian, the term "poverty" does not designate simply a privation and marginalization from which we ought to free ourselves. It also designates a model of living that was already in evidence in the Old Testament, in the type known as "the poor of Yahweh" (Zeph. 2:3, 3:12–20; Isa. 49:13, 66:2; Ps. 74:19,149:4) [§1148].

Here we have the first two senses of the term "poverty," as distinguished in Medellín, and the necessary premise for understanding the gospel demand of poverty as "solidarity with the poor and as a rejection of the situation in which most people on this continent live" (§1156). Spiritual poverty permits one to live this solidarity, and all its consequences, in the insecurity of quest, and confidence in the Lord.

The Poor Christ

Medellín sought to base its vigorous summons to the witness of poverty and the reflection that accompanies it on the example of Christ.[23] Puebla also appeals to this christological foundation.

Here the nub is in Christ's identification with the poor as we find it in Matthew 25:31–46, that key text for Puebla and for the pope's addresses in Mexico. It is also a central passage, as we know, for the basic Christian communities, as well as for theological reflection on the commitment to liberation in Latin America. In a passage cited above, Puebla speaks of the "suffering features of Christ," and then goes on to enumerate the concrete form these features take in the faces of the poor of Latin America (§31–40).[24] As a consequence of this identification, Puebla tells us:

> [This] Christian message . . . will also be lived by those who renounce a life of ready pleasure and dedicate themselves to serving others in a realistic way in today's world. For that is the criterion and gauge that Christ is going to use in passing judgment on human beings, even on those who had not known him (Matt. 25)[§339].

Puebla repeats the idea that service to the poor, and involvement with them and commitment to their cause, are the "privileged . . . gauge of our following of Christ" (§1145). And this service demands "constant conversion and purification among all Christians. That must be done if we are to achieve fuller identification each day with the poor Christ and our own poor" (§1140).

"The poor Christ" is an expression that has been acquiring more and more meaning and power among the poor of Latin America.[25] In it they see expressed their faith in the Son of God become a human being, become poor— "poor like us," as the "preferential option document" phrases it. In this expression, which is so closely linked with that of "Christ the Liberator" (of whom Puebla speaks in its "Message"), Jesus is seen as the Word made flesh, the one who "pitched his tent in our midst," as John's Gospel puts it (1:14).

Yes, in the midst of his people—a people poor and exploited, but believing and hoping in him.

One must be very far removed from the life of the people to fail to be able to perceive—here in this profession of faith in Christ's nearness as manifested in the expression "the poor Christ"—a profession of the presence of God in the concrete history of humanity, a profession that Jesus is the Son of God. I do not mean an external profession, with the lips, but one that springs from the everyday sufferings, struggles, and hopes of the poor; not an "orthodoxy" that exhausts itself within itself, but the affirmation of a vital, extremely intimate, and yet conscious and reflective truth. The masses receive but very little from those obsessed with the formal theses of the Christian faith. For Christ's poor in Latin America, these professions are part of daily life, prayerful practice, and of authentic theological reflection.

The term "following of Christ," in the text above, is a classic expression from the annals of ascetical literature, and one become current again today in Latin American theology.[26] It means walking the road Christ himself walked. That road, of course, is the one of "commitment to those most in need," according to the program mapped out in Luke 4:18–21 (§1141; cf. §190). Here Puebla strikes root in the fertile christological soil of solidarity with the poor. Another text says, concerning members of religious orders:

> Radically denying themselves, they accept the Lord's cross as their own (Matt. 16:24) and shoulder it. They accompany those who are suffering from injustice. . . . Sharing in the death of those who suffer, they joyously rise with them to newness of life. Becoming all things to all human beings, they regard the poor as privileged beings, as the Lord's favorites [§743].[27]

Here I should like to make an observation. Puebla published a document devoted to christology. It was well intentioned. But its general, basic statements are calculated to assure a broad and pacific consensus. It avoids major questions and fails to afford any stimulus for practice and reflection. Still it would be mistaken to see Puebla's doctrine on Christ as limited to this one document. There are rich christological observations scattered throughout the Puebla texts, and sometimes they touch on concrete problems, even disputed ones, facing the people of Latin America. Puebla sought fertile inspiration in the deeds and words of the Lord—and therefore it manifested a creativity abundantly deserving of our attention.

LIBERATION AND EVANGELIZATION

From a number of points of view, evangelization and liberation are closely connected in the life of the Latin American church. But this link runs the risk of taking off for the blue sky of the abstract unless it maintains its orientation toward the concrete poor. This is a point that had been made with precision and force in Latin American practice and reflection for a number of years. Then it was taken over by Medellín, and now we find it in Puebla.

Poverty and Integral Liberation

A Polemical Question. Liberation has been a key term in the experience of the Latin American people for some years now. At the economic and political level, it expresses a breach with compromise and reformism.[28] But the term "liberation" also means, at the theological level, an effort to cut to the very roots of the social injustice rampant in our part of the world—to go all the way to an understanding of the notion of salvation in present historical conditions, as a free gift of the Lord who becomes flesh in the life of a people fighting for its human dignity, and its status as offspring of God.

The synthetic, complete—and demanding—perspective expressed in this term immediately gave rise to a lively polemics. At first it was said we were running the risk of reducing Christ's liberation to its historical and social implications. Then it was said, without batting an eyelash and without taking the trouble to read what was actually written, that these historical and social consequences were the only thing in which the Christians involved in the liberation process were interested. Finally, with all the foregoing as a self-evident premise, the term "integral liberation" came into currency, as a "response" to this alleged reductionism. What was curious in all this was that "integral liberation," as understood by the proponents of the new term, was no more integral, for all its vaunting, than the reductionism they were themselves alleging. For they were *reducing* liberation to the so-called religious or spiritual—spiritualistic—plane.

As had happened with the preferential/nonexclusive option for the poor, now too the only aim was to win the argument by dint of sheer insistence, with little concern for the truth. One had the impression these guardians of the spiritual might even be seeking to convince themselves. At best, they began with ambiguous and sporadic assertions, and then generalized from them without attention to the complexity of the subject. Here again, then, putting aside any false sense of shame, we must energetically confront and belie these declarations. For they twist and distort the truth.

One of the oldest themes in the theology of liberation is the totality and complexity of the liberation process. This theology conceives total liberation as a single process, within which it is necessary to distinguish different dimensions or levels: economic liberation, social liberation, political liberation, liberation of the human being from all manner of servitude, liberation from sin, and communion with God as the ultimate basis of a human community of brothers and sisters. As I have written elsewhere:

This is not a matter of three parallel or chronologically successive processes, however. These are three levels of meaning of a single, complex process, which finds its deepest sense and its full realization in the saving work of Christ. These levels of meaning, therefore, are interdependent. A comprehensive view of the matter presupposes that all three aspects can be considered together. In this way two pitfalls will be avoided: first, *idealist* or *spiritualist* approaches, which are nothing but ways of evading a harsh and demanding reality, and second, shallow analyses and programs of short-term effect initiated under the pretext of meeting immediate needs.[29]

Paradoxically, then, integral or total liberation, presented in this polemic as an alternative to its supposedly lopsided antithesis in the theology of liberation, is actually one of the latter's most classic themes. But—and this is important—one must be careful to conceive of it as *really integral*. That is, one must keep account of the complexity of the subject, avoid sidetracking any of its dimensions, and understand it in conjunction with all the exigencies and demands from which it cannot be divorced. This, at bottom, is what those who deny that they see the historical implications of Christ's salvation have refused to do, and will so continue.

The Cry for Liberation: A Threat. Medellín had spoken of the mute cry for liberation of millions of Latin Americans (Document on Poverty, §2). Puebla asserts that, ten years later, things have changed: "The cry might well have seemed muted back then. Today it is loud and clear, increasing in volume and intensity, and at times full of menace" (§89).

Puebla recognizes that the yearning for liberation in Latin America has become even more urgent and demanding than before. In his addresses in Santo Domingo and Mexico, the pope had already spoken in this vein more than once, and now Puebla takes up the theme—frequently employing the adjective "integral." Hence it is important to see what Puebla means by "integral." One text is especially interesting. It expatiates on the integral character of true liberation, and makes some important precisions. This passage, part of the contribution of the Commission on Human Dignity, is so long (§§321–29) that we can cite only a few extracts, paraphrasing and condensing the rest.

After asserting that freedom is a gift and a task, which "cannot be truly achieved without integral liberation (John 8:36)," and which "in a real sense . . . is the goal of human beings, according to our faith," Puebla cites a text from St. Paul that has played an important role in our reflection on liberation—Galatians 5:1. The apostle says, "When Christ freed us, he meant us to remain free" (§321). Puebla goes on to say that fashioning a community, a participation, having its roots in the freedom that is the capacity to dispose of ourselves—fashioning our lives in their concrete reality—is something that must be done "on three inseparable planes: our relationship to the world as its master, to other persons as brothers or sisters, and to God as God's children" (§322). There follows a detailed presentation of these three planes (§§323–25). Finally, their intimate links with one another are expounded, as based upon a profound unity:

Through the indissoluble unity of these three planes, the exigencies of communion and participation flowing from human dignity appear more clearly. If our freedom is fully realized on the transcendent plane by our faithful and filial acceptance of God, then we enter into loving communion with the divine mystery and share its very life (*Gaudium et Spes*, 18). The opposite alternative is to break with filial love, to reject and despise the Father. These are the two extreme possibilities, which Christian revelation calls grace and sin respectively. But these two possibilities do not occur without simultaneously extending to the other two planes and having enormous consequences for human dignity [§326].

The last two points are an effort to identify the relationship between the third plane—one's relationship with God—and the other two: the relationship among persons and the relationship between persons and the material world (§323). The link between the third and second planes will be "first and foremost a labor of justice":

The love of God, which is the root of our dignity, necessarily becomes loving communion with other human beings and fraternal participation. For us today it must become first and foremost a labor of justice on behalf of the oppressed. The fact is that "one who has no love for the brother he has seen cannot love the God he has not seen" (1 John 4:20) [§327].

This "labor of justice," then, means the effort of liberation. The link with the first plane is expressed in a transformation of the material world with a view to the construction of a just lordship there—one that will consist in a true communion of sisters and brothers:

Authentic communion and participation can exist in this life only if they are projected on to the very concrete plane of temporal realities, so that mastery, use, and transformation of the goods of this earth and those of culture, science, and technology find embodiment in humanity's just and fraternal lordship over the world—which would include respect for ecology [§327].

Next, the document reaffirms the inseparability of the planes, following the schema of grace and sin indicated above. First, grace: the document sets forth the concrete social and historical demands of the love of God, of friendship with God:

Confronted with the realities that are part of our lives today, we must learn from the Gospel that in Latin America we cannot truly love our fellow human beings, and hence God, unless we commit ourselves on the personal level, and in many cases on the structural level as well, to serving and promoting the most dispossessed and downtrodden human groups and social classes, with all the consequences that will entail on the plane of temporal realities [§327].

There is no love for God without love for one's brothers and sisters, particularly those who are most poor, and this means—the document could not be clearer—a commitment on the level of social structures, "with all the consequences that will entail on the plane of temporal realities."

Now the document looks at what happens in the other half of the schema: sin. Of course the picture just presented is only reinforced. The concrete, historical consequences of sin—breach of friendship with God—are inevitable:

Sinfulness on the personal level, the break with God that debases the human being, is always mirrored on the level of interpersonal relations in a corresponding egotism, haughtiness, ambition, and envy. These traits produce injustice, domination, violence at every level, and conflicts between individuals, groups, social classes, and peoples. They also produce corruption, hedonism, aggravated sexuality, and superficiality in mutual relations (cf. Gal. 5:19–21) [§328].

All this is a description of the creation of a situation of sin, a notion that, as we have already mentioned, was central in Medellín, and which Puebla here resumes with greater force and insistence: "Thus they establish sinful situations which, at the worldwide level, enslave countless human beings and adversely affect the freedom of all" (§328).

Sin, the breach with God, is not something that occurs only within some intimate sanctuary of the heart. It "always" translates into interpersonal relationships, the document says, and hence is the ultimate root of all injustice and oppression—as well as of the social confrontations and conflicts of concrete history, whose existence among us the document makes no attempt to sidestep.

This is how far one must go if one wishes to grasp the meaning of Christ's liberation and all its implications. As Medellín says, in a now familiar passage:

It is the same God who, in the fullness of time, sends his Son in the flesh, so that He might come to liberate all men from the slavery to which sin has subjected them: hunger, misery, oppression and ignorance, in a word, that injustice and hatred which have their origin in human selfishness [Justice, §3; CELAM-LAB trans.]

Puebla takes up the same idea, in the conclusion of this long passage on the manner of understanding the expression "integral liberation"—and reasserts from this viewpoint the inseparability of the three planes that have now been so carefully expounded:

> It is from this sin, sin as the destroyer of human dignity, that we all must be liberated. We are liberated by our participation in the new life brought to us by Jesus Christ, and by communion with him in the mystery of his death and resurrection. But this is true only on the condition that we live out this mystery on the three planes described above, without focusing exclusively on any one of them. Only in this way will we avoid reducing the mystery to the verticalism of a disembodied spiritual union with God, to the mere existential personalism of individual or small-group ties, or to one or another form of social, economic, or political horizontalism (John Paul II, Opening Address at Puebla, III, 6) [§329].[30]

Puebla has the perspicacity to insist on the pope's integral focus—which condemns not only horizontal reductionism (the shibboleth of the polemicists) but the vertical as well, so frequently passed over in silence.

The passage is crystal clear. And the precision of its language recaptures the best of Latin American reflection on the point at issue. Puebla does not fall prey to the terrorist attitudes of those who undertake to ignore the complex, rich meaning of the term "liberation" as it has been used during recent years—years of increasing commitment, in the form of Christian practice and reflection, to the struggles of an exploited community of believers to build a humane and just society. Their communion with the death and resurrection of Jesus Christ, at the heart of this battle, is the magnificent witness of this people during these years.

To live the love of Christ to the point of giving one's life for one's sisters and brothers, affirming one's hope in the life of the resurrected Christ who vanquishes all death and injustice, is the central element of the power of the poor in history. This is why the aspirations and struggles of the poor for liberation are a threat to the great ones of this world, those who reap the benefits of a social order where they sow death—but fail to stifle hope.[31]

This long passage, then, is the key to the correct understanding of the term "integral liberation," so frequently used in Puebla.[32] It is in light of this notion of integral liberation that the whole series of Puebla documents on the subject should be read.[33]

The Evangelizing Potential of the Poor

When Puebla was in preparation, there was a great deal of searching to identify the primary and most urgent challenge to the task of evangelization in the church. After all, this would be the theme of the conference itself. But when the conference convened, there was no hesitation. Puebla stated its position at the very beginning. Hence we too may enter at once upon the point that interests us here—the relationship between gospel and liberation, from the perspective of the poor:

> The situation of injustice described in the previous section forces us to reflect on the great challenge our pastoral work faces in trying to help human beings to move from less human to more human conditions. The deep-rooted social differences, the extreme poverty, and the violation of human rights found in many areas pose challenges to evangelization. Our mission to bring God to human beings, and human beings to God, also entails the task of fashioning a more fraternal society here [§90].

Bringing God to human beings presupposes the building of a society of brothers and sisters. A dominant theme in Puebla will be this relationship between the proclamation of the gospel and the struggle for justice—the relationship between salvation, and that "justice for the poor" that is the teaching of the Magnificat (§1144).[34]

Puebla takes up a position from one of the richest gospel perspectives when it recalls:

> The poor are the first ones to whom Jesus' mission is directed (Luke 4:18–21), and . . . the evangelization of the poor is the supreme sign and proof of his mission (Luke 7:21–23) [§1142].

But given the concrete situation of the poor in Latin America, this evangelization will make an option for liberation. This is why, after pointing out that service rendered to the poor is the "privileged gauge" of the following of Christ, Puebla asserts:

> The best service to our fellows is evangelization, which disposes them to fulfill themselves as children of God, liberates them from injustices, and fosters their integral advancement [§1145].

The passage is brief but precise. It explains the meaning of a liberating evangelization by placing it within the context of the three planes of integral liberation, which we saw above and which we saw to be inseparable. This is the context in which the preferential option for the poor is situated:

> The objective of our preferential option for the poor is to proclaim Christ the Savior. This will enlighten them about their dignity, help them in their efforts to liberate themselves from all their wants, and lead them to communion with the Father and their fellow human beings through a life lived in evangelical poverty [§1153].

The option is demanded by the "scandalous reality of . . . Latin America," as we saw (§1154). It "should lead us to establish a dignified, fraternal way of life together as human beings and to construct a just and free society" (§1154). The proclamation of the gospel is a contribution to liberation from whatever oppresses the poor in the here and now of the social injustice in which they live. It summons them to live as children of God and to enter into communion with the Father. The condition for this proclamation of the gospel is "the lived experience of evangelical poverty" (§1157)—which we now know to be solidarity with the poor and rejection of the situation of spoliation in which the vast majority in Latin America live.

But Puebla goes a step further along these lines, echoing the rich experience of the Latin American church in recent years. In the document "The People of God Are in the Service of Communion," the conference asserts that the postconciliar years have been marked in Latin America "by a rising awareness of the masses of the common people" (§233). This and other considerations lead the Puebla bishops to demand in another document that the Latin American poor "be taken into account as responsible people and subjects of history, who can freely participate in political options, labor-union choices, and the election of rulers" (§135).

Accordingly, conscious of the fact that "the common people . . . construct the pluralistic society through their own organizations," the church must contribute to the construction of "a new society for and with the common people" (§1220). These observations and demands, concerning the people as agent of its own history, are also expressed in a most meaningful way in a context of evangelization. The "preferential option document" says:

> Commitment to the poor and oppressed and the rise of grassroots communities have helped the Church to discover the evangelizing potential of the poor. For the poor challenge the Church constantly, summoning it to conversion; and many of the poor incarnate in their lives the evangelical values of solidarity, service, simplicity, and openness to accepting the gift of God [§1147].

This notion had been expressed with great lucidity in the contribution of the Peruvian episcopate to Puebla's preparatory phase, in a section devoted to "the poor in Latin America as addressees and agents of evangelization" (§§435–41). There we find a discussion of the "evangelizing charism of the poor":

> The church's commitment to the poor and oppressed, and the growing importance of the basic church communities among the masses, from Medellín on, have led it to discover, and recognize the value of, the evangelizing charism of which the poor and oppressed are the bearers. For they constantly call the church to conversion, and many of them

live a life of evangelical values themselves—solidarity, service, simplicity, and openness to receive the gift of God.[35]

The similarity of the two texts speaks for itself. The Peruvian statement helps us better understand what Puebla means. What is being reflected here is a deep and fertile experience of the Latin American church, proceeding, as the text says, from a practice that intimately intertwines two elements: a commitment to the poor and oppressed, and the growth of the grassroots church communities. It had been in this solidarity, and in the rise of active and responsible Christian communities in the popular sectors, that the church had had the experience of the poor actually evangelizing—proclaiming the gospel themselves. To them, and not to the learned and prudent, is the love of the Father revealed (cf. Matt. 11:25). It is the poor who receive it, understand it, and announce it, in their own distinctive, demanding way. This is what Puebla means when it says that the ones the Bible calls the poor are not only the privileged recipients of the gospel; they are also, by that very fact, its messengers.[36]

Puebla's conviction is the fruit of praxis. Here we have an expression of the life of the Latin American church that bureaucracy and fear did not succeed in suffocating.

In this same connection, some observations on the basic Christian communities, the grassroots Christian communities, will not be out of place.[37] This was a bone of contention in Puebla. Persons unfamiliar with concrete pastoral work, and perhaps influenced by connotations that certain terms have in other parts of the world, looked on this phenomenon—one of the most fertile in the life of the church in recent years—with a certain diffidence at first. But here again, life is not easily ignored.

There is nothing more massive and bruising than reality itself, and any effort to conjure it away or counterfeit it eventually ends up in smithereens. This is what happened at Puebla. And here the Brazilian bishops—without a doubt one of the most outstanding delegations present—along with others (both bishops and nonbishops—members of the Latin American Conference of Religious [CLAR], for example) gave the doubters to understand the meaning of these Christian groups. They are groups born in, and committed to, the world of the common people. By whatever name they are called, they express a gospel experience, in communion with the church, of great wealth and promise for the presence of the church of Jesus Christ in Latin America. Hence Puebla notes with approval: "The poor, too, have been encouraged by the church. They have begun to organize themselves and to live their faith in an integral way, and hence to reclaim their rights" (§1137).

Latin Americans have found, in their grassroots community life, a rich vein of faith and vitality, and have found a way to carry forward their combat against social injustice, their struggle for liberation, and their experience of the gospel. And they have done so with ability, courage, and a sense of realism. The Puebla bishops declare their approval and patronage in a passage from the document "Evangelization and the People's Religiosity":

> The gap between rich and poor, the menacing situation faced by the weakest, the injustices, and the humiliating disregard and subjection endured by them radically contradict the values of personal dignity and solidary brotherhood. Yet the people of Latin America carry these values in their hearts as imperatives received from the Gospel. That is why the religiosity of the Latin American people is often turned into a cry for true liberation. It is an exigency that is still unmet. Motivated by their religiosity, however, the people create or utilize space for the practice of brotherhood in the more intimate areas of their lives together: e.g., the neighborhood, the village, their labor unions, and their recreational activities. Rather than giving way to despair, they confidently and shrewdly wait for the right opportunities to move forward toward the liberation they so ardently desire [§452].

Puebla's viewpoint—the evangelizing potential of the poor—constitutes a definite advance over that of Medellín. Puebla has sought out a stance in creative continuity with its predecessor, and this position enables us to comprehend better the meaning of the liberating evangelization so much insisted upon, in recent years, by Medellín, by Puebla, and especially by the praxis of the Latin American church.[38]

CONVERSION FOR EVANGELIZATION

In order to receive the kingdom of God one must undergo what the gospel calls "conversion." But conversion is also a prerequisite for the proclamation of the good news without telling a lie. Puebla is sensitive to this tandem of truths, and hence demands, on more than one occasion, the conversion of the church itself.

From the very beginning, in their opening "Message" (§2), the bishops ask themselves, "Are we really living the Gospel of Christ on our continent? . . . We are still far from living all that we preach." Then they frankly beg forgiveness: "For all our faults and limitations we pastors, too, ask pardon of God, our brothers and sisters in the faith, and humanity."

Acknowledgment of one's faults, and contrition for them, is an important element in conversion. It implies the desire to take a new path. This exordium establishes a theme whose thread is woven all through the Puebla texts—the conversion of the church and the reform of its structures.

"This Witness, Nascent but Real"

The bishops' opening question is concretized in terms of their commitment to the poor. What is done for the poor will witness to the authenticity of a life according to the gospel:

We wish to take note of all that the Church in Latin America has done, or has failed to do, for the poor since the Medellín Conference. This will serve as a starting point for seeking out effective channels to implement our option in our evangelizing work in Latin America's present and future [§1135].

The church's commitment to the poor has a connection with the efficacy of the activity of evangelization. Significant sectors of the church—with a might and a sense of reality that will always seem illusory to the defenders of a situation advantageous to themselves—have begun to take on a solidarity with the poor, and to denounce the unjust structures that make and keep them poor:

> We see that national episcopates and many segments of lay people, religious men and women, and priests have made their commitment to the poor a deeper and more realistic one. This witness, nascent but real, led the Latin American Church to denounce the grave injustices stemming from mechanisms of oppression [§1136].[39]

We have already seen that, along the lines traced by Medellín and the discourses of John Paul II, Puebla underscored the structural causes of Latin American poverty. It is on account of these structural causes that involvement with the poor must go beyond good-heartedness and social work. It must now become denunciation and battle. For it is the *social order* that is unjust.[40]

This has been the experience of numerous Christians in Latin America, this has been their involvement, during these years. It is an involvement, a commitment, that has brought many of them slander, prison, torture, and even death. These are the martyrs—the witnesses to the faith in God in the hearts of the poor—of recent Latin American history. Puebla does not give this the attention it deserves. Nevertheless there are some clear allusions. The "preferential option document" says:

> The Church's prophetic denunciations and its concrete commitments to the poor have in not a few instances, brought down persecution and oppression of various kinds upon it. The poor themselves have been the first victims of this oppression [§1138].

This last bears repeated emphasis. Puebla is certainly to the point when it says that it is the poor themselves who have been the first victims of these reprisals on the part of those who hold economic and political power in Latin American society. This is important. These persons—"history's anonymous ones"—often pass by unnoticed.

Another text comes right out and says that the church has had "to endure the persecution and at times death of its members in witness to its prophetic mission" (§92)—a profound recognition of the reason for the murder of so many sisters and brothers of ours in witness to the faith. Puebla also makes allusion to the reservations entertained in the dominant sectors toward the stance the church has taken regarding service to the poor.[41]

Latin America today is full of manifestations of these reservations. They are by no means divorced from the anxieties aroused by the prospect of an episcopal conference in Puebla in the first place. Fearing a "second Medellín," elements in the dominant sectors undertook harsh attacks upon the sectors most committed to the process of Latin American liberation. They also sought in various ways to bring pressure to bear on the course of the conference itself. In this sense Puebla's day was both painful and instructive. Conservative groups, many of them calling themselves Catholics, carried out a campaign of defamation before and during the conference. When the conference was in progress, even bishops of great pastoral experience, who were playing an important role at Puebla, were attacked and calumniated.[42]

With great lucidity, Puebla itself gives the profound reason for this attitude:

> The enormously positive activity of the Church in defense of human rights and its dealings with the poor have led groups with economic power, who thought they were the front ranks of Catholicism, to feel that they have been abandoned by the Church. As they see it, the Church has forsaken its "spiritual" mission [§79].

The analysis is clear. There is no mistaking the bishops' meaning. By "spiritual mission" the dominant sectors mean something that not only does not call their interests into question but actually protects them.[43]

Solidarity with a People Organizing Itself

Resistance encountered in the privileged sectors was thus due to the church's involvement with the poor. And it had been long in brewing. The church had been expressing great interest in organization of the people, in defense of legitimate interests, as far back as Medellín. It was not a matter of a sudden turn toward the poor on the part of the Latin American church.

Traditional Christian circles often have a concern for the poor, provided always that it not raise any questions. What was novel in Medellín and Puebla was the concrete nature of their interest. In a text we have cited above, the Puebla bishops express their satisfaction with the attempts the poor have made to organize themselves, in recent years, so as "to live their faith in an integral way, and hence to reclaim their rights" (§1137).

The preferential option, then, is not in favor of one or another individual poor person, nor again of the poor who are "grateful and good," as one is wont to hear in affluent social circles. Poverty as we have it in Latin America has a collective dimension, and leads ineluctably to a situation of social conflict.

We have seen this in our examination of the Puebla texts on the situation of poverty in Latin America. It is the result of unjust structures, which have created broad strata of poverty, broad strata of poor. Hence the "preferential option document" will say that the church should "understand and denounce the mechanisms that generate this poverty" (§1160). Only thus, by uniting its efforts to those of other churches and "with those of people of good will," will the Catholic Church be able "to uproot poverty and create a more just and fraternal world" (§1161). Indeed this is what the whole discussion is about—doing away with a poverty that dehumanizes, that tramples underfoot these persons' condition as children of God.

But, then, the people must organize. The pope stressed this point powerfully on his visit to Mexico, and Puebla echoes him:

> We support the aspirations of laborers and peasants, who wish to be treated as free, responsible human beings. They are called to share in the decisions that affect their lives and their future, and we encourage all to improve themselves [§1162].

To this end it is essential that they defend "their fundamental right 'to freely create organizations to defend and promote their interests, and to make a responsible contribution to the common good' " (§1163; cf. Monterrey, 3). The Puebla document will repeat the pope on this point. The workers of Latin America, it will say, "should not forget what Pope John Paul II told them in his talk. It is the right of workers 'to freely create organizations to defend and promote their interests, and to contribute to the common good in a responsible way' "(§1244). This is a repeated concern of Puebla, and the conference denounces every obstacle to these efforts of the popular classes to organize themselves:

> In many places labor legislation is either applied arbitrarily or not taken into account at all. This is particularly true in countries where the government is based on the use of force. There they look askance at the organizing efforts of laborers, peasants, and the common people; and they adopt repressive measures to prevent such organizing [§44].

In contrast with these preventive measures, and this hostility to such popular organizations, Puebla now unmasks the type of social order prevailing in our region of the world and denounces the present state of affairs: "But this type of control over, or limitation on, activity is not applied to employer organizations, which can exercise their full power to protect their interests" (§44).

The first step toward authentic resolution of social confrontations resulting from an unjust socio-economic system is not to hide them.

And so the commitment to which Puebla, in the footsteps of Medellín, summons us is hard and demanding. Nor therefore is it to be wondered at that, in these years:

> All this has produced tensions and conflicts both inside and outside the Church. The Church has frequently been the butt of accusations, either of being on the side of those with political or socioeconomic power, or of propounding a dangerous and erroneous Marxist ideology [§1139].

For we already know that if the church were to take seriously what John Paul II said about the defense of human rights being "an authentically *evangelical commitment* which, like that of Christ, is primarily a commitment to those most in need" (Opening Address at Puebla, III, 3), if we were to concretize the "preferential concern to defend and promote the rights of the poor, the marginalized, and the oppressed" (§1217), the church would be accused, as we saw, of forsaking its "spiritual" mission. It would even be accused, as we saw just a few lines above, of "a dangerous and erroneous Marxist ideology." This is exactly what has occurred in recent years. The accusations have come from those who see any denunciation of the *fact* of misery and exploitation as motivated by *ideology*. They would have liked to see preparation for Puebla take the form of an ideological dispute. They were crestfallen when it dealt instead with the massive facts. "How wonderful things would be," someone has ironically claimed they said, "if it weren't for reality."[44]

In addition to these "tensions and conflicts" outside the church, Puebla is not afraid to admit their existence inside the church as well. Once again we find ourselves reading language that is clear and outspoken, not afraid to call a spade a spade. What is happening is that the demands made on Christians in solidarity with the poor and oppressed are so serious that they are leading the whole church to a radical change in its way of life—to a conversion. Efforts along the lines of an involvement with the despoiled, marginalized sectors of society are vitally in evidence today, in the ongoing history of the Latin American people as well as in that of a church with such deep roots in that people. And yet the Puebla conference does not declare itself satisfied with this initial solidarity with the poor.

Inadequate Identification with the Poor Christ and a Poor People

Nascent and real, our commitment to the poor is insufficient, in the eyes of the bishops gathered in Puebla. "Not all of us in the Latin American Church have committed ourselves sufficiently to the poor. We are not always concerned about them, or in solidarity with them." Medellín's call was answered by important sectors of the church, but much remains to be done. The "preferential option document" has already referred to the "disregard and even hostility" (§1134) of many toward Medellín. Puebla now seeks to reaffirm its predecessor's demands of solidarity with the poor and oppressed. This is obviously one of its key themes. Hence Puebla notes: "Service to them really calls for constant conversion and purification among all Christians. That must be done if we are to achieve fuller identification each day with the poor Christ and our own poor" (§1140).

This conversion is presented as the means par excellence for concretizing the preferential option (§§1157-58). The criterion by which the evangelizing activity of the church is to be judged will be its similarity to Christ's own proclamation of his gospel:

> As the Pope has told us, the evangelical commitment of the Church, like that of Christ, should be a commitment to those most in need (cf. Luke 4:18–21; Opening Address, III, 3). Hence the Church must look to Christ when it wants to find out what its evangelizing activity should be like [§1141].

The conversion that arises out of this comparison will permit the church to acquit itself of its task of witness and proclaim the gospel. This conversion involves two things.

First, it requires a reexamination of the church's own structures and of the life of its members:

> To live out and proclaim the requirement of Christian poverty, the Church must re-examine its structures and the life of its members, particularly that of its pastoral agents, with the goal of effective conversion in mind [§1157].[45]

Effective conversion is a demand of an efficacious evangelization, a condition of the authenticity of the pastoral word. "Without the witness of a converted Church, our word as pastors would be futile" (§1221; cf. Paul VI, *Evangelii Nuntiandi*, 41). If the church is defined by its proper task, that of evangelization (§4), it need not fear to reexamine its structures, in order the more efficaciously to place them at the service of the proclamation of the message. The reexamination of these structures is therefore presented in the Puebla documents as a facet of the conversion of the church.

The dynamic standpoint taken here by Puebla is an expression of *parrhesia* —the Christian audacity of the Acts of the Apostles. It contrasts with the zealous defense of particular historical forms and structures, a defense undertaken rather in the service of one's vested securities than in view of a true sense of the presence of the Spirit in the church. The gospel tells us that the Spirit will lead us to the full truth (John 14:26), but there are those who cannot resign themselves to not knowing in advance which road to the truth will be the one to take.

Secondly, the Puebla document emphasizes the demands of an authentic lifestyle:

Such conversion entails the demand for an austere lifestyle and a total confidence in the Lord, because in its evangelizing activity the Church will rely more on the being and power of God and his grace than on "having more" and secular authority [§1158].

Reliance on the strength of the gospel, rather than on the powers of this world, for the accomplishment of the church's mission is one of Puebla's deep concerns. For example:

The Church must become more and more independent of the powers in this world. Only thus can it enjoy a broad area of freedom that will enable it to carry out its apostolic work without interference. That work includes the practice of cultic worship, education in the faith, and the fostering of those many and varied activities that lead the faithful to implement the moral imperatives deriving from the faith in their private, family, and social life. Thus, free of compromising and vested only with its witness and teaching, the Church will be more credible and better heard [§144].

Independence from vested interests is a condition of credibility for the proclamation of the gospel. To have said this of Latin American society, where there are still so many different modes of intimacy between "the powers of this world" and important sectors of the church, was an act of courage. And a commitment. A commitment made before the Lord, and before the poor of Latin America.[46] Finally, it is an act of confidence and faith. As the bishops say in their profession of faith at the end of their "Message to the Peoples of Latin America": "We believe in the power of the Gospel."

A church free of these entanglements will be a church that is poor and open to the poor and oppressed:

In this way [the church] will present an image of being authentically poor, open to God and fellow human beings, ever at their disposal, and providing a place where the poor have a real chance for participation and where their worth is recognized [§1158].

This was one of Medellín's great concerns, and the motive of some of its best and most courageous statements. After recognizing with honesty and Christian humility the reasons that "have helped create this image of a rich official Church" (§2), the Medellín Document on Poverty continues:

The poverty of the Church and her members in Latin América should be a sign and a commitment: a sign of the inestimable value of poverty in God's eyes, and a commitment to solidarity with those who are suffering [§7].

This is the church that will be both "sign and commitment." This is the church that will strike root in the world of poverty, the world of those who "intuit . . . in a privileged and forceful way" that "Kingdom brought to us by Christ" (Puebla, §132). In order to open itself to them the church need only recognize them, see them already present—with "their poverty on their backs," as Bartolomé de las Casas described them. For the church in Latin America, to be poor means to take on the life, the struggles, the sufferings, and the aspirations of the majority of its own members—the poor who are within the church indeed, but whose voice, especially if they are claiming their rights, sounds foreign to many within that same church.

Puebla, like Medellín, is neither a beginning nor an end. It is a stage along the historic march of the people of God in Latin America, an important moment in a life where, as Puebla itself says, the spirit must not be quenched or prophecy killed. Without this life of the church community, so evident in the preparation of the conference as well as during the course of its deliberations, there is no understanding the fact of Puebla. Its documents are an expression of everything within that church community at that time, including the nuances, the tensions, and the differences in perception on many a matter that are always present in a complex reality. But withal there is that solid, unshakable core, that basic, total option, maintained with courage and energy in spite of all the fears and calumnies.

Nor can the next stage be understood without first understanding the life of this Christian community. A meeting of pastors produces texts. But it also, and especially, creates attitudes and involvements—without which the texts would be a dead letter. What is important now, more than anxiously to defend the documents and argue over this passage or that one, is to do an exegesis of them within the actual praxis of the Latin American church. A facile "war of texts" must be avoided. Any passages brought into confrontation with one another should be examined against a background of authentic commitment to the poor of Latin America, in whom we are called to discover the face of the Lord. Otherwise we will only have a kind of "star wars."

No, if we want to step down to earth from outer space—where perhaps some have mounted in the hope that the silence reigning there will allow their voice, drowned out in the din of the earth, to be heard at last—we must take up the great options of Puebla in our everyday practice. With our feet firmly on the earth, and amid the tumult of our daily round, we must accept the fact that our voice is but one among many in Latin America. The documents of Puebla have not changed things in Latin America. Our hope is that they change things in the church.[47]

Puebla has allowed us to see that Medellín's program has not been completely carried out. And this is one of Puebla's great demands. In placing itself in continuity with Medellín, Puebla has reissued Medellín's call and challenge. For that call and challenge have not been sufficiently heard, and the Puebla documents remind us of this repeatedly. The new subjects taken up serve only to render the demand more urgent. It is a demand that must be answered with creativity—the creativity to which John Paul II exhorted us at the close of his opening address at Puebla. What precise and particular paths will be taken in carrying forward this resolution will depend on the decisions and work of the Christian community as a whole. The rich pastoral experiences of these past years—our experience of solidarity with the poor and oppressed—have opened a furrow that we must now continue to plow, with might and imagination.

Puebla addressed itself to many topics. It opened many promising paths. Other points are left for the future. In these pages we have sought only to shed light on two great themes: the perspective of the *poor*, and, in relationship with it, the subject of *liberation*. This is why we took the document "A Preferential Option for the Poor" as our guide. We have left many other themes out of consideration here. We trust that the points selected will afford access to what is fundamental in Puebla's option and thereby shed light on other important and controverted questions as well.

In solidarity, then, with the poor and oppressed of Latin America in their life, their sufferings, their struggles to break free of an unjust social order, and their longing for liberation, let us now address ourselves to a task that we shall surely find to be rigorously demanding: that of entering into, taking upon ourselves, the reality of the misery and exploitation in which the great majority of our people live. But we shall also find in it a communion— communion in the profound hope of the people in God as their Liberator, as the "Avenger of the Lowly," Rescuer and Vindicator of this exploited Christian people. This is what Puebla meant when it said that with a preferential option for the poor, and in the footsteps of Medellín, it was opening "new horizons of hope."

NOTES

1. "God always takes his stand unconditionally and passionately on this side and on this side alone: against the lofty and on behalf of the lowly; against those who already enjoy right and privilege and on behalf of those who are denied it and deprived of it" (Karl Barth, *Church Dogmatics* [New York: Scribner's], vol. 2/1 [1957], p. 386).

2. This is the same viewpoint as that expressed in a widely distributed brochure (March 1978) in defense of the Preparatory Document by A. López Trujillo, "Los pobres—¿olvido o rescate?"

3. An earlier draft, whose wording was very close to that of the final text, although approved, received forty-three negative votes—making this document, along with those of the First Commission (on the Latin American situation), the ones most heavily opposed in the balloting. (For precise data, see *CELAM*, 135 [Feb. 1979]: 48.) It is common knowledge that "A Preferential Option for the Poor" encountered further difficulties as well, at the hands of certain members of the conference, even after approval by the conference.

4. The present article will incorporate extensive citations from the Puebla documents. The advantages are evident. The version I cite [in the Spanish original of this article —ed.] is the *Texto Oficial*, which is known to contain numerous variant readings as compared with the text actually approved by the bishops in Puebla. English quotations are from *Puebla and Beyond*,

John Eagleson and Philip Scharper, eds. (Maryknoll, N.Y.: Orbis, 1979), a collection of documents including the NCCB-authorized translation of the Final Document from Puebla, as well as the major addresses of Pope John Paul II in Mexico, together with commentaries by specialists on Puebla.

5. A good many other texts in the same vein declare Puebla's fidelity to Medellín. See, for example, §§ 24, 88, 142, 143, 235, 480, 1165.

6. The "Message to the Peoples of Latin America," introducing all the other Puebla documents, recalls this classic biblical theme: "all that infringes upon human dignity somehow wounds God too" (*Puebla and Beyond*, p.118). Puebla speaks more than once of the charism of prophecy, in the sense in which we have just used the term. For example, the document "The People of God Are in the Service of Communion" states: "[The people of God] are sent out as a prophetic People to announce the Gospel or discern the Lord's calls in history. They are to announce where the presence of the Lord's Spirit is manifested; and they are to denounce where the mystery of iniquity is at work through deeds and structures that prevent more fraternal participation in the construction of society and in the enjoyment of the goods that God created for all" (§267). Then this document adds (contradicting an opinion commonly held in conservative circles in Latin America): "In the last ten years we have seen a definite increase in the function of prophecy" (§268).

7. The pope explicitly asserts that Medellín itself understood the privilege of the poor in this way. See his "Homily at the Basilica of Guadalupe" on the occasion of the solemn opening of the Puebla conference, Jan. 27, 1979, in *Puebla and Beyond*, pp. 72–76.

8. Unless otherwise noted, English quotations from the Medellín documents are taken from *Between Honesty and Hope* (Maryknoll, N.Y.: Orbis, 1970).

9. For a comprehensive study of this document, see chap. 5, above.

10. The *Texto Oficial* seems to have missed the meaning of the text actually approved in Puebla. The latter had said, "the situation of violence—institutionalized, subversive, and repressive. . . ." But the official text (and translation) reads, "the situation of violence—which can be called institutionalized violence (either as subversion or as repression). . . ." The wording softens the characterization of violence as the primary attribute of the overall situation in Latin America.

11. For example: "In recent years we have also seen deterioration in the political sphere. Much harm has been done to the participation of citizens in the conduct of their own affairs and destiny. We also frequently see a rise in what can be called institutionalized injustice" (§46; cf. §509). The expression "institutionalized injustice" had already been employed by Cardinal Lorscheider to describe the situation in Latin America (*Osservatore Romano*, Sept. 24, 1978).

12. Another passage runs in the same tenor: "But so long as huge segments of society cannot manage to satisfy these legitimate aspirations while others indulge themselves to excess, the tangible goods of the modern world will turn into a source of growing frustrations and tragic tensions. The blatant and striking contrast between those who possess nothing and those who show off their opulence is an insuperable obstacle to establishing the Reign of peace" (§138; cf. §§1260, 1264, 1269).

13. See the Homily in Zapopán.

14. See, for example, §§70, 185–86, 281, 452, 515, 1032, 1269.

15. The text approved by Puebla had said: "the extreme poverty that reigns on our continent."

16. The actual Puebla text had put it, expressively: "This denunciation is a summons to (*es convocadora de*) the church."

17. The condition of women is treated in several places in the Puebla documents, and the treatment constitutes without a doubt one of the conference's remarkable contributions. The passage cited here is one of the conference's clearest statements of the particularly oppressed condition of women in the despoiled and exploited populous sectors.

18. The actual Puebla text had said: "even before taking account of their moral or personal situation."

19. "Aporte de la conferencia episcopal peruana al documento de consulta del Celam para la tercera conferencia general del episcopado latinoamericano" (Lima, 1978), no. 421. Various regional assemblies of the Peruvian bishops had insisted on this perspective in their contributions to the preparation of this document.

20. See, for example, Leonardo Boff, "Maria, Mulher Profética e Libertadora: A Piedade mariana na Teologia da Libertação," *Revista Eclesiástica Brasileira*, 149 (March 1978): 59–78.

See also my *Theology of Liberation*, pp. 207-8; and Edmundo Leon, *María y la Iglesia profética* (Lima: CEP, 1977).

21. See, for example, §§12, 196, 268, 385, 695, 696, 711, 965, 1143.

22. To cite but two authors: Jacques Dupont, *Les Béatitudes* (Paris: Gabalda) is exhaustive on the theme (vol. 1, *Les Béatitudes: le probléme littéraire* [1969]; vol. 2, *Les Béatitudes: la bonne nouvelle* [1969]; and vol. 3, *Les Béatitudes: les Evangélistes* [1973]); and the shorter work by Julio de Santa Ana, *Good News to the Poor: The Challenge of the Poor in the History of the Church* (Maryknoll, N.Y.: Orbis, 1979).

23. "Christ, our Saviour, not only loved the poor but became poor ("he was rich, but he became poor"—2 Cor, 8:9). He lived in poverty, focused his mission around proclaiming the liberation of the poor, and founded his Church as a sign of this poverty among men" (Medellín Document on Poverty, 7—*Honesty and Hope*, p. 213).

24. In his opening address at the Puebla conference, John Paul II stated: "There can be no doubt that all this imposes exacting demands on the attitude of any Christians who truly wish to serve the least of their brothers and sisters, the poor, the needy, the marginalized: i.e., all those whose lives reflect the suffering countenance of the Lord (*Lumen Gentium*, 8)" (*Puebla and Beyond*, p. 60). And later he adds: "In the parable of the Good Samaritan, the Lord outlined the model way of attending to all human needs (Luke 10:30 ff.); and he said that in the last analysis he will identify himself with the disinherited—the imprisoned, the hungry, and the abandoned— to whom we have offered a helping hand (Matt. 25:31 ff.)" (ibid., p. 66). In the document entitled "The Truth about Jesus Christ, the Savior We Proclaim," Puebla says that, thanks to "the efforts at renewal that have taken place mainly since the Medellín Conference," there has been a "labor and growth" that has "brought many segments of the People of God closer to the Gospel and has prompted their search for the ever new face of Christ, who is the answer to their legitimate yearning for integral liberation" (§173). Matthew 25:31-46 is an important text in the pope's teaching. He appeals to it once more in his encyclical *Redemptor Hominis* and reaches a demanding conclusion: "This eschatological scene must *always* be 'applied' to man's history; it must always be made the 'measure' for human acts as an essential outline for an examination of conscience by each and every one . . ." (§16; emphasis added). Just above, he had spoken of a "confrontation" and a "contrast" between "rich, highly developed societies" and "the remaining societies, or at least broad sectors of them," which suffer hunger, "with many people dying each day of starvation and malnutrition" (ibid.). According to the pope, this is owing to prevailing "mechanisms" and "structures," and the textual apparatus refers us to his addresses in Santo Domingo and Mexico. This analysis lends very concrete content to the passage we have referred to from Matthew 25.

25. An entire paragraph of the "Aporte de la conferencia episcopal peruana," the Peruvian bishops' document drawn up in preparation for Puebla, was devoted to the subject of "Christ Poor" (nos. 456-60).

26. See Leonardo Boff, *Jesus Christ Liberator: A Critical Theology for Our Times* (Maryknoll, N.Y.: Orbis, 1978); and Jon Sobrino, *Christology at the Crossroads: A Latin American Approach* (Orbis, 1978). See also J. I. González-Faus, *La humanidad nueva: Ensayo de cristología*, 2 vols. (Madrid, 1974).

27. The actual Puebla document had said, forcefully: "They, and those crucified by injustice, accept the Lord's cross as their own and shoulder it."

28. Puebla speaks of "changes" that "either have not taken place, or else they have been too slow in coming in the concrete life of Latin America" (§30). And elsewhere: "In particular we must note that since the decade of the fifties, and despite certain achievements, the ample hopes for development have come to nothing. The marginalization of the vast majority and the exploitation of the poor has increased" (§1260).

29. *Theology of Liberation*, p. 37. The importance for the theology of liberation, ever since it began, of understanding Christ's salvation to include these different dimensions has been very well pointed up by R. Oliveros, *Liberación y teología: Génesis y crecimiento de una reflexión (1966-1976)* (Lima: CEP, 1977), and Miguel Manzanero, *Teología y Salvación-Liberación* (Bilbao, 1978).

30. Elsewhere, resuming the old classic distinction between freedom *from* and freedom *for*, a distinction used in the theology of liberation as well, the bishops say: "There are two complementary and inseparable elements. The first is liberation from all the forms of bondage, from personal and social sin, and from everything that tears apart the human individual and society; all this finds its source to be in egotism, in the mystery of iniquity. The second element is liberation for progressive growth in being through communion with God and other human beings; this

reaches its culmination in the perfect communion in heaven, where God is all in all and weeping forever ceases" (§482). And then, still in a perspective embracing all the various dimensions of a human being: "This liberation is gradually being realized in history, in our personal history and that of our peoples. It takes in all the different dimensions of life: the social, the political, the economic, the cultural, and all their interrelationships" (§483).

31. Puebla asserts: "From the depths of the countries that make up Latin America a cry is rising to heaven, growing louder and more alarming all the time. It is the cry of a suffering people who demand justice, freedom, and respect for the basic rights of human beings and peoples" (§87).

32. There are echoes here of a passage from *Evangelii Nuntiandi*, which it will be worthwhile to reproduce in its entirety:

It is well known in what terms numerous Bishops from all the continents spoke of this at the last synod, especially the Bishops from the Third World, with a pastoral accent resonant with the voice of the millions of sons and daughters of the church who make up those peoples. Peoples, as we know, engaged with all their energy in the effort and struggle to overcome everything which condemns them to remain on the margin of life: famine, chronic disease, illiteracy, poverty, injustices in international relations and especially in commercial exchanges, situations of economic and cultural neo-colonialism sometimes as cruel as the old political colonialism. The Church, as the Bishops repeated, has the duty to proclaim the liberation of millions of human beings, many of whom are her own children—the duty of assisting the birth of this liberation, of giving witness to it, of ensuring that it is complete. This is not foreign to evangelization [no. 30].

33. The media made a great deal of what they liked to see as a "condemnation of the theology of liberation." Wishful thinking indeed. For one thing, as everyone knows, the magisterium of the church, and the papal magisterium especially, is not exercised in unverifiable oral statements made to journalists. Secondly, the pope certainly did not use the words "condemn" or "condemnation" in any of his addresses in Santo Domingo or Mexico. Thirdly, the imagined condemnation was denied on more than one occasion by bishops in Puebla who had great influence at the conference. Finally, if any doubts remain, they must be dispelled by Pope John Paul II's catechetical address of Feb. 21, 1979, in which he spoke directly of the theology of liberation in terms calculated to put an end to a stubborn campaign that had only betrayed again what interests it represented. How uninformed the representatives of those interests are when it comes to knowing how such matters are dealt with in the church today!

34. See also the document "Evangelization, Liberation, and Human Promotion" (*Puebla and Beyond*, pp. 188–94). All these approaches frequently have as their backdrop the notion of "integral development" as presented in *Populorum Progressio*, 21.

35. A timid, ambiguous anticipation of this text is to be found in the Working Document, in a position midway between the Preparatory Document and the Peruvian contribution: "The poor are the riches of the church. It is in relationship with them that one discovers the evangelizing charism of the church of Latin America for our time." Puebla itself stops beating about the bush and espouses the unadulterated Peruvian position.

36. It is a pity that the documents "The Hierarchical Ministry" and especially "Lay People" (*Puebla and Beyond*, pp. 215–27, 227–35), failed to profit by this rich perspective.

37. Several passages in the Puebla documents take note of the expansion and maturation of these communities since Medellín. Puebla emphasizes the promise they hold for the Latin American church: "In 1968 base-level ecclesial communities [CEBs: *comunidades eclesiales de base*] were just coming into being. Over the past ten years they have multiplied and matured, particularly in some countries, so that now they are one of the causes for joy and hope in the Church. In communion with their bishops, and in line with Medellín's request, they have become centers of evangelization and moving forces for liberating and development. The vitality of these CEBs is now beginning to bear fruit. They have been one of the sources for the increase in lay ministers, who are now acting as leaders and organizers of their communities, as catechists, and as missionaries" (§§96–97). See also, of course, the document "Base-Level Ecclesial Communities" itself (§§617–57), which has a great many worthwhile things to say about these grassroots communities. Numerous other passages throughout the Puebla material make other contributions. It is this grassroots experience that forms the basis for that bone of contention, the church as "born of the people under the influence of the Spirit." A Puebla text laments the use of the *expression*

"people's church," or "church born of the people," as "rather unfortunate" (§263)—but then the very same passage goes on to endorse the actual *content* of these expressions (as the Working Document had already done, tenuously): "The problem of the 'people's Church,' the Church born of the People, has various aspects. The first obstacle is readily surmounted if it is interpreted as a Church that is trying to incarnate itself in the ranks of the common people on our continent, and that therefore arises out of their response in faith to the Lord. This rules out the seeming denial of a basic truth: i.e., that the Church always arises from a first initiative 'from above,' from the Spirit who raises it up and from the Lord who convokes it" (§263). Actually John Paul II himself had already opened up this approach when he said that one should not understand "people" here as a "mental category," and explicitly maintained that "the church is *born* of the faith response we make to Jesus Christ." And indeed the point is precisely the faith response that persons make to the convoking, summoning, message of Christ, of which they are the privileged addressees. A "church born of the people under the action of the Spirit," all arbitrary interpretations by its enthusiasts or its adversaries notwithstanding, is a challenging vocation for the whole church, not a sterile alternative to the church that already is. Viewed in this light, commitment along these lines becomes all the more urgent, given the conditions of the life of the Latin American church today.

38. This is Puebla's emphasis right from the start. After recalling that "evangelization is the very mission of the Church," the conference presents the evangelizing task as seeking "to contribute its services to a better future for the peoples of Latin America, to their liberation and growth in all of life's dimensions" (§4).

39. Concerning the involvement of members of religious orders in this area, Puebla had already stated: "Pastoral openness in one's labors and a preferential option for the poor represent the most noticeable tendency of religious life in Latin America. Indeed religious increasingly find themselves in difficult, marginalized areas; in missions to the indigenous peoples; and in silent, humble labors. This option does not imply exclusion of anyone, but it does imply a preference for the poor and a drawing closer to them. This has led to a re-examination of traditional works in order to respond better to the demands of evangelization. It has shed clearer light on their relationship with the poverty of the marginalized. Now this does not imply simply interior detachment and community austerity; it also implies solidarity with the poor, sharing with them, and in some cases living alongside them" (§§733-34). The activities of CLAR (*Conferencia Latinoamericana de Religiosos*, Latin American Conference of Religious) receive clear support in this passage. CLAR is known to have initiated, and courageously maintained, this involvement with the popular and marginalized sectors, while seeking to base it on solid theological reflection. See CLAR, *Pobreza y vida religiosa en América Latina* (Bogotá, 1970); and Equipos de Teólogos CLAR, *Vida religiosa en América Latina a partir de Medellín: Nueva situación* (Bogotá, 1976).

40. Underscoring this aspect of service to the poor, Puebla quotes Vatican Council II: "The demands of justice should first be satisfied, lest the giving of what is due in justice be represented as the offering of a charitable gift. Not only the effects but also the causes of various ills must be removed. Help should be given in such a way that the recipients may gradually be freed from dependence on others and become self-sufficient" (Decree on the Apostolate of the Laity, 8) [§1146]. The document from the Peruvian episcopate makes the same citation.

41. "The collective voice of the bishops has been awakening a growing interest in public opinion; but frequently it also runs up against reservations in certain sectors with little social sensitivity. This is a sign that the Church is carrying out its role as Mother and Teacher of all" (§160).

42. Cardinals Juan Landázuri and Paulo Evaristo Arns, and Bishops Hélder Câmara, Marcos McGrath, Leonidas Proaño, and Luis Bambarén, among others.

43. At bottom, the dominant groups understand very well what is at stake. A newspaper noted for its coarse and offensive campaigns against progressive elements during the Puebla conference ran this revealing headline over an article on a meeting of business executives: *"Dañina a la Empresa Teología de Liberación"* ("Theology of Liberation Business in Trouble") (*La Voz de Puebla*, Feb. 10, 1979)—not the gospel, not the Christian faith, but some "business" or other.

44. Puebla indicates one of the reasons for these accusations: "Fear of Marxism keeps many from facing up to the oppressive reality of liberal capitalism. One could say that some people, faced with the danger of one clearly sinful system, forget to denounce and combat the established reality of another equally sinful system (cf. Pope John Paul II's Homily in Zapopán)" (§92). This distinction between *existing reality* and *potential danger*, and especially the importance of

the poor and their liberation for an understanding of the mission of the church—our subject in these pages—affords a better appreciation of what Puebla means when it talks about the thorny problems of the relationship between faith and politics, theology and the social sciences, or social reality and Marxist analysis. When these problems are handled on the doctrinal level they are subjected to more of an ideological approach, whereas they actually deserve an ad hoc examination in their own right.

45. The text actually approved in Puebla had spoken of a reexamination of the life of "all" of the members of the church, and had concluded: "Thus, once converted, it will be able efficaciously to evangelize the poor." The official text in the section entitled "Witness" reads: "This is our first pastoral option: the Christian community itself—its lay people, pastors, ministers, and religious—must be converted more and more to the Gospel so that they will be able to evangelize others" (§973).

46. This is actually a ratification of the commitment made in Medellín, where that conference had said: "We want our Church in Latin America to be free of worldly tie-ups, conniving relationships, and ambiguous hallmarks. We want her to be 'free in spirit from the bonds of wealth' (Paul VI, Opening Address to the Latin American Bishops' Conference, Aug. 24, 1968), to make her mission of service more transparent and solid, and to live in the world reflecting Christ's light and participating in its betterment. We wish to stress and acknowledge the value and legitimate autonomy of temporal tasks" (Medellín Document on Poverty, 18: *Honesty and Hope*, p.216).

47. Bishop Proaño, a prelate of broad pastoral experience, put it this way, both inside and outside the Puebla conference: "We are duty bound to submit this document to the faithful and see how they react. They will know whether we have interpreted them correctly or not."

PART IV
FROM THE UNDERSIDE OF HISTORY

7

Theology from the Underside of History

For many a Latin American Christian, new involvement in the popular struggles for liberation has been, and is, the beginning of a new way of living, sharing, and celebrating the faith. Whether these Christians come from the popular classes, or are from other sectors of society, in either case, in spite of different breaks they must make with the past and different roads they must take for the future, they all share a conscious, clear identification with the interests of the embattled oppressed of Latin America. This is the major phenomenon affecting the Christian community in Latin America in recent years. This is what has been, and continues to be, the springboard of theological clarification that has led to the theology of liberation. Apart from this relationship to practice, the theology of liberation is incomprehensible.

The liberating practice of the popular classes today, with all its advances and all its setbacks, poses new questions. First of all it poses them in the social and political field. Then as a consequence it poses them in the area of current Christian and theological consciousness. By definition, the challenges of practice are the foremost concern of the theology of liberation. These are the challenges that constitute the initial locus and criterion of discernment of all the other questions that arise in the course of its endeavors.

It is only against this background—or, better, only from this solid standpoint—that we shall be able adequately to comprehend the various attitudes taken toward the theology of liberation. Whether it be a matter of systematic hostility, as in some sectors,[1] or diffidence, as in others,[2] or even the shrewd attempts of those who have sought to co-opt this theology for their own system[3]—in no case can one coolly dismiss a theological engagement so closely tied in with what may be the most courageous undertaking in Latin America, and in the Latin American church, in recent years. But there are

Spanish original, *Teología desde el reverso de la historia,* published by Centro de Estudios y Publicaciones, Lima, 1977. The text has been revised and amplified.

also observations and critical discussions of quite another nature to be considered, and from quite another direction: that of the most advanced currents in progressivist theology today.[4]

The first requirement for keeping one's feet on the hard ground of practice, with a view to entering into theological discussion with these various critical positions from a concrete point of departure, is not to mistake the adversary. The most lethal assaults on the theology of liberation have been mounted from quarters holding aloft the banner of orthodoxy and fidelity to the magisterium of the church (quite a novelty in the case of some of the more illustrious figures here). These assaults are the expression of a sudden defensive reaction by a social order that feels its foundations shaken, and once more has appealed to religion in the hope of shoring up its position. But in our day and age it cannot do this without attacking, tiresomely and with a remarkable absence of any personal thought, the Christian element in the threat to this social order. Here is where the hardest battle, and the most important one, is to be waged. One cannot afford to lose sight of this.

To be sure, the unsubstantial argumentation and penchant for distortion that characterize these sectors scarcely invite theological discussion. But in view of the political function these groups perform in today's society, and in the church in Latin America, one must realize that deeper things are at stake: life or death for countless Latin Americans and the hope of a Christian community bearing witness to a God of liberation.

On the other hand, taking a stand on the field of practice—in the situation of oppression and repression in Latin America today and the combat being waged to break free of that situation—will also mean taking our bearings with respect to other currents of thought in theology today. Of course we must be wary of slipping into excessive concern over attacks on our rear, or exhaustive bouts of theological hairsplitting. But it will nonetheless be important to pinpoint our differences with—and, where need be, our leave-taking of—contemporary theology. The clarification will be necessary in its own right. But it will contribute as well to an affirmation and review of our particular standpoint.

We shall try to keep account, then, of these various levels of opposition and confrontation as we attempt in the following pages to sketch out two theological perspectives: that of progressivist theology and that of the theology of liberation. More precisely, we shall be seeking to pinpoint the nature of the breach between the two. For, owing to the concrete context in which the theology of liberation locates itself today, what we shall have to say will necessarily bear more directly upon the points of opposition between the two currents of thought. Still, for the reasons given above, we shall make every attempt not to forget what the conservative positions mean for both perspectives in the present situation in which the churches find themselves.

I think it important first of all to situate these lines of theological thinking in their social and historical contexts. For it is their concrete situations that constitute the soil that nurtures them. Any attempt to do this in the space of a few pages will occasionally involve certain oversimplifications, but it is difficult to see how this can be avoided.[5]

THEOLOGY AND THE MODERN SPIRIT

The eighteenth century ushered in a revolutionary era in a number of fields of human endeavor. This was the age in which it began to be a commonplace to hear that human beings were acquiring a clear consciousness of their capacity to know and to transform nature and society. Humanity was learning to alter the course of history, by taking history into its own hands. For contemporary men and women this exercise of their reason became the experience of freedom inasmuch as they now saw themselves capable of changing the conditions of their lives, capable of taking a new position with respect to their social relationships.

This was the context in which bourgeois society—the social class whose interests and values are stamped on modern society—arose. But it was also the context in which the antithesis of that social class arose—the proletariat, which little by little would come to form the vanguard of the popular classes impoverished by the economic and social situation prevailing from the nineteenth century onward.

New challenges now appeared for the Christian faith. The church and theology reacted, initially, with thought categories developed in centuries gone by. Later came still other questions, questions broached by the revolutions of the bourgeois class and the ferment of ideas that surged in their wake. These left their mark on the theology of their time, first in its Protestant, then in its Catholic version, lasting through Vatican Council II. Postconciliar theology, especially the new political theology, seeks to respond to the same challenges as before. But it does so more explicitly, facing them directly, and with a creativity that merits special attention.

Modernity

The modern spirit is the result of a historical process in the world of events and ideas alike, a process that suddenly and radically altered a mentality that had been linked to a feudal world. Events took place at a more rapid tempo, and a new, revolutionary era was underway. A new rhythm had been scored for the history of humanity, especially in the West.

Bourgeois Revolutions and the Enlightenment. What we today call the industrial revolution began, in the classic conception, in the middle of the eighteenth century. The industrial revolution was the inception of an era of rapid, broad production and distribution of consumer goods, based on a hitherto unknown potential for the transformation of nature. Forces of production now transcended all foreseeable limits, and the economic activity of society underwent a substantial change. Before all else the industrial revolution was a revolution in production. It gave the dominant social sectors of the modern era a consciousness of their capacity to modify profoundly the conditions of their life. It was a resounding and exhilarating affirmation of freedom vis-à-vis the forces of nature.[6]

Linked to this phenomenon was another historical process. Its origins were in the same era but reveal a different side of the transforming activity of the human being. This was the social movement in quest of the so-called modern freedoms. Finally concretized in a special way in the French Revolution, this same ground swell had found expression earlier, in less aggressive form, in mid-eighteenth-century England, and then, a few years before the French Revolution, in the North American bourgeois revolution.[7] The hue and cry was for individual liberties within society. Jean-Jacques Rousseau's famous distinction between the "citizen" and the "man"—the public and the private spheres—became the great watchword.[8] Among these modern liberties we find religious freedom—that ancient, thorny problem that henceforth will be answered by the demand for religious freedom as an elementary human right, indissolubly linked to all the other freedoms and rights of a human being.

These two historical events were not only contemporaneous; they were mutually dependent, and they came to intellectual consciousness in the complex of thought currents that we know under the name of the Enlightenment. In France it was the Encyclopedia that most brilliantly represents it. But it was equally at home in Germany and England. In a celebrated passage, Kant characterizes it as follows:

> The Enlightenment represents the emergence from immaturity. Immaturity is cradled in the incapacity to make use of one's own understanding without another's direction. One is oneself responsible for this immaturity when its cause lies not in a defect of understanding, but in a lack of decisiveness and spirit for making independent use of it without another's guidance. *Sapere aude!* Have the courage to make use of your own understanding! This is the motto of the Enlightenment. . . . Nevertheless, the only thing required for this Enlightenment is liberty, and surely the least offensive of all the things that bear that name—that is, the liberty to make public use of one's own reason in any domain whatever.[9]

For Kant, then, the Enlightenment means that, thanks to the free use of reason, humanity has come of age, has attained its majority. Reason and freedom will permit it to twist free of the grasp of all authoritarian tutelage—especially in religious matters, where, Kant says, to remain in one's minority is "most dishonorable." This critical position vis-à-vis religion will be a mark of the theological perspective that we shall shortly be examining.

The phenomena that we have been tracing in such broad strokes are the result of a fermentation of events and ideas that first saw the light of day in the waning moments of the Middle Ages. In the sixteenth and the seventeenth centuries we witness the birth of a new society, the bourgeois society. Here science, politics, philosophy, and religious consciousness will set up new and different relationships among themselves.

Experimental, or modern, science arose in the sixteenth century, with Galileo's physics. Science was a new sort of knowledge, different from philosophical knowledge. Science was "methodologically atheistic." The "God hypothesis" was unnecessary for the furtherance of an experimental knowledge of nature. As persons gradually became aware of this, science became a key factor in the secularization process. It would now not be long before they would discover the meaning of science for the transformation of the concrete conditions of their lives. This would provide a new orientation for restless spirits in search of a "practical philosophy."[10]

At the same time important changes were occurring in the area of politics. The rift in Christendom occasioned the rise of the modern state, and this in turn sent political reflection speeding down new pathways. Machiavelli would be one of the first to seek to introduce a new rationality into these questions, representing a break with traditional thought patterns: he conceived of the state as autonomous vis-à-vis any religious tutelage and he analyzed political decisions according to purely political criteria.[11] This opened up new vistas. Two centuries later, the French Revolution would usher in the lay state.

In isolation from modern science and politics, there is no understanding modern philosophy. The birth of science posed grave epistemological questions, which ultimately yielded to a critical theology of knowledge most aware of its presuppositions. I am referring, of course, to Immanuel Kant. But even before Kant, experimental science had served clear notice that it meant to challenge philosophy itself. Science and philosophy (more precisely, idealistic philosophies) had long since taken up their respective positions—mutual opposition. This unstable equilibrium would be expressed in philosophy itself—for example, in Cartesian dualism.

Modern science represented a new structure of knowledge, one different from the philosophical, as Hume was at pains to point out—and here is where Kant took his cue, with a vigor and lucidity that made him the father of a whole new stage of philosophical thought. Next, scientific reason and politics became philosophy's modern interpreters, to the point where they take it down new paths on one of its own classic terrains: ethics. Kant, again, will be a name to reckon with here, and his perspective will strongly mark Protestant theology from his time on. Finally, these same interpreters will escort philosophical reflection into new and unfamiliar territory as well, in the "philosophy of history." Here, although we meet Kant once more, Hegel will erect the system that will become the obligatory point of reference for all subsequent efforts. All these projects will bear the imprint of a search for the "practical philosophy" to which I alluded above.[12]

Another important factor in this total process is the Reformation. In many respects, of course, the roots of the Reformation are in a bygone, medieval age. But the Reformation gave birth to a powerful current of religious individualism, as befitted the mentality of the modern era. As Hegel will say:

This is the essence of the Reformation: Man is in his very nature destined to be free. . . . It is a fact of the weightiest import that the Bible has become the basis of the Christian Church. Henceforth each individual enjoys the right of deriving instruction for himself from it, and of directing his conscience in accordance with it. We see a vast change in the principle by which man's religious life is guided: the whole system of Tradition, the whole fabric of the Church becomes problematical, and its authority is subverted.[13]

The Reformation originated in Germany in the sixteenth century, as a criticism of church institutions, and gave rise to religious reforms that recognized the validity and value of the subjective. Reformation ideas also established themselves in England, although in more moderate guise. That country underwent other forms of liberalization as well—in the political sphere, through the English Revolution.[14] Eighteenth-century France, by contrast, had had none of these experiences. And so it was in this Catholic country, so long accustomed to a centralization of power, that the anticlerical, libertarian explosion would be all the mightier. What happened in France, with its repercussions in Italy, would condition the life of the Catholic Church all through the nineteenth century.

Individualism and Rationalism. Individualism is the most salient characteristic of modern ideology and bourgeois society. For the modern mentality, the human being is an absolute beginning, an autonomous decision-making center. Individual interest and initiative are the point of departure and motive force for economic activity. The French Revolution's Declaration of the Rights of Man proclaims:

> Every man is free to use his physical strength, his industry, and his capital as shall seem to himself to be good and useful. He may produce what he pleases, and produce it as he sees fit.

The various interests of individuals will encounter their regulatory agent in the marketplace itself: they will have to contend with the law of supply and demand. Thus the free play of individual interests will bring them into convergence with the general interest, and the result will be a natural order of things, instead of something forced upon nature by an authority that steps in and decides what ought to be done. Hence springs the notion that capitalism is the natural economic system for human beings.[15]

The individual now becomes the absolute principle of economic activity, and thereby also the absolute principle of the organization of society, which is made up of individuals. Individual liberty is the prime consideration. The social order is not imposed from without, by way of authority, as in the ancien régime. It is the result of free activity on the part of human beings. Society presupposes a free association, a "social contract," which will produce a "general will" alongside the plurality of individual wills.[16] But a contract can be entered into only by equals. Hence a principle of social equality is needed.

Both the demand for individual freedom and the demand for social equality, then, have ties with the new economic forms. Fundamental to bourgeois society is the right to private ownership, which will be primarily a matter of private ownership of the means of production. "The freedom of industry is the child of modern individualism, indeed its favorite child," writes a liberal historian.[17] Actually, freedom of industry is more nearly individualism's mother than its child. Social equality also has a clear economic reference. At the moment of the mercantile transaction, all human beings are equal. Indeed, their formal equality is actually a condition for the activity of the marketplace.[18]

This same individualism is reflected in the area of knowledge. Each individual's reason is the starting point of all knowledge. Truth does not come by way of divine revelation or human authority. Everything must be submitted to the judgment of the critical reason, and it is thus that human beings become lords of the world—and their own masters into the bargain. In the individual's free use of his or her own reason, Hegel saw the essence of the Enlightenment:

> The independent authority of Subjectivity was maintained against belief founded on authority, and the Laws of Nature were recognized as the only bond connecting phenomena with phenomena. Thus all miracles were disallowed: for Nature is a system of known and recognized Laws; Man is at home in it, and that only passes for truth in which he finds himself at home; he is free through the acquaintance he has gained with Nature. Nor was thought less vigorously directed to the Spiritual side of things: Right and [Social] Morality came to be looked upon as having their foundation in the actual present Will of man, whereas formerly it was referred only to the command of God enjoined *ab extra*. . . .
>
> These general conceptions, deduced from actual and present consciousness—the Laws of Nature and the substance of what is right and good—have received the name of *Reason*. The recognition of the validity of these laws was designated by the term *Eclaircissement (Aufklärung)*.[19]

As L. Goldmann perceptively observes, empiricism itself is an expression of this individualism.[20] Like rationalism, empiricism is an affirmation that one's individual consciousness is the absolute origin of knowledge and activity—the only basic difference being that rationalism posits innate ideas and empiricism experience as the starting point of this knowledge and this activity. But in neither case does knowledge seem to have any limits, and it is against this broad horizon that human beings know and affirm themselves in their individuality. The ability to reason eliminates the mysterious and leads to a towering confidence in humanity's capacity for knowledge and progress.

The Bourgeoisie in Control. A great deal of water has flowed under the bridge since all this began. The facile optimism rapidly faded as Enlightenment aspirations and illusions went unfulfilled. Internal contradictions came to light very early. Even Hegel could speak of the "unsatisfied Enlightenment."[21] But in spite of all, the grand claim of the Enlightenment continues to mark the modern spirit. One of the reasons is that, like any ideology, modernity has a historical subject, or carrier: the new dominant class, the bourgeois class.

The bourgeoisie is the social class that arose in the cities of a dying feudal world. Little by little this class established itself as the dominant one, and henceforward it would constitute the driving force of the economic system we know under the name of capitalism. Reaching the peak of its power in the industrial revolution, the bourgeoisie would now be in control of an economy based on private enterprise—and on the vicious exploitation of workers (in Europe) and the poor (in colonial and neocolonial lands).[22] Shortly the bourgeois class would become the driving force in politics, too.

Any attempt to separate the ideology of modernity from its historical agent, the bourgeois class, is to make a game of ideas and persons by ignoring social realities. This is the idealist view of history, and it will not fail to have heavy consequences in theology.

The New Critique of Religion

Bourgeois ideology, with its rationalism and its optimism, will level a severe critique at traditional religion, especially Christianity.

The Social Function of Religion. For the modern spirit, religious peoples simply live in a cloud of obscurantism and superstition. Religion is the enemy of human progress. Dogma is the enemy of science. Machiavelli and Montaigne had already sketched out a critique of the social function of religion, which the Enlightenment would sharpen: religion is no solid base for a real ethics or a just society.[23] In fact, religion implies immorality and social injustice.

Traditional religion, by preventing human beings from taking their destiny into their own hands, contravenes the liberty and autonomy of the human person, and in this consists its profound immorality. Hence the choice will now be, for the people of these times: faith or science. On this, deists and atheists can agree.

This critique of the function of traditional religion in society, and especially of the role played by Christianity, was carried on in the case of the deists from the standpoint of a natural, rational religion. This attitude had had antecedents in Renaissance humanism: intellectual circles of the fifteenth and sixteenth centuries had sought a universal religion, a religion that would accord a value to the world of nature then being discovered, and thus place human beings before God in a new light. This new religious consciousness did not at first express itself in hostility to Christianity. On the contrary, it considered that Christianity, if properly understood, could be just this religious form that seemed so needful.

But the eighteenth century meant to replace the revealed, authoritarian, Christian religion with a rational religion—one that, being rational, would be the only valid religion for every human being. After all, the universality of reason is one of the characteristic traits of the modern spirit. Reason would provide a religion that could be embraced freely, without dogma and without authority.

Original sin seemed one of Christianity's aberrations: the principle of individualism found it inadmissible that one person could be responsible for another's sin, just as the democratic spirit found it inadmissible that God would arbitrarily bestow grace and salvation on some and not on others. Such a God seemed tyrannical. The modern mind postulated a universal salvation and thereby contradicted a theological tenet that had come down from the church of the fourth century.[24]

This rational religion was seen as the religion of philosophers, of the heirs of the Enlightenment, of human beings who had attained their majority and now dared to use their reason. It was an elitist attitude, for the other side of the coin was that the popular masses were considered to be wallowing in superstition and ignorance.

Along the same lines of thought, the grand postulate of the era was religious tolerance—not in the negative sense of tolerating an evil, but as Bayle demanded it: out of respect for the religious convictions of others. Every person is free to believe or not, to take up this religion or that. Here again, in matters of religion as well, the individual is seen as an absolute point of departure. What is to be combated is superstition, which denies the value of science and reason, or intolerance, which denies human beings their liberty. To be sure, this attitude of tolerance vis-à-vis religious convictions was accompanied by a note of skepticism regarding the possibility of arriving at the truth in such matters. And it was accompanied by concerns of a practical order, due to the new forms of social experience that prevailed: in the marketplace, religious convictions were without importance. One exchanged goods not with someone who believed in someone, but with someone who had something. In capitalist economies, in spite of certain links with the sacral order, there is, as Max Weber observes, a desacralizing factor at work.

Henceforward the demand for respect for religious liberty will be closely linked with the defense of the other modern freedoms. Religion in European bourgeois society will now become increasingly relegated to the private domain.[25] Political theologies, ancient and modern, will now rise up together— though from opposing positions—against this dislodging of the Christian faith from society's public domain.

Radicalization of the Critique of Religion. In its origins, this critique of religion was undertaken from deistic or skeptical positions. Only in a few instances did it have its basis in atheism. But it soon became radicalized, in thinkers such as Feuerbach, whose questions now constituted a major challenge for theology.[26] It will not serve our purpose to examine this radicalization process in detail. Its basic themes are already present in what we have discussed above. The bourgeois unbeliever, atheist, and skeptic have become the principal interpreters of modern theology.

Of course it must be pointed out, as we conclude our bird's-eye view of the origin of the critique of religion, that in the new society created by the bourgeois class, Christians and non-Christians will often share the same economic, social, political, and cultural world. The hiatus dividing them will be found mainly in the realm of the religious. Their differences will be mainly in respect of faith and the philosophical presuppositions of faith.

Theology and the Modern Spirit

The challenge thrown at the feet of the Christian faith by the modern spirit was the turning point of theology. The most advanced efforts of theological reflection throughout the nineteenth and twentieth centuries have developed under the rules of play posited by this challenge.

The Essence of Christianity. The response of theology to the challenge—a theology born in another historical context, that of the ancien régime—was simply to reject the modern world and its questions.[27] At first conservative sectors of Christianity, as expressed in this theology, nourished the hope of a restoration of the old social order—and eliminated or reduced to silence, by way of condemnation, groups that had demonstrated a relative openness to the movement of modern freedoms and critical thought. But when it became evident that the new social class was going to continue firmly in power, conservative Christian factions fell back and began a reluctant accommodation. The bourgeoisie, for its part, shaken by the first assaults of the masses, began to moderate its belligerence against the church. And suddenly the way was open for compromise—and the overt or covert introduction of modern values in old wrappings. Of course, it was always an unhappy marriage, dictated by resignation and need, and with little love lost between the uncomfortable partners.

Protestant thought, on the other hand, was joined to the modern spirit from the very start. The association was a stormy one, but in the sixteenth century these toddlers were taking their first steps together, and the Protestant churches were more willing than Catholicism had been to try to comprehend the new world that was dawning. The vanguard of Protestant theology would become the great Christian theology of modernity, for it was a current that would lend an attentive ear to the questions asked by critical reason and individual liberty in this society forged by the bourgeoisie. For a number of historical reasons, this theology would center in Germany, the land of the Reformation.

The modern spirit's philosophical and critical predilection was for classic German philosophy. A number of the first great moderns were at once En-

lightenment figures and Christians, as in the case of two of the most tower-
ing, whose weighty influence is still felt in theology today—Kant and Hegel.
Both of these thinkers sought to bring the tools of reason into the service of
Christian faith, in the context of a bourgeois society. In the field of ethics,
Kant bent his efforts to demonstrate the reasonableness of Christianity. Later, Hegel would remark that the Kant of the *Critique of Practical Reason* is
more impressive and valuable than the Kant of the *Critique of Pure Reason*.
Hegel, for his own part, would choose, as the locus of encounter of philosophy and Christian faith, an area as rich in potential as it was complex: history.

Then Schleiermacher, who was more of a theologian in the classic sense
than either Kant or Hegel had been, stepped forward, as another interrogator
of the modern spirit. Indeed it is to the representatives of the Enlightenment
that he addressed his first and greatest book *Discourses on Religion*. His
work had a deep apologetical character: his theological efforts were concentrated on demonstrating the essential religious dimension of every human
being. The critical rationalist in Schleiermacher will feel constrained to posit
the expression of this dimension in what he called "religious sentiment."[28]
But religion, he held, ought to be recognized in its value and stature by human
reason. Rational criticism ought to be capable of delimiting the essence of
religion. Hence, more concretely, it ought to be able to isolate the essence of
that superior form of religion known as Christianity.

Liberal theology, more an attitude and climate than a school properly so
called, arose against a background of the great syntheses of Hegel and
Schleiermacher. It will honor Kant's epistemological questions and ethical
concerns with a great attention. Indeed it will exert an enormous effort to
build up a theology in the intellectual framework of the Enlightenment and in
the social context of a modern, bourgeois society. To take up the historical
and critical methods means to accept modernity. Some will consider this acceptance to be tantamount to capitulation—as if the rational and the modern
could ever become the criterion of what is authentically Christian!

Faith and Religion. Indeed this was precisely the charge leveled against
liberal theology by a brilliant group of thinkers who would soon represent the
best in twentieth-century Protestant theology—and whose influence is felt
everywhere in theology today. I refer, of course, to Barth and Bultmann, as
well as Tillich. Liberal theology, these writers declared, had capitulated to
modern thought. Their energetic reaction now dislodged liberal theology
from the primacy it had enjoyed in the teaching of theology.

The new historical and social context exercised a directive influence on this
reaction. World War II threw hard questions in the face of the old facile
optimism. The *belle époque* was no more. The socialist movement had just
appeared on the scene and had come to power in Russia. A little later, fascism
rose up against the freedoms proclaimed by the bourgeois ideology.

In one of the most perceptive pages of his prison diary, Bonhoeffer draws
up the balance sheet for this new theological current. Tillich's insistence, in

the footsteps of Schleiermacher, on the religious dimension does not seem to Bonhoeffer to take into account that the modern world has no need of an interpretation from without—a religious interpretation, for example. The world's understanding of itself is self-sufficient.

Barth had seen this, and therefore situated Christian faith on the level of the freely revealed word, rather than in a religious effort on the part of the human subject. But Barth had fallen into what Bonhoeffer called a "positivism of revelation." He had left the world to itself. When all was said and done, Barth, in Bonhoeffer's eyes, was still within the framework of a liberal theology—whatever may have been his intentions to the contrary. Bultmann, to Bonhoeffer, was even more frankly within the liberal purview: his impossible and ultimately useless demythologizing was but a prolongation of liberal theology's typical effort—the reduction of Christianity to its "essence."

Bonhoeffer thought the question of modernity had to be grasped more by its roots. The challenge of modernity is how to live and think the Christian faith in a nonreligious way. His thematic of "irreligiousness" will earn Bonhoeffer the reputation of having given the theology of secularization its original impetus. Today this interpretation appears reductionist. It fails to do justice to the depth and richness of the Lutheran theologian's thought.

It seems to me that, for Bonhoeffer, the notion of religion is bound up with the idea of power: the human being's power over God (the idea Barth had already rejected)—but God's power over the human being as well. Bonhoeffer gives full attention to this second form of understanding Christianity and considers it important to combat it as well. To believe in an almighty and omniscient God is to believe in a religious manner, and this is what the modern world finds unacceptable. To believe "irreligiously" is to believe in the weak and suffering God of the Bible:

> God lets himself be pushed out of the world and on to the cross. He is weak and powerless in the world, and that is precisely the way, the only way, in which he is with us and helps us. Matthew 8:17 makes it quite clear that Christ helps us, not by virtue of his omnipotence, but by virtue of his weakness and suffering.[29]

Bonhoeffer's own direct and cruel experience of suffering, as victim of the Nazi repression, and martyr—witness—of God's helpless love in the political conditions of his time, was a factor of vital importance in molding this perception.

Bonhoeffer's incisive question as to how to speak of God in an adult world takes on a deep meaning here. The modern world, like Bonhoeffer's own experience of suffering and impotence, poses a more important question than the one that asks whether the human being is or is not religious, whether the human being is or is not capable of believing in God. It poses a question concerning God himself. And Bonhoeffer sharpens this question with another: Who is Jesus Christ for us today? The second question contains a hint of the answer to the first.

The God of the Christian faith is the God who suffers in Jesus Christ.[30] To speak of God in a world come of age means to speak of a God who suffers. To live in a world without God ("before God, with God, and without God") demands that a Christian "share in God's suffering." No one else, perhaps, has appreciated the challenge of modernity as profoundly as has Bonhoeffer. The very depth of his posing of the question grasps the thinking of the spirit of modernity by its stalk and its roots start cracking.

Faith and Politics. As early as the middle of the nineteenth century, alongside the simple authoritarian rejection of the modern world, there arose in Catholic circles a minoritarian current that was open to dialogue with the new bourgeois society. It was called liberal Catholicism.[31] After many a vicissitude, its more moderate wing found an echo in the political doctrine of Leo XIII, and little by little certain other modern values began to be recognized as well, in other areas of Catholic theology. The search was undertaken for a language that would be understandable to the contemporary human being.

The first movements of openness to the modern world took place out on the margin of official church teaching. But they soon received support from an evolution in the social and political domain. And indeed the attitude of the dominant bourgeois class toward religion in the great countries of Europe was itself in a process of evolution. Religion, and the aristocracy that took refuge in it, were no longer important adversaries. In principle, liberal governments and political parties maintained their demands—individualism, religious freedom, the lay state, and so on. But in practice there were concessions. Difficulties with religion persisted, it is true. But it was clear that the bourgeoisie had a new enemy now: the movement of the popular masses.

John XXIII's great intuition in convoking Vatican Council II can be expressed in an image he himself used. The purpose of the council would be to "shake off the dust of empire." The hostility of the church toward the modern world, born at the beginning of the sixteenth century and maturing and peaking toward the end of that century, had riveted the church in the orbit of empire, in the world of Christendom. And so the challenges of the modern spirit occasioned the church's retreat; they did not spur it down new avenues in the proclamation of the gospel. Vatican Council II undertook to respond to the great questions of the movement for modern freedoms—the movement of the Enlightenment.

Thus it is scarcely to be wondered at that everything in the council's aggiornamento that seemed so urgent to the Christians of lands ruled by the old revolutionary social class, the bourgeois agent of the ideology of modernity—in Central Europe or the United States, for example—appeared as a dangerous novelty to those who had not had this historical experience, or had not had it to the same degree—Spain, Italy, or the Roman Curia, for example.

This also explains the interplay of the elements that came to be known as the "majority" and the "minority." Before the council opened, in the preparation of the schemata for discussion, it was the "minority" who had the greater influence. But once the debates were underway the minority progressively lost ground. Its strength had lain in the cohesiveness of a theology that had been developed over the course of centuries and was quite at home with a defensive attitude toward "modern ideas." Its weakness lay in its being out of step with contemporary society.

The Dogmatic Constitution on the Church in the Modern World—which had not been envisioned in the council's planning stage—presents a new horizon for the activity of the church. It is an optimistic view of the world and its progress, of contemporary science and technology, of the human person seen as the agent of history. And it is optimistic as to the possibilities for liberation. True, the fathers have some slight reservations. The recognition of these human values carries its risks, especially if it were to be forgotten that they attain their fulness only in relationship with the Christian message.

But all in all the document's view is encouraging and confident. It recognizes the existence of atheism in the world today, but points out the responsibility Christians have for it and issues a call for collaboration between believers and nonbelievers in the "just upbuilding of this world in which they live in common." The Lord of history is present, the council declares, in this world, a world distinct from the church but not necessarily hostile to it, and it is from this world that he calls the Christian community to greater fidelity to the gospel. This is the world in which the church is summoned to carry out its mission as "universal sacrament of salvation."

With moderation and reserve the great demands of modernity are accepted: the rights of the human person, subjective values, freedoms, social equality, the value of human progress. Social conflicts, on the other hand, are touched upon only in general terms of the presence of misery and injustice in the world. Although a certain distance is taken from some aspects of the individualistic roots of bourgeois society, there is no serious criticism of the implications of the monopolistic domination of the popular classes, especially the poor, by capitalism. The council is concerned with something else. The moment has arrived for dialogue with the modern world. The fact that this society, far from being a harmonious whole, is shot through with confrontations between social classes, is not a circumstance falling in the council's direct line of sight.

In an effort to recoup centuries of misunderstanding, Vatican II demonstrated a moderate openness to modern society. Oxygen was injected into an atmosphere that was becoming more and more asphyxiating. The "new political theology" of Johannes Baptist Metz is intended as a response to the questions of an expanded world. The explicit point of departure in this courageous theological effort is the problematic of the Enlightenment, especially in its critique of religion and society. In a recent article Metz says:

> The need and opportunity for a new political theology is born of the question of the possibility of a theology of the world that will take account of the world of the modern era—with its processes of Enlightenment, secularization, and emancipation. Ultimately the question

is identical with the question of the possibility of a theology, and of the working out of a theological systemization, dealing with the world of the modern era in general. This is the primary theological and theoretico-theological locus of a new political theology.[32]

Political theology, then, is a theology of the world. This is the form a fundamental theology must assume today if it seeks to take account of the modern mentality—and especially if it seeks to be understood by the modern mentality. Political theology underscores the public character of the Christian message, in reaction to the privatization of the faith to which the churches have fled before the critical assaults of the Enlightenment. This public character is not a rehash of the old "political Catholicism."[33] It is not, then, a theological attempt to rehabilitate what Moltmann calls "political religion." The new political theology steps forward rather as a criticism of these positions—perhaps indeed their only effective, radical criticism. To this end it seeks to take its position, however independently, within the very process of modern enlightenment and emancipation.

Metz distinguishes three theologies of the world in connection with these contemporary processes. The first is represented by the theology of secularization:

A theology face to face with the modern era is possible because theology for the first time has perceived itself in its radical otherness with respect to the world, in its own "unworldliness" *(Weltlosigkeit)*.

This is the focus in which faith may recognize the world in its "basic secularity" and bind itself to that world only by the fact of having contributed historically to the world's consciousness of this shortcoming. For Metz, this is the theology that privatizes faith, gives rise to an "ahistorical anthropological model," and perhaps even initiates the dissolution of theological reason. For Metz, this is the theology that, in the area of politics, manifests a predilection for the "doctrine of the two kingdoms."

The second theology of the world represents a new version of "liberal theology." It is marked by an uncritical conformism with today's world. "Christian," for this theology, will be whatever the modern spirit considers rational. This purely apologetical identification, like its antithesis, the "two-kingdom" theology, leads to the "self-dissolution of theological reason into the emancipatory and abstract reason of the modern era." Faith exercises no critical function over this new liberal anthropological model of the human being as "nature's dominating agent." Human realities such as suffering, play, and joy are solemnly left out of account.

Between these two theologies of the world, political theology appears on the scene as "an attempt to express the eschatological message of Christianity in relation to the modern era as a function of critico-practical reason." It therefore emphasizes the politico-eschatological, and interprets Christianity as a provocative "critico-liberative memory in the process of the emancipation, secularization, and enlightenment of the modern era." Like the theology of secularization, and like the new liberal theology, Metz's theology states its intent to take into account and assimilate the advances and the questioning of the modern spirit. But in this case the intent is critical, and for two reasons. First, the very process of emancipation, secularization, and enlightenment contains an internal dialectic that may not be lost sight of with impunity. Secondly, the Christian message *is* liberating and critical. It cannot be denied public notice. In this way theology will assist critical reason to become practical reason. This last step is of capital importance in the enlightenment process. Political theology, Metz asserts, seeks to express "the theologico-Christian version of practical reason in its relationship with the modern era."

The recovery of this provocative, critico-liberative memory will at last permit us to acquit ourselves of "the ancient and ever new task of the Christian message: the task of speaking of God." And it will enable us to do so in the manner Bonhoeffer demanded: so as to be intelligible to the human being of today. As Bonhoeffer himself implied, with his theme of God's weakness, it is a matter of the memory of the message of salvation, pardon, and reconciliation in Jesus Christ, publicly proclaimed in radical form in his death on the cross.[34] The cross here symbolizes the mortal combat waged by Jesus with the public powers of his time. The crucified Christ is the foundation of the human being's liberation by means of faith and hope. The cross rips the mask from the face of all political idolatry, deprives the powers that be of the justification "from above" they thought was their refuge.

From this point of departure, Metz has mined a most rich vein for theology in the form of "narrative." According to Metz, the history of death and resurrection is accessible to us in a special manner via "narrative."[35] The language of narrative must be a language that leads us to the memory of persons in their suffering, a memory of the suffering of the poor of this world. Theology and the theologians have kept aloof from this "pain of the people." They must "permit themselves to be interrupted by the mute pain of a people."[36]

Thus political theology seeks to face up to the questions of the modern story of freedom, enlightenment, and a Marxist critique of religion. It is a new kind of fundamental theology, one that takes its stand deep within the modern spirit and demands public notice for the Christian message. Until now this public character of the Christian message has been lost sight of by a "political Catholicism," which, being precritical, was not only incapable of speaking to today's world, but incapable even of rethinking its own Christian faith and its own church.[37] It was this incapacity that led to the privatization of faith—to liberal theology, a theology of secularization, and so on. These theologies gave more attention to the demands of bourgeois society, but ended by accepting the place that that society assigned them—the sphere of the private. This entailed a renunciation of the dimensions of faith that political theology now resumes within a new mentality, revalidating the critical dimension of the gospel message and thereby giving it a role to play in the process of the modern freedoms.

Jürgen Moltmann has expressed his adherence to the program of political theology, which he prefers to call a "political theology of hope."[38] Taking his distance from Luther's doctrine of the two kingdoms (a doctrine "secular, realist, and conservative") and Barth's political ethics ("seeking parables and signs of, and references to, the kingdom of God in history"), Moltmann considers political theology something to be shared by Catholics and Protestants equally, for "both churches are faced with the same problem of the irrelevance of their teachings for modern life and find no key in their respective traditions for the solution of these problems." The key to the response to the modern world will consist in a grasp of the fact that concern for the future has now caused the experience of transcendence to quit the field of metaphysics for that of eschatology. "Political theology," Moltmann avers, "sinks its roots in the theology of hope."[39]

Thus the new political theology takes its stance, altogether frankly but with fertile originality, within the parameters marked out by humanity's so-called adulthood. Its context is the challenge of bourgeois revolution and the Enlightenment, together with the criticism of religion by reason and its consequent relegation to the private sphere—just as they were the context of its two predecessors, whose theology we sketched in rapid strokes above.

Today political theology has entered into fruitful dialogue with the theology of liberation, and interesting points of convergence are emerging. The first encounters, however, were uncomfortable—perhaps because the theological undertaking centered on the liberation process comes from a different purview, and not only from a different purview, but from an essential opposition (and not a lack of attention) to the principal elements of the historical process we summarized at the beginning of this article.[40] It is this opposition to some concrete aspects of history that we shall attempt to explain and clarify in the following pages.

THEOLOGY IN A WORLD OF OPPRESSION

For the nascent bourgeois society of the cities of a feudal world, the discovery of new worlds in the fifteenth and sixteenth centuries was a decisive factor in the development of mercantile capitalism and hence in the development of the new mode of production that would go on consolidating its claims to exclusivity in centuries to come. The participation of the first representatives of capitalism in the conquest and colonization of the "West Indies" is a matter of record.

The encounter with the American Indian posed Western Christendom a series of new problems, in which politics and religion were neatly intertwined. And Western Christendom attempted to meet those problems with its old categories. But the impact of the Indian, this stranger, this "other" with respect to the Western world, gave rise to practices and reflection that called the prevailing theology into question. This disquieting discovery of the "other" has continued to our own day.

Today we clearly see that what was a movement for liberty in some parts of the world, when seen from the other side of the world, from beneath, from the popular classes, only meant new and more refined forms of exploitation of the very poorest—of the wretched of the earth. For them, the attainment of freedom can only be the result of a process of liberation from the spoliation and oppression being carried on in the name of "modern liberties and democracy." Here faith is lived by the poor of this world. Here the theological reflection seeking self-expression has no intention of being a palliative for these sufferings and refuses integration into the dominant theology. Here theology is ever more conscious of what separates it from the dominant theologies, conservative or progressive.

Before we attempt to trace the routes and uncover the milestones of this theological reflection—this theologizing from the standpoint of the exploited of this world—it will be useful to call in a representative. We shall want to hear a word from "history's absent ones." For it is precisely in their absence from history that they question the socio-economic structures that oppress and marginalize them, and it is this totalistic questioning that calls for a faith reflection.

Absent from History

Oppression and marginalization of the poor—of the Indians, originally—is an old Latin American tradition. It goes all the way back to colonial times. Later, with the frank insertion of our countries into the world of capitalism, new forms of exploitation came into being. Indeed the nineteenth century marks the beginning of a new stage in the history of the peoples of Latin America—a stage dominated by the bourgeoisie of the great industrial countries, in complicity with local elites.

Let us reverse the chronological order of events, and begin with this more recent era. Here we shall see again, in Latin America, the ideology of modernity that we examined earlier, along with its repercussions on social concern in the Christian sectors of the petty bourgeoisie. We shall then be better prepared to speak of the historical antecedents of today's popular movement against both the old and the new forms of colonialism and exploitation.

Bourgeois Democracy and the New Domination. Latin America was born dependent. Any change taking place in Europe wrought changes in Latin America. The eighteenth century was the beginning of the end for Spanish power, both economically and politically. England was becoming a match for Spain, as well as for Holland, on the high seas, and this meant international trade. The nascent industrial revolution was strengthening the hand of the European bourgeoisie. It was gradually asserting its hegemony over international trade and by the end of the eighteenth century had succeeded in penetrating the Spanish colonial market itself—though it had to leap the hurdles the Crown still managed to place in its way.

Colonial independence favored English domination. Thus after emancipation from Spain the so-called neocolonial pact was established, whereby the lands of the New World would furnish raw material and the industrialized countries would sell them finished products. The old colonies had come unequivocally within the capitalist system.

Liberal utopianism now led these new nations to a political organization based on "liberty" and "modernity." A more or less liberal ideology would echo ambiguously in the new national constitutions. The break with Spanish domination, and the onset of a new oppression at the hands of the large capitalist countries, was the work of a white colonial elite, in collaboration with certain other elements that had been won over to the new "liberty." The poorest—Indians, blacks, and *mestizos*—generally had no share at all in the advantages of the new arrangement, although some did profit peripherally or even shared sporadically in the spoils. The freedom guaranteed in the new constitutions did not reach society as a whole, but was limited to favoring the privileges of dominant groups in the service of the nascent international bourgeoisie.

For several decades these dominant groups were divided among themselves. The liberals represented an intellectual, progressivist echelon, favorable to ideas from Europe or the United States, and serving as the mouthpiece of commercial and financial interests linked to English or other European capital. Culturally their goals sprang from the Enlightenment, and they strove to overcome the remaining traces of barbarism among the poor of Latin America.[41] The conservatives, for their part, struggled to keep the old colonial economic model alive within the new political forms, merely transferring their allegiance from the bureaucracy forged during the colonial era to that of the large landholders. They also had ties with the Catholic Church, which continued to be important to the majority of the population.

Opposition between the liberals and the conservatives was a feeble reflection of what was occurring in Europe during those same years. It lost momentum, as it did in Europe, when popular movements began to threaten privileges shared by both sectors. Meanwhile the center of economic and political decision-making passed from England to the new capitalist power, the United States of America, whose "manifest destiny" was to transport it across the North American West, handing it dominion over South and Central America into the bargain.

The liberal era in Latin America turned out to be merely a cheap imitation of what was happening in the North Atlantic world. The social and economic structure actually underwent very little change. The only important one was that now that structure was at the service of the new international capitalism. The bourgeois interest of the industrialized countries, in complicity with dominant groups on the local scene, only instituted a more refined exploitation of the Latin American masses—some of whom actually found themselves in conditions worse than under the old colonial domination.

Of course, the whole situation was dissimulated and beautified with language about political liberties and modernization, and this deceived some popular sectors. But little by little it was given the lie. What had been a movement for modern freedoms, democracy, and rational, universal thought in Europe and the United States, in Latin America only meant new oppression, and even more ruthless forms of spoliation of the populous classes. The exploitation carried on among us by the modern nations—those shining knights of "liberty"—occasioned a traumatic experience not easy to forget about when we hear of "freedom and democracy."[42]

Openness to the Modern World and Social Problems. By 1930, economic and political structures in certain Latin American countries were undergoing changes owing to the international economic crisis. In countries whose economy was more solid, first steps were taken toward industrialization. No longer would manufactured goods have to be imported. New questions arose for Catholic Church circles in the southern part of the continent—Argentina, Chile, Uruguay, and the south of Brazil, whose populations were racially and culturally more European and more European-minded.

The Christian social current, which was awakening the social conscience of certain groups in Europe, was beginning to reach Latin American shores. This current had issued from the modern wing of liberal Catholicism, from certain ideas of French social Catholicism, and from the social doctrine of the church launched by Leo XIII. Jacques Maritain was its principal framer, as he welded these different lines of thought along an axis of Thomistic philosophy. It was an attempt to infuse some breadth and flexibility into the mentality of Christendom—to open Christianity up, in moderation, to the values of the modern world and the bourgeois ideals of liberty and democracy.

The misery of the vast majority of the Latin American population was now no longer seen simply as their historical lot, and the persons living in this misery were no longer thought of simply as objects of the works of charity. An awareness of social injustice as the basic cause of their circumstances arose. How could one continue to be a Christian without becoming involved in correcting this state of affairs? Individuals felt challenged by this harsh reality. But few noticed that it was the whole of society, with its system of values, that had come radically into question. Indeed, the nature of Christianity itself must now come under scrutiny, and even more totally and urgently than that of society itself.

Hence it is not surprising that, in some countries (in Chile, for example, in spite of recent setbacks), socio-Christian political parties saw fit to ally themselves with more conservative elements. In the socio-Christian perspective, creating a more just and more Christian society means correcting it—integrating the marginalized and attending to the most flagrant injustices. Sometimes a specific project might go further, but socio-economic analysis was lacking in scientific method, and in spite of all its good intentions could undertake only a general, vague defense of the dignity of the human person. Then too all this was set in the framework of the "concrete historical ideal" (Maritain's expression) of a society inspired by Christian values, values now seen as compatible with a modern demand for democratic liberties and social justice.

The socio-Christian perspective did not take the same direction in all Latin American countries. In some countries the most committed groups opposed the use of the Christian label in political activity. Their route to involvement in the liberation process was not the same, and some eventually made a radical break with the socio-Christian political parties.

The Underdogs. From the very beginning of the *Conquista* the native American peoples rebelled against their dominators, just as the black slaves would rebel against their new masters.[43] Recorded history has little to say in this regard. Nevertheless, little by little we are recovering the memory of the struggles for liberation in Latin America. Depending on the moment, Christian motives might well have been present in those rebellions.

Indians, blacks, and *mestizos* who had received the gospel found reasons in it for resisting the oppression to which they were subjected. Reading the gospel from within their own situation and culture, they sometimes departed from traditional orthodoxy, but often times their understanding of the Bible enabled them to grasp the depth of its meaning of justice.[44] Frequently the ideological basis for a movement would be in a politico-religious messianism—a precarious but rich vein to follow, in pursuit of the liberation of the poor in Latin America.[45]

Certain popular elements played a part in the wars of emancipation, only to be disappointed at the outcome. Then in the second half of the nineteenth century, Latin America began to feel the influence of the first currents of French socialism, with its sensitivity to the misery of the new proletariat created by industrial capitalism. A few protest documents, but not much in the way of organized activity, appeared in Latin America. The masses were heavily *campesino* in composition. Miners and urban laborers were still in the process of forming a social class. The first union organizations, and first militant union activity, toward the end of the century, would take place under the anarchist banner, and that influence would continue well into the twentieth century.

As the new century opened, the socialism of the Second International made its influence felt in laboring and intellectual circles and made a powerful contribution to the organization of workers' locals. Meanwhile it was giving birth to political parties as well. From 1920 on, however, the socialist current suffered the reverses of a confrontation between a moderate line and a more revolutionary one. Among representatives of the latter, the most outstanding example of action and thought was José Carlos Mariátegui. Mariátegui sought to think through the reality of Latin America in creative Marxist terms. A native of Peru, one of the oldest nations of the South American continent, he saw the Indian question as a demanding and permanent theme for reflection.[46]

Except for occasional, isolated figures, such as Clotario Blest, founder of the *Central Unica de Trabajadores* (CUT, "Consolidated Workers Union") of Chile, few Christian leaders participated in these first beginnings of political organization and consciousness among the popular classes of Latin America. Later, a greater number did become involved in important, if often only short-lived, populist, and national movements. In some countries the socio-Christian current guided them toward the organization of socio-Christian labor unions. Years later, after a great deal of progress in social awareness, these same Christian energies were harnassed for projects, organizations, and political parties that carried no Christian label, and some of which opted for a socialist approach to our problems.

Recent years in Latin America have been marked by an increased awareness of the world of the "other"—of the poor, the oppressed, the exploited class. In a social order drawn up economically, politically, and ideologically by the few for the benefit of the few, the "others"—the exploited classes, oppressed cultures, and ethnic groups that suffer discrimination—have begun to make their own voice heard. Gradually they are learning to speak without interpreters, to have their say directly, to rediscover themselves, and to make the system feel their disquieting presence. They are becoming less and less an object of demogogy and manipulation, or an object of half-heartedly disguised "social work," and more and the more the agents of their own history—forgers of a radically different society.

The revolutionary ferment in Mexico (in its more popular aspects), as well as in Bolivia and Guatemala, in the 1950s, played a preparatory role. The socialist revolution in Cuba—whatever analysis some observers may make today—opened up new outlooks. The year 1965 marked a high point in armed struggle in Latin America and hastened a political radicalization even of persons who had hoped to find other avenues for their revolutionary activity. Camilo Torres and "Che" Guevara symbolized so many others—anonymous, committed, setting an indelible seal on the Latin American process, raising questions and exerting definitive influence in Christian circles.

Indeed from these years onward, an increasing number of Christians—in Brazil especially, at first—have become active agents in this process, and consequently in the process of discovery of the world of the exploited of Latin America. In most instances this has simply meant becoming aware of their own world. This commitment, this involvement, constitutes the greatest single factor in the life of the Latin American Christian community today. It is giving rise to a new way of being a person and a believer, a new way of living and thinking the faith, a new way of being called together, and calling others together, in an *ek-klesia*, a church—the assembly of those called apart for a task. This commitment is the dividing line between two experiences, two times, two worlds, and two languages, in Latin America, and hence in the Latin American church.

This participation by Christians—of various confessions—in the liberation process exhibits varying degrees of radicality. It has different nuances in each Latin American country. It is expressed in experimental languages, which grope along by trial and error. At times it becomes lost in detours and blind alleys along the way. At other times, some special occurrence will encourage it, and its pace quickens.

Latin America has always been a land of oppression and repression. At the moment, after the socialist experiment in Chile, after the mass movements in

Argentina, and the reformist and nationalist ferment in other countries, repression has only become more massive and more refined.[47] What Medellín so appropriately characterizes as "institutionalized violence" is on the increase, and now resorts to the indiscriminate use of force—imprisonment, massacre, torture, and so on—and a systematic violation of the most elemental human rights, in order to keep the popular movements "in check."[48]

But the popular movement is consolidating its base. The political awareness of the dispossessed masses is deepening and maturing. Autonomous organization is becoming more common. New ways of working are being learned. Both the gains and the failures are instructive experiences. The spilled blood of those (whose photos may or may not appear on the front pages of newspapers) who have risen up against a secular injustice, bestows unlooked-for titles of ownership, more and more rapidly now, over a land more and more foreign, and yet ever more insistently laid claim to by the ones the Bible calls "the poor of the earth." Yes, the popular movement knows its retreats and its vacillations—what historical process does not? But it knows its constancy, as well, its hope, and its political realism. And it knows its capacity for resistance—which the defenders of the established order find perplexing. It surprises even the revolutionary elite, who have been conducting their projects amid such harsh frustrations during these recent years in Latin America.

This is the context in which the theology of liberation was born and grew. It could not have come to be before the popular movement itself and its concrete, historical liberation praxis had achieved a certain degree of development and maturity. These struggles are the locus of a new way of being men and women in Latin America, and thereby as well of a new manner of living the faith, a new mode of encounter with the Father and with one's sisters and brothers. It is this spiritual experience (in Paul's sense of "living according to the spirit"), at the very heart of social conflict, that is, in solidarity with "history's absent ones," the very spring and source of our new theological effort.[49]

The System Questioned

The poor, the wretched of the earth, are not, in the first instance, questioning the religious world or its philosophical presuppositions. They are calling into question first of all the economic, social, and political order that oppresses and marginalizes them, and of course the ideology that is brought in to justify this domination. Only within this framework can we appreciate the challenges to the faith that come from within the world of the exploited.

Their questioning seeks to go to the very root of the misery and injustice in which millions in Latin America and other parts of the world live. This is why they take the road of social revolution and not of reformist palliatives. This is why they go in search of liberation, not developmentalism; they call for socialism, not some updating of the system in effect.

To "realists," these options may seem utopian, romantic. And well they should. They form part of a rationality that is new and foreign to "realists"—the rationality of a concrete thrust in history, no longer originating with the dominant classes but with those on the underside of that history. It is a work of denunciation of a society built to benefit the few, and of proclamation of a social order established in favor of the poor and oppressed. It is a project just underway, nourished by the daily struggle of the people to live in spite of oppression—and to resist oppression and struggle for liberation.

The theory of dependency, in the social sciences, has contributed in recent years to a new political awareness in Latin America. According to these analyses the social structures of Latin America are structures of "external dependency and internal domination." Early researchers perhaps failed sufficiently to point up that the confrontation is not in the first instance between nations or continents, or between a "center" and a "periphery" (understanding these terms geographically), but between social classes. In the dependency framework one can analyze other confrontations as well. These have their own dynamisms, and it will not do to underestimate them—nationalism, for example, or racial confrontations. The role of the multinational corporations, too, in the economic and political control of the poor countries, becomes clearer when analyzed in the light of the theory of dependency.[50] Today all of this is at our fingertips, and it permits us to sketch a better outline of the nature of the dependence on capitalism that characterizes Latin American social configurations.

Here at the heart of a concrete historical process, and not in the peace and quiet of a library or a dialogue among intellectuals, there arises for the popular movement an encounter with the social sciences and Marxist analysis. They have their importance for understanding the mechanisms of oppression imposed by the prevailing social order. More than anything else, it is the system itself that is being called into question by the exploited, and it is impossible to live the faith outside the framework of this questioning. This is why the popular movement is also the locus of encounter of the social sciences and Marxist analysis with theology—an encounter, to be sure, involving criticism of theology, and an encounter undertaken within the dynamics of a concrete, historical movement that transcends individuality, dogmatisms, and transitory enthusiasms. Hence any and all intellectual terrorist tactics simply miss the mark.[51]

The project of creating a new and different society includes the creation of new human persons, as well, who must be progressively liberated from whatever enslaves them, from whatever prevents them from acting as the agents of their own lot in history. This is the reason for the challenge to the dominant ideologies of our day, with their model of the human person that they attempt to impose on our society.

There are certain religious elements present in these ideologies. It is only within the framework of a challenge to the established order *in toto* that it is possible to understand the critique of religion on the part of the oppressed;

for religion is being criticized precisely as a factor purporting to justify the domination under which the exploited and marginalized suffer. This recognition of the importance of social conditioning for our Christian life and theological reflection leads the theologian to a serious concern with the relationship between theology and ideology. The question is one that cannot be sidestepped by anyone who intends to engage in a theological reflection from the perspective of "history's absent ones."[52]

However, the building of a different society, and of a new human person, will be authentic only if it is undertaken by the oppressed themselves. Hence the point of departure for this undertaking must be the values of these persons. For it is from within the people that the prevailing social order is being so radically questioned. It is from within the people that the culture of oppression is on its way to being abolished. Indeed this is the only way in which a genuine social and cultural revolution can be carried out.

One of the values of the people of Latin America is popular religion. Popular religion is something beyond the comprehension, and beneath the contempt, of the "enlightened" bourgeois mentality. And yet of course the representatives of this mentality do not hesitate to manipulate it in defense of their privileges. Hence the presence of elements of the dominant ideology in popular religion. But the religious experiences of the people are also charged with values of protest, resistance, and liberation.[53]

This is why our question is not how to speak of God in an adult world. That was the old question asked by progressivist theology. No, the interlocuter of the theology of liberation is the *"nonperson,"* the human being who is not considered human by the present social order—the exploited classes, marginalized ethnic groups, and despised cultures.[54] Our question is how to tell the nonperson, the nonhuman, that God is love, and that this love makes us all brothers and sisters.

The faith experience and faith reflection welling up here are not only on the religious plane, as when the critique originates on the part of nonbelievers. Here the hiatus is not primarily between believer and nonbeliever, but between oppressor and oppressed. And among the oppressors are those who "hold themselves forth as Christians," as Bartolomé de Las Casas would say.

The case is not the same when the critique of religion is made by the modern spirit, where the religious element creates a division among persons sharing the same quality of life and the same social world. Here the oppressors and the oppressed share, superficially at any rate, the same faith, and what differentiates them is precisely their economic, social, and political levels. Indeed, some are actually exploiting others on this level. The contradiction is clear as can be. A like divorce between the area of faith and the historical realities in which faith must be lived crumbles at the touch of even a rudimentary analysis in the light of the word of God. And yet this lie has shown itself to be extremely tenacious in circles calling themselves Christian.

Theology and the "Scourged Christs of the Indies"

Living and thinking the faith from within the culture of "history's absent ones" demands a new mode of understanding the salvific message of the gospel. Taking one's stand in the very midst of the world of oppression, sharing the popular struggles for liberation, leads one to reread the faith. But this rereading presupposes that we move to a different history from that of society's dominant sectors.

The breach between the traditional and the progressivist theologies, and the theology of liberation, is not purely theological. There is first of all a political breach—without which it is impossible to understand the effort of liberation theology to rethink the struggles of the poor and oppressed of this world. This political breach, rooted in the differences between social classes, enables us to see that the central issue is not between European theology and Latin American theology.[55] We have a traditional, and a modern, theology in Latin American, too. They are the theologies of the dominant sectors in our societies. The locus of liberation theology is elsewhere—among the poor, among the native masses, among the popular classes, as agents and creators of their own history. The place where the theology of liberation materializes is in the expressions of their faith, in their hope in the poor Christ, and in their struggles for freedom.

All this was clearly perceived by certain sixteenth-century missionaries. For reasons of brevity, we shall restrict ourselves here to the theological efforts of Bartolomé de Las Casas.

The presence and scope of the viewpoint of the poor in theology in later centuries could be studied as well, of course. There one would have to take into account not only the efforts of traditional rational theology, but especially of the symbolic language in which the people expressed their resistance, their combats, and their religious experiences.

On the other hand, as we have already pointed out, the liberal ideology was being assimilated in Latin America at this same time. The popular outcry was loud then, especially during the struggles for emancipation, but it would soon be stifled.

Theologically, modernity has been rather unfruitful in Latin America. Modernity's disciples, now as in the past, have never managed to do their thinking from within, and with, the Latin American people. But the past decade has seen changes in the situation of the popular movement. Conditions have arisen that favor the initiation or, to be more exact, the reinitiation of a rereading of the faith from within the struggles and hopes of the poor. We shall be referring to these efforts in later sections of this article.

The Indian: Heathen or Pauper? The conquest and colonization of the lands Columbus discovered were promptly presented as a missionary endeavor. The salvation of the "heathen" there, by their incorporation into the church, soon became the ostensible reason for Spain's involvement in the Americas. Christian considerations were brought forward in order to justify the colonial enterprise. But they were also brought forward to indict it. Thus Christianity, in this double function, became the center of the "controversy of the Indies."

For Bartolomé de Las Casas, salvation—that great, lifelong concern of his, the ultimate motive for his missionary activity—was bound up with the establishment of social justice. And the link between the two was so profound, as he saw it, that he was led to invert the hierarchy of problems traditionally posed by missionaries, on at least two points.

First, Las Casas pointed out that the Spaniards were placing their own salvation in jeopardy by their behavior toward the Indians. If they did not cease their degradation, spoliation, and exploitation of the Indians, Las Casas said, they would without a doubt be damned: "for it is impossible for anyone to be saved who does not observe justice."[56] For Las Casas, the salvation of the "faithful," the salvation of those who claimed to be Christian, was more in jeopardy than that of the "heathen."

Secondly, Las Casas had the prophetic depth to see the Indians more as poor persons, in the gospel sense, than as heathen. Thus in a letter to the emperor he says that if the Indians' conversion to Christianity "could not take place without their death and destruction, as has happened until now," it would be better "for them never to become Christians."[57] A live heathen Indian, in other words, was better than a dead Christian Indian. This is the attitude we hear characterized today as a "materialistic viewpoint." But Las Casas thought that salvation in Christ had to include social justice.

His positions were shared by many who worked, as did he, actively and in an organized fashion in defense of the Indian.[58] But these positions also had determined enemies. One of the most renowned apologists of the *Conquista* and colonialization was Juan Ginés de Sepúlveda. The heavy cannon in Sepúlveda's arsenal was the argument that the Indians were natural slaves, inferior to the Europeans, their natural masters. This distinction between two classes of human beings was based on a celebrated text of Aristotle, along with some unclear texts of Thomas Aquinas, on slavery. The subjection of the Indians to the Spaniards, for Sepúlveda, was in conformity with human nature. Hence wars to achieve this subjection were fully justified. Furthermore, these wars were necessary in order to be able to evangelize these rude, barbarous peoples, with their unnatural customs.

All this was expounded brilliantly, with abundant citations, and presented as traditional doctrine. It is a well-known strategy, and has been used in our own day. It is a theological justification for the oppression carried out by the *encomendero* class—who, as might be expected, roundly applauded this doughty defender of their privileges. We have had a good many Sepúlvedas since then in the Americas—advocates of the exploitation and enslavement of the majority in the name of "Western Christian civilization." But it is only in recent years, perhaps, that they have become as frank and plainspoken as he in their attempt to justify the oppression and massacre of the Latin American poor and exploited as they struggle for liberation.

Las Casas's position is familiar to us. We have no need of pursuing all the convolutions of his argumentation. It will be worth the effort, however, to make certain observations here—not all equal in importance, to be sure—that will help us better situate the later theological approach of which he was the herald and forerunner.

Before launching his copiously referenced argumentation, full of subtle distinctions, against Sepúlveda's theses, Fra Bartolomé makes an observation that disqualifies his adversary's position from the standpoint of sheer practice. The theses Sepúlveda defends, Las Casas writes, have been the cause of unspeakable death and destruction:

> The so-called *conquistas* and *encomiendas* have wiped out human populations without number and devastated the land over more than two thousand leagues, by new and various manners of cruelty and inhumanity on the part of the Spaniards in the Indies.[59]

One of the best ways to refute a theology is to look at its practical consequences, not its intellectual arguments. This text is not an isolated one. Many times Las Casas reproaches Sepúlveda for his intellectualism, his lack of familiarity with the Indies, and the concrete implications of his theological tenets. Bartolomé de Las Casas was a man of action. His theological work is but an element of this action of his—part of his commitment to and involvement with the Indians.

This way of doing theology is different from that of more classic and academic theologians. A case in point is the most famous theologian of his time, Francisco de Vitoria. It seems to us to be an error to seek to reduce the arguments of Las Casas in the controversy of the Indies to Vitoria's positions. To be sure, it was thanks to a solid Thomistic training, together with the timely warnings of Dominican missioners in the Indies, that Vitoria was able to bring his reflections on the theology of law to the point where a law of nations, an international law, could be framed.

It is equally clear that there are many points of convergence between the two great Dominicans and that Las Casas had much respect for the Master of Salamanca. But on the questions posed by the conquest of the Indies, Vitoria only goes half-way. He energetically refutes the reasons brought forward for making war and subjugating the Indians. But he reintroduces the possibility by drawing up a list of hypothetical reasons that would justify such wars in other, theoretical, cases. He works with abstract hypotheses, as is typical of a theologian not in direct contact with the facts. Anyone familiar with the situation of the Indies knew the hypotheses were false.

Francisco de Vitoria was a centrist theologian, a representative of the most advanced and modern wing of the dominant sectors. Bartolomé de Las Casas took a different viewpoint. His point of departure is the Indian—despised, exploited humankind. This is why he very rarely cites Vitoria, or bothers to criticize his intellectual positions, estranged as they are from experiential reality.[60] All centrism, political or theological, opens the door for more reactionary positions. Thus Vitoria's centrism permits warlike conduct, if not war itself, against the Indians.

And this brings us to a third consideration. Is it really true that a theology that is more closely bound up with practice, with a commitment to the struggles of the people, with planning for effective action, and with the witness of faith, is less serious and scientific? For this is often what differentiates Vitoria and Las Casas. I think the answer is no. Rather, it would seem that the scientific rigor and rationality of a concrete theology is something so unfamiliar to the system's dominators, and to those who depend on the ideology of the dominators, that it seems to *them* to lack rigor and reason. In any case it is certainly a fact that direct participation in a concrete historical process, in the struggles of the poor and in popular expressions of the faith, afford a perception of aspects of the Christian message that escapes other approaches. We have seen this in Las Casas's exposition of his ideas on salvation and justice. This, we suggest, is the result of his having seen the Indian not as just a heathen to evangelize, but as a poor person, in the gospel sense—as an "other," who is calling Western Christianity to account.

The depth of Las Casas's perception is due to one of his greatest insights: that Christ speaks to us from among the Indians. This is already apparent in his account of his own conversion, and it is something he will repeat many times. In the Indies, he writes, he had seen "Jesus Christ, our God, scourged and afflicted and crucified, not once, but millions of times."[61] How inconceivable for the theology of a Sepúlveda, for whom the Indian was born to be a slave. Identified with Christ! The masters, perhaps; but surely not the Indian. Not even Vitoria would have allowed such a concept to creep into his theology. Here is what is deepest and most profound in the theology of Las Casas: Christ calls us, summons us, challenges us, from within the mass of the oppressed.

Bartolomé de Las Casas, and those who, like him, take the Indian's part, bear witness to medieval Christianity's confrontation with someone "other" than what it had known until then. These thinkers had been trained in traditional theology. And yet they break new paths in theology, once they have read the gospel from the viewpoint of the "scourged Christs of the Indies."[62]

Modernity and Dependent Theology. The thrust of involvement and theological reflection that began with Las Casas had its protagonists all through the colonial period. But it never had the breadth and assertiveness it had in the sixteenth century. Only well into the twentieth century will this same outlook return to the theological scene. In Las Casas, and those who like him allow themselves to be summoned and challenged by the Indian, liberation theology recognizes its pioneers. For they blazed the trail the theology of liberation would follow.

The theology of liberation seeks continuity, on another horizon and in another age, with this sixteenth-century theology. And it seeks to break with the dominant theology marked by the modern spirit. Hence before resuming the thread of a theology that comes up from among the "scourged Christs of the Indies," it will be appropriate to say something about the influence of the modern spirit on theological reflection in Latin America. Our digression will be brief, however, because, as already indicated, the modern mentality has not produced any creative theological reflection, properly so-called, in Latin America.

In the nineteenth century, and during the first decades of the twentieth, it was the traditional sectors that maintained the theological upper hand in the church. Their attitude was very defensive. Then too, the ideological weakness of the nascent bourgeois class failed to provoke any theological response. Everything was reduced to a faint, infertile repetition of the confrontations between liberals and conservatives taking place in Europe. Protestant circles were closer to the modern spirit, but in Latin America were so thinly scattered, minoritarian, and foreign, that they, too, failed to produce any theological reflection in the framework of modern ideas.

Later, from 1930 up to Vatican II, more advanced Catholic theological circles merely followed the French theology then in the vanguard of Catholic thought. Their work was enthusiastic, but not very creative. This meant, first, a socio-Christian political influence, and later the theology of the distinction of planes. The socio-Christian element, searching for a middle road between capitalism and socialism, espoused a social-reform approach, and demonstrated an openness to the modern world, as well as, guardedly, to the liberal ideology whose genesis and characteristics were presented in the first part of this chapter. Overlaid on the base of this theological reflection was a veneer of social concern, but it was always the prisoner of a Christendom mentality and a political middle-of-the-road stance.

Today, hoping to profit by the political situation in Latin America, defenders of the socio-Christian position are attempting to rejuvenate it and present it once more as the Christian solution to Latin America's problems. Anxious to avoid extremes, the socio-Christian doctrine, in this markedly more conservative version, feels called to fill the gap constituted by the absence of ideologies capable of being translated into effective political programs. Its theoreticians believe that there is presently a great disunity among the Christian groups of Latin America, and that their version of the socio-Christian doctrine could provide them all with the cohesiveness and direction they need. Actually there is little to be hoped for from this attempt to turn the clock back. But its advocates dispose of sufficient economic means to convince some that these projects have managed to escape the ivory towers of authors and editorial offices for the world of concrete reality.

The theology of the distinction of planes was more seriously sensitive to contemporary values and had a broader theological scope. It was the link that bound certain Latin American circles to a preconciliar progressive theology. Its great themes, in function of its full acceptance of democratic government and a concern for social justice, were the presence of the church in a heterogeneous world and the corresponding diversity of Christian political involve-

ment. Its whole thrust received a great deal of encouragement from Vatican
II, which, as we have seen, sought to respond to the economic, social, political, and cultural world forged by the bourgeois classes of the large nations.

After the council it was the theology of development that briefly captured
the interest of those in search of modernization. Here, a recognition of the
value of human progress meant greater social concern for poor populations.
An optimistic, dynamic outlook, however, failed to make up for a myopia
with regard to the causes of misery and injustice or the meagerness of the
Christian experience underlying the theology.

The theology of revolution sought to break with these shortcomings. I
mention it here only as a step in the direction of a new stage. In some cases it
marked the first moments of a radicalized political involvement. This was the
theological outlook frequently appealed to by young persons from the socio-
Christian camp, for example, when they broke with their respective political
parties. But its limited purview soon came to light, in its tendency to "baptize" the revolution, import its problematic, broaden the notion of revolution almost to the vanishing point, and, especially, neglect a critical reflection
based on de facto praxis.

Theology and the Perspective of the Poor. The years from 1965 to 1968
were decisive ones in the experience of Latin America's popular movement.
They were also decisive for Christian participation in the movement. The
theology of liberation, born just before Medellín, is rooted in those years.

Apart from the life of Christian communities during this time, there is no
explaining what happened at the Second Latin American Bishops' Conference, in Medellín. For it was in Medellín that these Christians' experience
with involvement in the liberation process found expression. Medellín's acceptance and support of this experience was a matter of surprise to many. But
Medellín did even more. It set in motion new wheels of activity and reflection,
and thereby undertook one of the tasks assigned to the council by Pope John
XXIII, one that the council was unable to carry out: to take account of the
challenge of poverty in the world of today. In fact it is the viewpoint of the
poor that gives Medellín its character and originality, whatever may have
been its inevitable lacunae and shortcomings.

The principal theme of Medellín was "The Church in the Current Transformation of Latin America, in the Light of Vatican II." Thus the conference's professed intention was to take the principles of the council and
apply them to the situation in Latin America. But contact with reality had the
effect of reversing the order of the elements in the theme into something more
like "The Church of Vatican II in the Light of the Latin American Situation." This reversal, this expression of the maturity of the Latin American
Christian community—and, above all, this expression of the misery, hope,
and commitment in which the peoples of Latin America live—gave Medellín
its thrust and power.

It is this reversal that certain persons refuse to forgive Medellín for, as they
seek to blot it from the Latin American landscape. They err if they think they

can succeed. When you place your hope in the Lord and sink your roots into the concrete power of the poor in history, you are not living on nostalgia. You are living in a present moment, whose only direction is forward.

Latin America's difficult situation today, along with the changes undergone by the Latin American Episcopal Conference (CELAM) since 1972, have led some to glorify the past, and glibly parrot what they have heard about the birth of liberation theology at a time of euphoria and enthusiasm. "The good old days," of course, will always look better than life right now. But the years from 1965 to 1968 were more a time of struggles, successes, failures, and new experiments, than of euphoria. And 1968, the year the first formulations were worked out for a theology of liberation, was not, to be sure, a time like the time we are living through today, but it was certainly not a year of facile optimism either.[63]

Furthermore—and this may come as a surprise to superficial analysts—the reasons we had for hope in 1968 are ultimately the same reasons we have today. This bears repeating in a difficult moment such as the present. Scramble as they may, the puppets of repression will not be able to drive the Latin American people back down the road, away from the liberation toward which they have begun to march. For this is the road that, in the circumstances of today, one must follow as a condition and requirement of a life of authentic faith and hope in the Lord.

From the beginning, the theology of liberation had two fundamental insights. Not only did they come first chronologically, but they have continued to form the very backbone of this theology. I am referring to its theological method and its perspective of the poor.

From the beginning, the theology of liberation posited that the first act is involvement in the liberation process, and that theology comes afterward, as a second act.[64] The theological moment is one of critical reflection from within, and upon, concrete historical praxis, in confrontation with the word of the Lord as lived and accepted in faith—a faith that comes to us through manifold, and sometimes ambiguous, historical mediations, but which we are daily remaking and repairing.

It is not a matter of setting an inductive method over against the deductive method of such and such a theology. This would be an oversimplification.[65] It is rather an attempt to situate the work of theology within the complex and proliferous context of the relationship between practice and theory.

The second insight of the theology of liberation is its decision to work from the viewpoint of the poor—the exploited classes, marginalized ethnic groups, and scorned cultures. This led it to take up the great theme of poverty and the poor in the Bible. As a result the poor appear within this theology as the key to an understanding of the meaning of liberation and of the meaning of the revelation of a liberating God.[66]

This second point, of course, is inseparable from the first. If theology is to be a reflection from within, and upon, praxis, it will be important to bear in mind that what is being reflected upon is the praxis of liberation of the oppressed of this world. To divorce theological method from this perspective would be to lose the nub of the question and fall back into the academic.

It is not enough to say that praxis is the first act. One must take into consideration the historical subject of this praxis—those who until now have been the absent ones of history. A theology thus understood starts off from the masses and moves from within their world. It is a theological reasoning that is *veri-fied*—made to be true—in a real, fertile involvement with the liberation process.

The inseparability of these two prime intuitions, furthermore, is what enabled liberation theologians to see from the very beginning that they were not going to be able to build a theology of any substance if the poor had no grasp of the hope that was theirs. Any attempt to make progress in theology apart from the hope of the poor—a hope from within their world and in their own terms—could well gain a little here and a little there, perhaps, but would not give us the quantum leap we were looking for.[67] This is important. The only way to come to a new theological focus and language was to sink our roots in the social life of the Latin American people—this people whose own roots are geographically, historically, and culturally so deep in this land; this lowly people who had so long kept silent and now suddenly wished to speak, to cry out.

A historical process of vast implications is underway. If what we have today in the way of a theology of liberation, with all its limitations, can make a contribution to this process, and thereby open up the possibility of a new understanding of the faith, then it will have accomplished its interim task. For the task of any theology is a transitional one, and liberation theology, like any other, is only a new generation's new awareness of its faith, in ecclesial communion, at a given moment of history. Our own generation has only just begun to cut the many ties that bind it, consciously or unconsciously, to the prevailing system and to discover the "other" in the world in which it continues to live. Our own generation has only just begun to discover the presence of the Lord at the heart of the history of the Latin American people.

The Other History: The History of the Other. Human history is indeed the concrete locus of our encounter with the Father of Jesus Christ. And in Jesus Christ we proclaim to all human beings the Father's love. We have indicated that this history is conflictual. But it is not enough to say this. One must insist on the necessity of a rereading of history. History, where God reveals himself and where we proclaim him, must be *reread from the side of the poor*. The history of humanity has been written "with a white hand,"[68] from the side of the dominators. History's losers have another outlook. History must be read from a point of departure in their struggles, their resistance, their hopes.

Many an effort has been made to blot out the memory of the oppressed and thereby deprive them of a source of energy, of historical will, of rebellion. Today downtrodden peoples seek to comprehend their past in order to build their present on solid foundations.

The history of Christianity, too, has been written with a white, Western, bourgeois hand. We must recover the memory of the "scourged Christs of the Indies" and, in them, the memory of all the poor, the victims of the lords of this world. This memory lives on—in cultural expressions, in popular religion, in resistance to the imposition of ecclesiastical apparatus. It is the memory of Christ present in everyone who hungers, or thirsts, or is taken prisoner, or is debased, the memory of Christ present in despised ethnic groups and exploited classes (see Matt. 25). It is the memory of Christ who, "when he freed us, meant us to remain free" (Gal. 5:1).

But the concept of a "rereading of history" can appear to be an exercise for intellectuals, unless we understand that it is the result of a remaking of history. It is impossible to reread history except in the midst of the successes and failures of the struggles for liberation. Remaking this history, redoing it, means we have to "subvert" it, turn it around, make it flow backward—make it flow not from above but from below. The established order has inculcated in us a pejorative concept of subversion: subversion is dangerous to the established order. But from the other viewpoint, the great wrong is to become—or, perhaps, to continue to be—a "super-versive," a bulwark and support of the prevailing domination, someone whose orientation of history begins with the great ones of this world. But a subversive history is the locus of a new faith experience, a new spirituality, and a new proclamation of the gospel.

This memory of the poor, and this remaking of history from beneath, have always been alive—in actions repressed by political power, in reflection marginalized by the dominant echelons—expressed in tentative formulations, hence in formulations not immune to impatience and ambiguity. All through history there has been a repressed but resurgent theology, born of the struggles of the poor. To follow in the footsteps of the poor in this history is the urgent task of liberation theology. It is the task of its own historical continuity.

The great milestones on this long journey have to be studied—the primitive Christian community, the great pastors and theologians of the first centuries, the Franciscan movement and Joachim da Fiore in the Middle Ages, the Hussite movement in the fifteenth century, the peasant wars in Germany and Thomas Münzer in the sixteenth, the defense of the Indian and Bartolomé de Las Casas, Bishop Juan del Valle, and so many others of the same era in Latin America, Juan Santos Atahualpa in the eighteenth century in Peru, and the peasant struggles and popular piety in more recent times in Latin America.

These subterranean streams gush up, at times unexpectedly, from the living fonts of poor persons' awareness of the God who sets them free. This is why the mystical and contemplative dimension is so often present in this current. This water from under the earth sometimes comes to the surface and forms pools, creating, in the midst of an academic theology, and in spite of unavoidable concessions and ambiguities, certain "oases"—the rights of the poor in scholastic theology (as against the property rights of others, or the tyranny the poor must suffer, for example), the beginnings of a heightened social awareness in French Catholicism in the middle of the nineteenth century, religious socialism in Germany and Switzerland in our own century, certain aspects of the "Social Gospel" in the United States, the early Reinhold Niebuhr, and many others.

Particularly meaningful in this respect are the contributions of Barth and Bultmann. We referred to these thinkers at the beginning of this article, following the line of thought furnished us by Bonhoeffer. But there is something else to be said about them. Recent studies have recalled how important for Barth was his experience as a pastor in a laboring community at the beginning of the century. This experience led him to an out-and-out militancy. He became a socialist and joined the Social Democratic Party in Switzerland before World War I—a political commitment that he renewed in Germany on the eve of the Nazis' coming to power. Whatever influence this option may have had on the actual development of the details of his theology, it cannot be denied that Barth himself demonstrated a great sensitivity to these questions, and to the socialist outlook, to the end of his days.[69]

This was not the case with Bultmann. His world is clearly the world of the modern spirit. His framework is that of bourgeois ideology. At first sight this can be surprising. Barth, the theologian of God's transcendence, unlike Bultmann, pays little attention to the hearer of the word. And yet he is sensitive to the situation of exploitation in which these broad segments of humanity live. Bultmann, on the other hand—the theologian who begins with the questions of those whom he considers to be today's human beings, the theologian concerned with the difficulty these human beings have in understanding the message of the gospel—ignores the questions that come from the world of oppression (a world created precisely by the modern person who constitutes his point of departure).[70] The one who starts with heaven is sensitive to those who live in the hell of this earth; whereas the one who begins with earth is blind to the situation of exploitation upon which the earth is built.

Many will find this paradoxical. But the paradox is only apparent. It rests ultimately on a false, but common interpretation of the categories at play here. For an authentic, deep sense of God is not only not opposed to a sensitivity to the poor and their social world, but is ultimately lived only in those persons and that world. The spiritual, as we say, is not opposed to the social. The real opposition is between bourgeois individualism and the spiritual in the biblical sense.

This irruption of the outlook of the poor into the modern problematic, where, after all, Barth's theology remains, is to be observed in Bonhoeffer as well.[71] Here too there is an oasis, watered by the current that wells up out of the poor. There is a beautiful text of Bonhoeffer in which he says:

We have learned to see the great events of the history of the world from beneath—from the viewpoint of the useless, the suspect, the abused, the powerless, the oppressed, the despised. In a word, from the viewpoint of the suffering.[72]

As with Barth, the depth of Bonhoeffer's sense of God leads him to a perception of what it means to read reality from the viewpoint of the poor. Bonhoeffer would have no time to make this intuition the center of his theological discourse. Most of his attention would continue to be preempted by the great challenges of the modern world. But his reflection would take a tack in function of a very profound personal experience. This is why his testimony, and the paths he indicates, are so fertile.[73]

To the extent that the exploited classes, poor peoples, and despised ethnic groups have been raising their consciousness of the oppression they have suffered for centuries, they have created a new historical situation. It is an ambivalent situation, as is everything historical. But at the same time it is a situation charged with promise—a promise that the lords of this world see rather as a menace. This is the situation in which the Christian communities of these downtrodden human cultures are endeavoring to live and think their faith. Their efforts have led them to read the biblical message—the liberating love of the Father—from the outlook of the poor of this world.

Various theologies of liberation have come along this path—black theology, Hispanic-American theology, African, Latin American, Asian theology, feminist theology. For the first time in many centuries, theological reflection rooted in the world of poverty and oppression is arising from many sides.[74] It is a theology being done primarily by history's nameless ones. Hence it makes little difference whose name appears on articles and books.

What had been a dominated, repressed theology, an underground spring working its own way to the surface, today has burst into the sunlight in uncappable geysers. Rivulets have formed, then streams, and now, in the rivers of this theology, we recognize not only the tributaries of the present situation, but waters flowing from the living wellsprings of a historical, concrete past as well. These torrents are thundering straight for the windows of the great ones of this world. They in turn peer out and see all this, only too well. The waters are mounting for them. Their time is up. The ill humor, the thinly-veiled contempt—even the occasional condemnations that these movements provoke—are not long for this world. The poor of the earth, in their struggles for liberation, in their faith and hope in the Father, are coming to the realization that, to put it in the words of Arguedas, "the God of the masters is not the same." Their God is not the God of the poor. For ultimately the dominator is one who does not really believe in the God of the Bible.

This is the historical and theological context of the theology of liberation in Latin America. As we have said, this theology could not have come into existence before a certain degree of maturity had been achieved in the popular movement in Latin America. But it is also inscribed in an experience and search that go beyond Latin America and plunge their roots in the past, a past filled with struggle and reflection both on the part of the dominated areas of our societies and on the part of the Christian communities that have sprung up in their midst.

Our discussion of Latin America as a whole is not intended to imply that life and reflection there does not vary from one national context to another. The intense political experience of Peronism, for example, has led certain Latin American theologians to distinguish, within the theology of liberation in recent years, a particular current, having its own traits, which they call the "theology of popular pastoral ministry." Juan Carlos Scannone has systematized this approach with clarity and penetration, centering it on the category of "people."[75]

Internal polemics will doubtless be of some use in charting positions and in avoiding the ambiguities into which an enthusiasm of the first hour often causes one to fall. I am not in agreement, however, with the way in which Scannone sets up an opposition between what he calls "two vectors in the theology of liberation." In doing so, he devitalizes—and indeed, without intending to, deforms—one of these vectors, by withholding from it elements (a reference to the popular movement, a sense of Latin American history, popular piety, and popular pastoral approaches) that swell the current to which he sees himself as belonging.

There is a difference. But the difference is not in the absence of these elements or in a denial of their importance and richness. The difference is in the manner of bringing them into focus. Many factors come into play here, and among them is the historical and political context to which we have alluded above. This context colors one's precise understanding of "people," and "popular classes," and even of the genuine nature of a popular evangelization and of the function of the church in this concrete moment in Latin America.

The theology of liberation is rooted in a revolutionary militancy. It is aware of the grave questions posed by social conflict, but it considers that these should be attacked and overcome in their roots, without turning one's back on the concrete situations in which they have arisen. Furthermore, this theological line of thinking not only does not neglect, but actually demands, the labor and proclamation of the gospel on the wavelength of the masses. It is not the perspective of an elite, or of little groups, but it is one of organizations—which the popular movement, and the Christian people within that popular movement, build for themselves.

On the other hand, when we speak of the maturity of the popular movement, we do not mean to imply that the popular movement is simply tumbling along from victory to victory. Things go deeper than that, and when we understand things more deeply than that we shall be able better to understand the vagaries of history. It is right to emphasize the situation of captivity and exile in which we live in Latin America today. This is a rich and fruitful approach, and it helps us see more clearly what the liberation process and its theological reflection actually mean today.[76]

Interpretations are arising here and there that demonstrate the importance of avoiding superficial analyses and facile categories, which with all the good will in the world run the risk of disarming and demobilizing a people in severe circumstances, but a people that resists, that fights. They err, therefore, who think that all is submerged by repression and fascism in Latin America to-day.[77] For this downtrodden people, suffering and captivity are nothing new. These have always been here. But the will to rebellion, and hope, have always been here too. Long has this people been in exile in its own land. But long, too, has it been in exodus, on the road to its redemption.

It is this dialectic—not enthusiasm for a liberation just around the corner—that has given birth to the theology of liberation. And this dialectic, living and vital at the heart of the history of a poor people, continues in full process today. It is true that new dimensions have been added to the secular captivity and exile of these popular classes. Not to keep these in account would betray the lack of an elemental realism and would mean taking the road to suicide. But to overestimate these dimensions, and present them as an altogether new stage, in the wake of some form of liberation that these classes are supposed to have enjoyed during the years before, shows an ignorance of the deep and ancient experience of oppression and marginalization so famil-iar to the masses of Latin America. It also shows an ignorance of the capacity for resistance and creativity and an ignorance of the hope of liberation, which these popular classes have always kept alive.

Let us beware of an elitist view of history. Let us not make our personal or group experiences, however important they may be, the point of departure for a sketch of Latin America as a whole. Those who live in the poorer coun-tries, which have had little occasion for illusions in recent years, are particu-larly sensitive to deformed, simplistic readings of recent history.

Then again, new and creative efforts are springing up in Latin America from all sides, right in the midst of today's cruel conditions. They are less well known, perhaps, and less bustling, than others in the immediate past. They may be carried on by persons who, for "Latin American observers," are anonymous. But they are nonetheless real for all that, nor are they any less deeply rooted in a lowly people. Today more than ever before, it is important to belong to those who resist, who fight, who believe and hope. Intellectuals may allow themselves extravagances and disquisitions the people may not. And what this people knows as a living experience, even more than suffering, and demands even more than compassion, is a will to affirmation in the midst of a situation that denies their condition as human beings.

Finally, what Christ came to proclaim and actualize is not captivity and exile, but liberation—a liberation that begins from within these oppressive situations. The heart of his message is the fulness of the saving and liberating love of the Father. This should also be the core of our Christian life and theological reflection.

The Poor Preach the Gospel. An understanding of the faith from within the concrete, historical practice of liberation leads to a proclamation of the gospel at the very heart of this practice. It is a proclamation that is at once vigilant deed, active involvement, concrete solidarity with the interests and battles of the popular classes—and word, which is rooted and verified in deed, which defines attitudes, and which is celebrated with thanksgiving.

Evangelization proclaims liberation in Jesus Christ. And the scope of this liberation is presented to us in the programmatic discourse recorded in a well-known text of Luke:

> He came to Nazara, where he had been brought up, and went into the synagogue on the sabbath day as he usually did. He stood up to read, and they handed him the scroll of the prophet Isaiah. Unrolling the scroll he found the place where it is written:
>
>> The spirit of the Lord has been given to me,
>> for he has anointed me.
>> He has sent me to bring the good news to the poor,
>> to proclaim liberty to captives
>> and to the blind new sight,
>> to set the downtrodden free,
>> to proclaim the Lord's year of favor [Isa. 61:1–2].
>
> He then rolled up the scroll, gave it back to the assistant and sat down. And all eyes in the synagogue were fixed on him. Then he began to speak to them, "This text is being fulfilled today even as you listen" [Luke 4:16–21].

For Jesus, then, liberation is total liberation. And thereby he identifies the root of all injustice and exploitation: breach of friendship, breach of love. We are not presented with a liberation open to a "spiritualistic" interpretation, still so tightly clung to in certain Christian circles. Hunger and justice are not just economic and social questions. They are global human questions, and they challenge our way of living the faith in its very roots.

We must radically revise our notions of matter and spirit. They are steeped in a Greek thinking and idealistic philosophy having little in common with the biblical mentality. As Berdyaev put it, reinterpreting these terms so lightly bandied about in Christian circles, "If I am hungry, that is a material problem; if someone else is hungry, that is a spiritual problem." Love and sin are concrete realities. They occur in concrete, living situations. This is why the Bible speaks of liberation and justice as opposed to the slavery and humiliation of the poor in concrete history. The gift of filiation, by which we become the daughters and sons of God, occurs in concrete history. We receive this free gift, which is not a gift in word but one in deed, when we make ourselves brothers and sisters to one another. This is what it means to live the love of the Father and give testimony to him. The proclamation of a God who loves all persons equally must take flesh in history, must become history.

The proclamation of this liberating love in a society scarred by injustice and the exploitation of one social class by another will transform this "emergent history" into something challenging and conflictual. Within the very heart of a society in which social classes, ethnic groups, and cultures are in conflict with one another, we verify God, we make God to be true, by taking the part of the poor, of the masses, of the despised ethnic groups, of the marginalized classes. It is from within them that we strive to live and proclaim the gospel. Its proclamation to the poor of this world gives them to perceive that their situation is contrary to the will of a God who makes himself known in events of liberation. This will contribute to a raising of their consciousness of the profound injustice of their situation—and a raising of their hope of liberation.

The gospel, read from the viewpoint of the poor, from the viewpoint of the militancy of their struggles for liberation, convokes a popular church—that is, a church born of the people, the "poor of the earth," the predilect of the kingdom, "God's favorites." It is a church rooted in a people that snatches the gospel from the hands of the great ones of this world. It prevents it from being utilized henceforward as an element in the justification of a situation contrary to the will of the Liberator-God.

Thus there comes into existence what for some time now has been called a "social appropriation of the gospel." It is one of the moments in what we also call a "militant reading of the Bible." The Bible must be restored to the Christian peoples who believe and hope in the God who reveals himself there. Otherwise all self-styled "scientific" exegesis loses its validity. We must reclaim a believing, militant reading of the word of the Lord, and rediscover the popular language needed to communicate it. It will be a reading done from within, and in function of, its proclamation by the people itself.[78]

At the point of departure of this communication of the gospel there is a spiritual experience. It is a collective experience, a popular experience. It is the experience of encounter with the Lord in the midst of the battles of the "condemned of the earth." It is a moment of silence, a moment of careful listening to the Lord and to the people. It is a time of contemplation, and an experience of joy. To evangelize is to communicate the silence and gladness that the word of the Lord creates within us. But the silence is a silence of rebellion, and the gladness is an Easter gladness. It is the conquest of death, which seems to be the dominator. It is the resurrection of hope, which the conciliator reduced to desperation. It is the presence of the free love of the Father, who takes up all things.

We are told in the gospel that the sign of the arrival of the kingdom is that the poor have the gospel preached to them. "Poor," for the Christian community that was the first audience for this gospel, meant the Christians themselves. But today may we not perhaps turn the expression around and say that "Christian" means poor?

In fact, must we not go further and understand that evangelization will be genuinely liberating only when it is the poor themselves who become the bearers of the message, the actual agents of evangelization? *Then* the proclamation of the gospel will be a rock of scandal, a stumbling block. *Then* we shall have a gospel that is "not presentable" in society, a gospel expressed in terms that the "educated" of this world will find "unrefined." The Lord, the

Servant of Yahweh, who "seemed no longer human" (Isa. 52:14), will speak to us from among the poor. Only if we listen to his voice shall we recognize him as the God who liberates, who calls persons together into a church, *Ekklesia,* the community of those called apart, as only he knows how to call them. This is where the poor of the earth have begun to develop their "historical credo," their creed of the concrete. From here, the poor of this earth are telling one another and the whole world why they believe in the God of the poor—together with a concrete historical past, and in the actual social conditions in which they are living.[79]

To see ourselves as a people of God means to pose all over again the question of who God is for us today. The God who reveals himself in concrete history is a God who is irreducible to our manner of understanding him, irreducible to our theology and even to our faith. This God cannot be appropriated. He cannot become anyone's private property, this God who makes himself present in events, this God who becomes history. God is a love that ever transcends us, "since it is in him that we live, and move, and exist" (Acts 17:28). He is the Utterly Other, the Holy One—"for I am God, not man: I am the Holy One in your midst" (Hos. 11:9). God manifests himself in time of trial as a God of might (Exod. 19:18), *but* he can also be heard in a gentle breeze (1 Kings 19:12). But ultimately he is a God who dwells in the heart that can love (Ezek. 36:26), and in the bosom of his people (John 3:16).

The God we believe and hope in comes to us as the God of the poor, the God of the oppressed. This is why he reveals himself only to the person who does justice to the poor. But a great deal of work needs to be done along this line of thought. A radical reflection on our idea of God is an urgent necessity if we wish to progress beyond our first insights and not become mired down in clichés. One of the tasks before us, as we subject the praxis of liberation to a theological reflection, is to arrive at a deeper grasp of what "God of the poor" means in a concrete history of oppression and struggle for liberation—in a world of adversity, but at the same time in a world of hope for the exploited.[80] This is the path marked out by what we called the "historical creed" in reference to the people of Israel. For it is precisely faith and hope in the God of the people that makes us a people of God: "I shall be your God, and you shall be my people."

We come to this God through Jesus Christ. The God we believe in is the Father of Jesus. In Jesus God not only reveals himself in history, he becomes history. He "pitches his tent" in its midst (see John 1:14). Being a Christian is not, first and foremost, believing in a message, but believing in *someone*. The gospel is the good news because it has been proclaimed by Jesus. The message must not cloud the fact that our faith, our confidence, reaches beyond its pronouncements to Christ himself. To believe in him is to enter into his kingdom, a kingdom of justice. By Jesus' life and death we know that the only possible justice is definitive justice. But we also know that now is the time to begin building it—from within our concrete, conflictual history, by accepting the kingdom in which the love of God will reign and all exploitation will be scattered to the winds:

They will build houses and inhabit them, plant vineyards and eat their fruit. They will not build for others to live in, or plant so that others can eat. For my people shall live as long as trees, and my chosen ones wear out what their hands have made [Isa. 65:21–22].

Ecclesiology and Latin America. Years of experiments and searching in Latin America have made theological reflection on the church more urgent than ever before. But it has also made it more concrete. To be sure, Vatican II gave fresh impetus to ecclesiology. But the world has kept turning, and the perspective of those on the bottom, on the underside of history, and of the Lord who speaks to us from among them—the viewpoint that began to come to light in Medellín—has become more and more necessary. It is easy to predict that the future will see ecclesiology become an ever more crucial area, difficult but fertile, in the life and reflection of the Christian peoples in Latin America.[81]

A Christian understanding of the church begins with christology.[82] I should like to recall this as we review certain ecclesiological considerations.

During the greater part of its long historical experience, all through the era of Christendom, the church studied itself from within, so to speak. Supernatural salvation appeared as an absolute value of which the church was the sole depository. Western Christendom was built pastorally and theologically in function of the believer, the Christian. In order to understand itself the church looked at itself. This is what we call "ecclesiocentrism." Here, Christ is viewed mainly as the founder of the church. The historical matrix of this attitude is easy to uncover and understand.

When new peoples were discovered, the task of incorporating them into the church was seen as a salvific mission. Linked historically to Western culture, white societies, and European values, the expansion of the church throughout the world bears the mark of the West.

It is a commonplace to say that Vatican II put an end to the Christendom mentality. Now is the hour of dialogue and service to the world. The church's consciousness of itself now begins from without, from the modern world. It is a world hostile to the church, a world centuries old now, prideful in its own values.

The Pastoral Constitution on the Church in the Modern World presents the new horizon against which Vatican II views the activity of the church. It is an optimistic view of the world, of its progress, of contemporary science and technology, of the person as agent of history, of liberty. Of course, it is a somewhat reserved endorsement, in view of the risks accompanying these human values. In particular, the pastoral constitution is concerned to recall that these modern values reach their fulness only when they are referred to the Christian message.

The document issues a call for collaboration between believers and nonbelievers in the "just upbuilding of this world in which they live in common." It is a world that is different from, but that need not be hostile to, the church.

It is a world in which Christ is present and active, and it is from outside itself, from the world, that he calls the Christian community, too, to the gospel. Hence Vatican II resumes the Pauline theme of Christ as Lord of history. This is the history in which the church must accomplish its mission as sign, as "universal sacrament of salvation." The church's openness to the world bears the mark of modern society.

In recent years it has seemed more and more clear to many Christians that, if the church wishes to be faithful to the God of Jesus Christ, it must become aware of itself from underneath, from among the poor of this world, the exploited classes, despised ethnic groups, and marginalized cultures. It must descend into the hell of this world, into communion with the misery, injustice, struggles, and hopes of the wretched of the earth—for "of such is the kingdom of heaven." At bottom it is a matter of living, as church, what the majority of its own members live every day. To be born, to be reborn, as church, from below, from among them, today means to die, in a concrete history of oppression and complicity with oppression.

In this ecclesiological approach, which takes up one of the central themes of the Bible, Christ is seen as the Poor One, identified with the oppressed and plundered of the world. Here new paths open wide, for this is what has been called the "underside of history." For example, in this approach one gradually comes to see that what is ultimately important is not that the church be poor, but that the poor of this world be the people of God—that disquieting witness of a God who liberates.

An ecclesiology whose point of departure is Christ calling out to us from the midst of the oppressed can furnish us with the guidelines we need to locate the function of the church in today's concrete situation in Latin America. Today, worsening hunger and exploitation, as well as exile and imprisonment (political prisoners all over Latin America, especially in Chile, or the case of the bishops arrested in Riobamba, Ecuador, for example), torture and death (the *campesinos* of Bolivia and Honduras, the priests of Argentina and Brazil), make up the price to be paid for having rebelled against a secular oppression. They are the price to be paid for having begun to understand what it is to be Christian, and to be church, in our day.[83]

These lives and this blood, apart from all questions about tactics or analysis or prudence or effectiveness, have placed the whole church (and not just the Latin American church) before a radical challenge. Now it will appear whether that church will be faithful to its own authentic tradition, and through that tradition to the Lord who "establishes justice and right."

Justice and right cannot be emptied of the content bestowed on them by the Bible. Defending human rights means above all defending the rights of the poor. It is a prophetic theme, and one deeply rooted in the tradition of the church. And it must be kept in mind in order to avoid falling into the liberal focus with regard to human rights. The liberal approach presupposes, for example, a social equality that simply does not exist in Latin American societies.

It is this approach, and not the defense of the poor, that inevitably leads to the particularisms and ideologization that some fear today within the Latin American church. Our understanding of the true meaning, and biblical requirement, of the defense of human rights will originate with the poor of Latin American society. Here is where we shall begin to grasp that this task is an expression of the gospel proclamation, and not some subtle form of power-grabbing, or presenting a program as a political alternative in Latin America. The church does not receive its prophetic inspiration from adherence to a liberal program, but from its roots in a world of poverty.

CONCLUSION

I have tried to show that theological reflection is tied to social processes. Part and parcel of other historical structures and mind-sets, theology cannot be understood apart from them. Like all thought, theology must be placed in its social context. Theologies do not follow one another like links of a chain floating in midair; they are responses to vast historical processes. They can and should be challenges to these processes.[84]

Theological reasoning is an effort on the part of concrete persons to form and think out their faith in determinate circumstances, to plan activities and make interpretations that play a role in the real-life occurrences and confrontations of a given society. The theologian does not work in some kind of ahistorical limbo. His or her reflection has a milieu, starts out from material bases, addresses us from a precise location, speaks the word of the Lord to us in the vernacular. This leads us, where the theology of liberation is concerned, to view the theologian as Gramsci does: as an "organic intellectual" —organically linked to the popular undertaking of liberation.[85]

I have also tried to indicate, along the same lines of thought, the point of breach between progressivist theology and the theology of liberation. Evidently they cross paths. But their points of intersection can be understood only in light of the point of breach.

The interlocuter of progressivist theology is the modern spirit and liberal ideology, whose agent—historical subject—is the bourgeois class. This point of departure distinguishes it from traditional theology, with its mark of the feudal world and its prolongation in the ancien régime. But it distinguishes it from the theology of liberation as well.

The theology of liberation begins from the questions asked by the poor and plundered of the world, by "those without a history," by those who are oppressed and marginalized precisely by the interlocuter of progressivist theology. The modern forms of this oppression must not deceive us, but rather show us the exact point of historical, political, and social breach between the two perspectives.[86] This is why we said that theologies of liberation could arise only after a popular movement had attained a certain maturity.

The modern spirit, whose subject frequently is the nonbeliever, questions the faith in a context of the meaning of religion. The critique from the standpoint of rationalism and the affirmation of the modern freedoms prefers a debate on the terrain of religion, and the philosophical presuppositions of religion, together with the role of the church in modern, bourgeois society. The questions asked by the "nonperson," the "nonhuman," by contrast, have to do with the economic, the social, and the political. And yet this does not make for a nontheological discussion, as some seem to think. That would indeed be a facile solution. It is a matter of a different theology. The difference is clearly seen in the real world, where persons live and die, believe and hope, and where it is reprehensible to obscure social conflict with generic affirmations and a false universalism.

Theology that attempts to come to grips with the challenges of the bourgeois nonbeliever necessarily enters into the problematic of modernity. We have seen this in some examples, especially from the advance wing of Protestant theology, the great Christian theology of modernity. By comparison, Catholic theology appears rather closely linked with traditional forms of thought. But the historical antecedents of the new society, and the assertiveness of the modern sector of the Catholic world, have been effacing this difference in recent years. The historical bloc to which reflection on the faith belongs determines both the material and the limits of the reflection.

Of course, when I say "belong" I do not mean to imply that modernity is accepted without critique. This is not a theology that mechanically translates the great modern themes into a reflection on the faith. An original rethinking of these themes is what gives this theology its breadth and importance. But it must be said that this is a theology situated in a context. To separate it from the social and cultural world in which it subsists is to render it incomprehensible, and this is recognized by its most competent representatives. This context, this social and cultural world, is the world of modern society and bourgeois ideology.

The point of departure of the theology of liberation is not only different from that of the progressivist theology, it is in contradiction with it. The contradiction can be grasped only in the real world of history. To speak of the "postmodern world" is a superficial response, and of little help. It is not a matter of chronological order, but of concrete historical and dialectical contradiction. This dialectical opposition to the bourgeois ideology and the dominant culture comes up out of the popular classes, and from their vanguard. The exploited strata of society are the concrete, historical agents of a new understanding of the faith. The God of the Bible reveals himself through those despoiled of their dignity as a people and as human beings. He manifests himself in those the gospel calls "the poor" and "the least."

There are a number of paths for life, and for one's understanding of the presence of the Lord, in a world of oppression and repression (but of resistance and hope as well). In their journey along these paths, "history's absent ones" make the free gift of the Father's love their own by creating new social relationships—relationships of a community of sisters and brothers.

Theological reflection along these lines of thought is just taking its first steps. Let us not overestimate its scope. What is primarily at issue is not a theology, but popular liberation. Theology comes only later. When intellectual discussion leads someone to invert the order of the stages, the liberation project finds itself in trammels, and the work of theology is inevitably sterile as well. In order for theology to be a part of, and a service to, a concrete process of liberation, it has to be liberated—as do we also—from every restraint that impedes solidarity with the poor and exploited of this world. Only in this way can the effort of reflection on the faith escape being coopted by the system.

Living and thinking the faith from within the immurement of the "wretched of the earth" will lead us along paths where we shall not meet the great ones of this world. Instead we shall meet the Lord. We shall meet him in the poor of Latin America and of other continents. And like the disciples at Emmaus, we shall interpret his words and his deeds in the light of Easter, and our eyes will be opened. Then we shall understand—to cite Arguedas once more—that "God is hope. God is gladness. God is daring."

NOTES

1. See, for example, *Tierra Nueva* (Bogotá)—any of a score of issues that have appeared to date, as the periodical reshuffles its arguments with dogged tenacity.

2. See the articles in the last issues of *Víspera*, since suspended by the government of Uruguay.

3. I refer to efforts to dress up wizened pastoral and theological attitudes with a vocabulary of liberation, or attempts to hitch up to a liberation-theology bandwagon while jettisoning all its real, historical cargo by means of a distinction between a "good, genuine current" and a "bad, spurious" one.

4. See Jürgen Moltmann's "Open Letter" to José Míguez Bonino, in *Christianity and Crisis*, March 1975. See also the talks given by Moltmann and Johannes B. Metz in Madrid in 1974, published in *Dios y la ciudad* (Madrid: Cristiandad, 1975). Claude Geffre's position is different: see his "Editorial: A Prophetic Theology" in *Concilium* 96 (New York: Herder and Herder, 1974).

5. In the following pages I shall attempt to develop certain concepts I presented initially in a course given at the Catholic University of Lima in the spring of 1974, and first published as "Liberation, Theology, and Proclamation," in *Concilium* 96. I shall incorporate some approaches originally developed in a seminar presented at the Bartolomé de Las Casas Center in Lima, in 1975, of which the reader will be able to fine an expanded version in Gustavo Gutiérrez and Richard Shaull, *Liberation and Change* (Richmond, Va.: Knox, 1977). I hope to have the opportunity to gather and systematize all these essays in a more extensive work at some future time.

6. For the industrial revolution, see the classic works of Paul Joseph Mantoux, *The Industrial Revolution in the Eighteenth Century* (New York: Macmillan, 1961); and Eric J. Hobsbawm, *The Age of Revolution, 1789–1848* (Cleveland: World, 1962); as well as Hobsbawm's *Industry and Empire* (Baltimore: Penguin, 1969).

7. It is interesting to note that democratic ideas properly so called did not originate in North America, but were part of the impact of what happened in France. See Vernon L. Parrington, *Main Currents in American Thought*, vol. 1 (New York: Harcourt, 1927).

8. On the difference between the "liberties" of antiquity and those of the modern era, see V. Cerroni, *La libertà dei moderni* (Bari: Donato, 1968), pp. 75–81.

9. "Ideen zur Philosophie der Geschichte," *Jenaische Litteraturzeitung*, 1785.

10. Francis Bacon played an important role here. See Benjamin Farrington, *Francis Bacon: Philosopher of Industrial Science* (London; repr. of 1951 ed., New York: Haskell, 1973).

11. Antonio Gramsci shows us the originality of Machiavelli's thought, but takes his distance from it in favor of his own view, in his well-known *The Modern Prince, and Other Writings* (New York: International, 1968). The "modern prince" is the political party.

12. It is interesting to note the echoes we find in Kant of the questions Duns Scotus asked about a practical knowledge of God. And it is a known fact that the theme of praxis is present in Hegel, if in a context of an idealist philosophy: see N. Lobkowicz, *Theory and Praxis* (University of Notre Dame Press, 1967).

13. Georg Wilhelm Friedrich Hegel, *The Philosophy of History* (New York: Dover, 1956), pp. 417–18.

14. See Christopher Hill, *Reformation to Industrial Revolution* (Baltimore: Penguin, 1969).

15. The great theoretician of this "liberal," or free, economics, based on the interplay of the interests of each individual, is Adam Smith. David Ricardo, working within a capitalist framework, will give more attention to the system's internal contradictions.

16. This will be one of Jean-Jacques Rousseau's great themes, and one of the reasons for his more critical attitude toward liberalism than that of his contemporaries.

17. Guido de Ruggiero, *The History of European Liberalism* (London: Oxford, 1927), p. 43.

18. Marx will severely criticize this. For him there is a real inequality between the buyer and the seller, from the moment the majority of the population must sell their physical labor in exchange for a wage.

19. Hegel, *Philosophy of History*, pp. 440–41.

20. L. Goldmann, *The Philosophy of the Enlightenment* (London: Routledge, 1973). Many of the observations I have been making on the relationship between the Enlightenment mentality and a capitalist economy have their inspiration in this work.

21. See W. Oëlmuller, *Die unabefriedigte Aufklärung* (Frankfurt: Suhrkamp, 1969). See also Max Horkheimer and Theodor W. Adorno, *Dialectic of Enlightenment* (New York: Herder, 1972). Alexis de Tocqueville had already remarked on the contradictions of this movement with respect to modern freedoms.

22. This process has been studied at length by Karl Marx. See, for example, chap. 25, "The General Law of Capitalist Accumulation," in *Capital* (Chicago: Britannica, 1955).

23. See Joachim Matthes, *Religion und Gesellschaft: Einführung in die Religionssoziologie*, vol. 1 (Hamburg, 1967), chap. 2.

24. See Ernst Cassirer, *The Philosophy of the Enlightenment* (Princeton University Press, 1951), chap. 5.

25. The reason we say "*European* bourgeois society" is that it does not seem to me that the situation in the United States is the same. It may be that the individualism of the bourgeois mentality is more deeply rooted, and more generalized, there, but this does not relegate religion to the private sphere there. On the contrary, religion in the United States performs an important public and political function. Individualism and privacy are not synonymous. The former *is* compatible with the public character of religion. Here the question is not the privatization of faith, but rather its individualistic interpretation—grounds for reflection on the part of the exponents of political theology.

26. Hence Karl Barth includes him in his history of nineteenth-century theology. Feuerbach's importance for theology has been emphasized by Bonhoeffer: "We actually find in Bonhoeffer's first Berlin lecture of 1931 the following sentence: 'Feuerbach put two questions to theology that remained unanswered: 1. about the *truth* of her propositions, 2. about their relevance to real life' " (Eberhard Bethge, *Bonhoeffer: Exile and Martyr* [New York: Seabury, 1975], p. 137). Henry Mottu had already called attention to this in his article in *Union Seminary Quarterly Review*, 25/1 (1969): 1–18.

27. See the pronouncements of the popes on "modern liberties" throughout the course of the nineteenth century. Is is a sad story, and one that bears repeating nowadays in view of the efforts of the everlastingly nearsighted to obtain new condemnations. Only, this time, those who attempt to vindicate the rights of this world's oppressed stand accused of threatening the very "modern liberties" the popes rejected!

28. Paul Tillich, a great admirer of Schleiermacher, will lament the use of this expression as ambiguous. Based on Schleiermacher's later works, insists Tillich, "religious sentiment" means "sentiment of unconditional dependency," not a subjective emotion. See Tillich's *A History of Christian Thought* (New York: Simon & Schuster, 1972), pp. 391–98.

29. Dietrich Bonhoeffer, *Letters and Papers from Prison*, rev. ed. (New York: Macmillan, 1967), p. 196. The passage is from a letter to Eberhard Bethge dated June 8, 1944. Wolfgang Pannenberg, on the other hand, criticizes Barth and Bultmann for their premodern and authori-

tarian notion of revelation and sees his own contribution as falling within the framework of the Enlightenment. See Pannenberg's "Response to Discussion," in J. M. Robinson and J. B. Cobb, eds., *Theology as History* (New York: Harper & Row, 1967), p. 226.

30. See Bonhoeffer, *Letters*, pp. 178–79 (letter to Bethge dated July 16, 1944). Bonhoeffer's work opened new perspectives for certain currents of contemporary theology: see Jürgen Moltmann, *The Crucified God* (New York: Harper & Row, 1974); and Kazoh Kitamori, *The Theology of the Pain of God* (Atlanta: John Knox, 1965).

31. There is an immense bibliography on liberal Catholicism. Among its major historians are R. Aubert and A. C. Jemolo. A good survey of the whole phenomenon is contained in the minutes of an international colloquium held in 1971, *Les Catholiques libéraux au XIX siécle* (Grenoble: Presses Universitaires, 1974).

32. "Teologia politica: questioni, scelte e prospettive," in *Ancora sulla teologia politica: Il dibattito continua* (Brescia: Queriniana, 1975). Our quotations from Metz are translations from this article.

33. In the sense in which it is presented in Carl Schmitt's celebrated work *The Necessity of Politics: An Essay on the Representative Idea in the Church and Modern Europe* (New York: Macmillan, 1932).

34. See Johannes B. Metz, *Theology of the World* (New York: Harper & Row, 1969); and Jürgen Moltmann, *Crucified God*.

35. See Metz, "Breve apología de la narración," *Concilium*, Spanish ed., May 1973, pp. 222–38.

36. Metz, "Iglesia y pueblo," *Dios y la ciudad*, p.141.

37. Metz's ideas have given rise to important considerations concerning the church and its social functions. See, for example, M. Xhaufflaire et al., *La pratique de la théologie politique* (Tournai: Casterman, 1974).

38. Rosino Gibellini's expression, from his fine, exhaustive work *La teologia di Jürgen Moltmann* (Brescia: Queriniana, 1975).

39. Jürgen Moltmann, "Fe y política," *Diálogo Ecuménico*, 1974.

40. In their introduction to the texts of the talks given by Moltmann and Metz in Madrid in 1974 *(Dios y la ciudad)*, A. Alvarez Bolado and J. Gómez Caffarena remark that liberation theology was on the minds of audience and speakers alike. Gómez writes: "It is safe to say that liberation was the contrasting backdrop against which many of the participants instinctively tended to see this new German way of theologizing. . . . If it is possible, then, to summarize in very broad strokes what is new in these approaches, we should perhaps have to say: Moltmann opts for a systematic, clearer, and more nuanced reaffirmation, and thus finds himself able to deal with situations such as that of Latin America or Spain—or at any rate he claims to be able to do so with greater maturity than liberation theology can. Metz opts for a powerful emphasis on a heretofore relatively neglected aspect in his theology, and thus he too finds himself able to handle situations as in Latin America or Spain, and claims to be able to do so with greater authenticity than can liberation theology—namely, the relevancy of the people as active subject" (ibid, pp. 14–15).

41. The liberal Argentinian, Domingo Sarmiento, is a good example. See his famous *Life in the Argentine Republic in the Days of the Tyrants: or, Civilization and Barbarism* (New York: Hafner, 1960). The title itself is indicative of his approach.

42. Moltmann, in his "Open Letter" to Míguez Bonino, seems unable to grasp the perspective from the other side of history. He expresses concern for what he considers the scant interest that liberation theology takes in freedom and democracy. My experience, on the contrary, is that it is the prevarications of bourgeois society that ought to be the object of concern, along with the routes the popular classes should take in order to attain authentic democracy and real freedom. This process is an aspect of what we call liberation. The same lack of comprehension is manifested in Moltmann's remark about a neglect of historical facts and of European thinkers in liberation theology. Surely both historical facts and European thinkers are necessary for a grasp of certain facets of our reality in Latin America. But given the historical and cultural facts of Latin America itself, what is important is not allusion to these events or ideas, but the viewpoint from which we read them. And it is this latter with which we are concerned in the present article.

43. In Latin America we have nothing to match H. Aptheker's *American Negro Slave Revolts* (New York: International, 1974). It would be most instructive to be able to follow the history of this important segment of overall history of the oppressed peoples of Latin America. There is some material in the articles and bibliography of Ann M. Pescatello's collection, *The African in*

Latin America (New York: Knopf, 1975); Leslie B. Rout, *The African Experience in Spanish America: 1502 to the Present Day* (Cambridge University Press, 1976); and for Peru, Denys Cuche, *Poder blanco y resistencia negra en el Perú* (Lima: IEP, 1975).

44. Here we find, for example, Juan Santos Atahualpa, who led a native rebellion in the middle of the eighteenth century, and even, in a way, Túpac Amaru, who rose in revolt toward the end of the same century.

45. The complex history of the Mexican *Cristeros* bears reexamination in this connection. For Latin American messianic movements, see María Isaura Pereira de Queiroz, *Historia y etnología de los movimientos mesiánicos* (Mexico City: Siglo XXI, 1969).

46. Thanks to Mariátegui, a political and ideological polemic was waged in Peru nearly fifty years ago between the social-class approach and the inter-classist efforts of that nation against the imperialism defended by Haya de la Torre. Decades later, the same polemic appeared in a new version in Peronism—with abundant repercussions for the interpretation of Latin American reality and theological reflection alike.

47. See the important work of José Comblin in his *The Church and the National Security State* (Maryknoll, N.Y.: Orbis, 1979). See also the criticisms brought forward by A. Methol Ferré in his mimeographed study "Sobre la actual ideología de la Securidad Nacional." Cándido Padin had already called attention to this problem several years earlier in "La doctrine de las seguridad nacional a la luz de la doctrina de la Iglesia," *SODOC*, 1 (Petrópolis, 1968), col. 432–34. But see also another viewpoint in Genaro Arriagada, José Manuel Santos, et al., *Seguridad Nacional y Bien Común* (Santiago de Chile, 1976); and an equally recent work, but one that puts more emphasis on economic factors in the national security state, Gerald and Patricia Mische, *Toward a Human World Order: Beyond the National Security Straightjacket* (New York: Paulist, 1977). We may hope for abundant literature on "national security," in time. If we are aiming for genuine realism in our study of this question, we shall have to come to appreciate the inadequacy of talk about "the state." The state does not parachute in from another planet. We must take account of the economic and social interests lying behind political power. For example, if we fail to grasp the role of the multinational corporations and the current structure of international capitalism, we shall scarcely be in a position to understand the political systems that have implanted themselves in Latin America in response to popular movements during recent years.

48. These actions have been denounced in courageous and clear documents by the episcopates of Paraguay and Brazil, for example. See also the collection of texts in *Bolivia 1971–76—Pueblo, Estado, Iglesia: Testimonios de Cristianos* (Lima: CEP, 1976).

49. This spiritual experience is distasteful to intellectuals formed in a stale scholastic rationalism that prefers to work with abstract theological hypotheses. For them a concrete faith, when all is said and done, is just a nuisance. But for the theology of liberation this experience is a capital theme. Many Christians have begun to see for themselves what Frei Betto hoped for when he was in prison: "Finding an appropriate way to live the gospel in Latin America today requires something else as well: a spirituality, a concrete form of docility to the Spirit who leads us to communion with God and with persons, in the history of this people so exploited and oppressed" (*Cartas do cárcere*, letter of Jan. 15, 1973).

50. See Stephen Hymer, *The International Operations of National Firms: A Study of Direct Foreign Investment* (Cambridge, Mass.: MIT, 1976); and Theotonio Dos Santos, *Imperialismo y empresas multinacionales* (Buenos Aires, 1973). See also John Eagleson, ed., *Christians and Socialism: Documentation of the Christians for Socialism Movement in Latin America* (Maryknoll: Orbis, 1975).

51. See the very significant book by José Míguez Bonino, *Christians and Marxists: The Mutual Challenge to Revolution* (Grand Rapids, Mich.: Eerdmans, 1976), especially the author's statement of his approach (p. 7) and his thesis (p. 19).

52. See Juan Luis Segundo, *The Liberation of Theology* (Maryknoll, N.Y.: Orbis, 1976); and James H. Cone, *The God of the Oppressed* (New York: Seabury, 1975).

53. Some years ago I began research on a project called "Popular Religion and Liberating Evangelization," at the Bartolomé de Las Casas Center in Lima, and the theoretical framework of this project appeared in a pilot work by Raúl Vidales and Tokihiro Kudó, *Práctica religiosa y proyecto histórico* (Lima: CEP, 1975). The importance of this question had already been emphasized in my *A Theology of Liberation* (Maryknoll: Orbis, 1973), and I had better point this out right now, before I am intercepted by overeager commentators! There I noted that "the relationship between evangelization and popular religiosity is beginning to appear in a different light," and I went on to indicate a preliminary bibliography on the matter (pp.74–75). This concern was

the consequence (and this will likewise contradict arbitrary interpretations) of my refusal simplistically to accept the validity of the secularization process in Latin America, in spite of the spirit then in vogue.

54. *Women* in these social strata are doubly exploited, marginalized, and looked down upon.

55. Pablo Richard has remarked this with precision in his excellent "Teología de la liberación latinoamericana: Un aporte crítico a la teología europa," *Páginas* (Lima), July 1976.

56. *Del único modo de atraer a todos los pueblos a la verdadera religión* (Mexico City: Fondo de Cultura Económica, 1942), p. 545.

57. George Sanderlin, ed., *Bartolomé de Las Casas: A Selection of His Writings* (New York: Knopf, 1971), pp. 180–81.

58. J. Friede has called attention to this aspect of Las Casas's undertaking in his *Bartolomé de Las Casas: Precursor del Anticolonialismo* (Mexico City: Siglo XXI, 1974), thereby giving the lie to the image so often presented of Bartolomé as an "idealist." See also Enrique Dussel's work on the early colonial bishops, *Les évèques hispano-américains, défenseurs et évangelisateurs de l'Indien 1504–1620* (Wiesbaden: Steiner, 1970); as also his well-known *Historia de la Iglesia en América Latina* (Barcelona: Nova Terra, 1974). In English see *A History of the Church in Latin America* (Grand Rapids, Mich.: Eerdmans, 1982). See also the excellent selection of texts in *La larga marcha de Las Casas* (Lima: CEP, 1975), with an introduction and commentaries by J.B. Lassègue.

59. "Aquí se contiene una disputa o controversia" (1552), in *Obras Escogidas* (Madrid: BAE, 1958), 5:293.

60. See the *Apologia*, which we hope we shall soon have in Spanish. For certain passages in English, see *Selection of His Writings*, pp. 114–46.

61. "Historia de las Indias," *Obras*, 2:356. It is interesting to note that, in taking up the cause of the Indians, Las Casas is no less earnest in the defense of the poverty-stricken Spaniards suffering under the lords of the Indies (see Friede, *Precursor*, p. 105).

62. Las Casas's defense of black slavery in the Indies has been the occasion of attacks and calumnies that call for a response. In 1516 Las Casas approved, and counseled, the introduction of black slaves in the Indies with a view to improving the condition of the Indians. He was not, however, the initiator of the project, as a royal order had already authorized it in 1501. Further—and most importantly—Las Casas has left us clear and painful testimony of his remorse for what he did in the beginning of his battle in the Indians' behalf. In a work of his maturity, the fruit of long toil and meditation, following a passage in which he criticizes his earlier decision, he writes that "the blacks have the same right to freedom as the Indians." Elsewhere he declares himself "not sure whether his ignorance and good intention will excuse him before God's judgment seat" (*Historia de las Indias* [Mexico City, 1951], 3:117, 275). Las Casas's final attitude on the matter is recognized by, for instance, the famous historian of black slavery in the United States, John H. Franklin, in *From Slavery to Freedom: A History of Negro Americans* (New York: Knopf, 1980), p. 36.

63. This is the year, 1968, when the Brazilian dictatorship became more harsh and repressive. In Argentina there was a military dictatorship, not Cámpora or Perón. In Chile we had not Allende, but Frei. And in Mexico hundreds of students were murdered by the government. Peru had a depressing and difficult year. The situation in the other countries of Latin America, with the exception of Uruguay, was by now more or less the same as it would be in the years immediately to come. Then too, the death of "Che" Guevara the previous year had dealt the armed struggle a rude blow. But most of all, the poor and lowly peoples of Latin America had enjoyed little improvement in their conditions during these years. In some countries political oppression had become even more refined and cruel; but the economic repression, known by the poorest, had always been so atrocious that there is simply no possible way to maintain that it had only just recently created, or caused a return to, an especially dehumanizing situation. It was a situation which had always obtained, and these people had never been really able to struggle free of it. May I be permitted to recall that, in a work presented in CICOP (Washington) in January 1970, I stated that the situation in Latin America was so harsh and difficult that one simply had to "Hope against hope" (De la Iglesia Colonial a Medellín," *Vispera* [April 1970], pp. 3–8)—surely not a very euphoric commentary on the times. For the historical context, and first steps, of the theology of liberation see Roberto Oliveros, *Liberación y teología: Génesis y crecimiento de una reflexión (1966–1976)* (Lima: CEP, 1977).

64. See my *La pastoral de la Iglesia en América Latina: Análisis teológico* (Montevideo: MIEC-JECI, 1968), chap. 1, a paper presented in one of our first meetings, in Pretópolis, Brazil, in

1964, where we were searching for a theological reflection with its point of departure in the reality of our situation. See also my *Theology of Liberation*, chap. 1.

65. For methodological questions within the theology of liberation, see especially Segundo, *Liberation of Theology*. See also Hugo Assmann, *A Theology for a Nomad Church* (Maryknoll, N.Y.: Orbis, 1976); and the August-September 1975 issue of *Estudios Centroamericanos* (San Salvador), devoted to theological method and Latin American christology, with articles by Ignacio Ellacuría, Jon Sobrino, and J. Hernández Pico; the suggestive piece by Raúl Vidales, *Cuestiones en torno al método en la Teología de la Liberación* (Lima: MIEC-JECI, 1974); and Beatriz Melano Couch, in John Eagleson and Sergio Torres, eds. *Theology in the Americas* (Maryknoll, N.Y.: Orbis, 1976), pp. 304–8. On the concept of praxis, see F. Castillo, *El problema de la praxis en la teología de la liberación* (Münster, 1976).

66. Poverty is one of the earliest great biblical themes of the theology of liberation—see my *Theology of Liberation*, chap. 13, and the commentary on Matthew 25 in chap. 10. I apologize for this and other references to my own writings. Here it would scarcely be worth the trouble, were it not for friends who, naively "buying" a distortion propagated by persons with other interests, have begun to repeat what they have heard to the effect that, in its beginnings, the theology of liberation was centered exclusively on the Old Testament theme of the exodus. This is altogether in error. (On the other hand, we are far from denying the central importance of the exodus theme throughout the Bible, and hence throughout theology.) Alejandro Cussianovich has called attention with force and originality, to the contemporary significance of the biblical theme of poverty for evangelization and the religious life (*Religious Life and the Poor* [Maryknoll, N.Y.: Orbis, 1979]).

67. This conviction is very deep-rooted among us (see my *Theology of Liberation*, pp. 307–8; and chap. 3, above, "Liberation Praxis and Christian Faith.") In fact it is the methodological point of departure for all our efforts of theological reflection in the Bartolomé de Las Casas Center in Lima. Our interfaces with other contemporary theology is always filtered through this point of departure as a principle of discernment.

68. Leonardo Boff's expression, referring to the history of Brazil. See his *Teologia do cativerio e da libertação* (Lisbon: Multinova, 1976).

69. See the challenging study by F. W. Marquardt, *Theologie und Sozialismus: Das Beispiel Karl Barth* (Munich: Kaiser, 1972). The same author has an article in the collection by G. Husinger, ed., *Karl Barth and Radical Politics* (Philadelphia: Westminster, 1976), which collection also contains some texts of Barth. Henry Mottu investigates the scope of Barth's socialist option in his excellent "Le Pasteur Rouge de Safenwill: Réflexions sur le socialisme du premier Barth," *Bulletin du Centre Protestant d'Etudes* (Geneva), Aug. 1976, pp. 15–30. For historical antecedents of Barth's socialism, see the parallel traced by Hugo Echegaray between Luther and Münzer, in "Lutero y Münzer: Dos concepciones antitéticas del proceso de liberación," *Páginas*, no. 7 (1976).

70. Dorothee Soelle (*Political Theology* [Philadelphia: Fortress, 1974]) has perceptively demonstrated the connections between Bultmann and political theology. Both are theologies of the Enlightenment. This corroborates what we are saying here—that progressivist theology springs from the political consciousness of the modern spirit, and not from that of the world of the oppressed.

71. Tillich's work should also be considered here. His commitment to "religious socialism" in the early part of this century is a matter of record. See the collection of his writings in Paul Tillich, *Political Expectation* (New York: Harper, 1971).

72. *Gesammelte Schriften* (Munich: Kaiser, 1959), 2:441. Editor Bethge dates this text 1942. Robert McAfee Brown has called attention to the passage in an excellent article in which he warns against a premature cutting of the ties with European theology in order to build a North American one; provided, of course, that the European theology be one that is willing to face the need for radical social change: "A Preface and a Conclusion," in Eagleson/Torres, *Theology in the Americas*.

73. Henry Mottu utilizes Gramsci's analyses to shed new light on Bonhoeffer's critique of religion. Mottu places that critique in relationship with Bonhoeffer's political experience to show us a Bonhoeffer capable of "keeping account of the healthy core of popular religion" ("Theologische Kritik der Religion und des Volkes," in *Genf '76: Ein Bonhoeffer-Symposium* [Munich: Kaiser, 1976], pp. 68–97). For Bonhoeffer's importance in Latin American Christian circles, especially among the ISAL Protestants, see Julio de Santa Ana, "Bonhoeffer und die Theologie der Befreiung," in *Genf '76*, pp. 151–70; and José Alemany, "La recepción de Die-

trich Bonhoeffer en Latinoamérica," *Teología y Vida* (Santiago de Chile, 1976).

74. See Sergio Torres and Virginia Fabella, eds., *The Emergent Gospel: Theology from the Underside of History* (Maryknoll, N.Y.: Orbis, 1978). For black theology, see James H. Cone's basic *A Black Theology of Liberation* (New York: Lippincott, 1970); and Allan Aubrey Boesak, *Farewell to Innocence: A Socio-Ethical Study on Black Theology and Power* (Orbis, 1976). For a feminist approach, see Letty Russell, *Human Liberation in a Feminist Perspective: A Theology* (Philadelphia: Westminster, 1974). For African theology, see the articles published in *Essays in Black Theology* (Johannesburg, 1972); and Kofi Appiah-Kubi and Sergio Torres, eds., *African Theology en Route* (Orbis, 1979). For Asian theology see Gerald H. Anderson, ed., *Asian Voices in Christian Theology* (Orbis, 1976); Virginia Fabella, ed., *Asia's Struggle for Full Humanity: Towards a Relevant Theology* (Orbis, 1980); and Kosuke Koyama, *Waterbuffalo Theology* (Orbis, 1974). For the Caribbean, see Noel Leo Erskine, *Decolonizing Theology: A Caribbean Perspective* (Orbis, 1981).

75. See the collection of articles in *Teología de la liberación y praxis popular* (Salamanca: Sígueme, 1976), especiaily the chapter "Teología de la liberación, cultura popular y discernimiento." Although not in agreement with Scannone here—he seems to have generalized too rapidly from a small number of cases—we must confess ourselves in his debt for important observations on the problematic of the theology of liberation, as well as for having so clearly posed questions that will contribute to a more lucid and critical resumption of our own points of departure. To this end we shall have need of a broad, critical study that will take account of the various lines of approach of liberation theology, as well as of the complex political and ecclesial panorama against which it is situated.

76. See Leonardo Boff's excellent work *Teologia do cativeiro e da libertação* (Lisbon, 1976).

77. Many of these "realists," having never either believed in or taken part in the liberation effort, easily regard it with an intellectualist skepticism, or even come out against it in frank opposition. They are not drawing up the balance sheet of these recent years. They have always thought this way. Only circumstances suddenly permit them to say aloud what they had but dared whisper before. Now they look askance at the new life and creativity beginning quietly to stir in Latin America once more.

78. See Ernesto Cardenal's efforts in this direction: *The Gospel in Solentiname*, 4 vols. (Maryknoll: Orbis, 1976–82). Another interesting report is given by Charlie Avila in his mimeographed "Peasant Theology: Reflections by the Philippino Peasants on their Process of Social Revolution." See also Alejandro Cussianovich and the Committee of JOCIST Female Domestic Servants, *Llamados a ser libres* (Lima: CEP, 1974); and articles in *Pastoral Andina* (Cuzco) and *Páginas*. This would be a most fertile area for further investigation. Recent years have produced quite an interesting approach in the form of a "materialist reading of the Bible"; see the path-breaking work by Fernando Belo, *A Materialist Reading of the Gospel of Mark* (Maryknoll, N.Y.: Orbis, 1981); and Michael Clévenot, *Approches matérialistes de la Bible* (Paris: Cerf, 1976). There would be a great deal to refine and qualify here, but it is a tack that affords access to perspectives that other approaches fail to reach. It would be a pity, though, were the whole undertaking to stick fast at the level of an intellectual reading of the Bible—were it to be relegated to the methods and modes of pure exegesis. If it, for instance, were simply to become a successor to the structuralist interpretation of the Bible. One must be clear about the breaches with tradition that this reading involves, surely. But this is exactly what should take us to the root of things and help us rediscover a framework of militancy and concrete commitments.

79. The popular expressions used in the present paragraphs have sprung up in the life of the Christian communities committed to popular liberation. Generally they are oral in their origin, even when they have eventually found their way into the written word. See, for example, ONIS, *Evangelización liberadora* (working documents, Lima, 1972).

80. Black theology has begun to face this problem with much perspicacity and excellent results. See William R. Jones, *Is God a White Racist?* (New York: Anchor/Doubleday, 1973); and Cone, *God of the Oppressed*. Porfirio Miranda has stressed the importance of the theme of justice for understanding the God of the Bible in his *Marx and the Bible* (Maryknoll, N.Y.: Orbis, 1974) and *Being and the Messiah: The Message of Saint John* (Orbis, 1977).

81. Let us hope that this reflection will have its point of departure in the practice of this people, as writ large on the horizon of popular liberation. Sometimes discussion of these subjects develops intellectual dynamics of its own that remove it from the humble but massive realities that actually constitute their authentic springboard. This alienation from reality only yields up the exhaustion of these subjects in a labryinth of endless intrachurch squabbling.

82. On the subject of christology from the standpoint of our Latin American problematic, see Jon Sobrino's important contribution, *Christology at the Crossroads* (Maryknoll, N.Y.: Orbis, 1978). On the relationship between evangelization and ecclesiology, see the Peruvian episcopate's 1973 document "Evangelización," in *Signos de lucha y esperanza* (Lima: CEP, 1978).

83. See Martin Lange and Reinhold Iblacker, eds., *Witnesses of Hope: The Persecution of Christians in Latin America* (Maryknoll, N.Y.: Orbis, 1980).

84. We welcome analyses of this involvement by theological reflection in concrete reality in the "theological models" laid out in David Tracy's well-documented *A Blessed Rage for Order* (New York: Seabury, 1975).

85. "He will be someone personally and vitally engaged in historical realities with specific times and places. He will be engaged where nations, social classes, people struggle to free themselves from domination and oppression by other nations, classes, and people" (Gutiérrez, *Theology of Liberation*, p. 13).

86. On the social conditioning required for theological work in Latin America, see Luis A. Gomes de Souza, "Los condicionamientos sociopolíticos actuales de la teología en América Latina," in *Liberación y cautiverio*, pp. 69–81; and the more historical approach of Enrique Dussel in his *Historia de la Iglesia*, pp. 19–66, "Sobre la historia de la teología en América Latina."

8

The Limitations of Modern Theology: On a Letter of Dietrich Bonhoeffer

Theological reflection is always carried on in a context of specific historical processes. It is accordingly bound up with these processes. The bourgeois revolutions and their intellectual consciousness, the Enlightenment, opened an age of important changes in the concrete life conditions of the Christian churches of the West. Simultaneously, therefore, they produced new challenges for systematic reflection upon the faith—challenges still charged with consequences in our own day.

The new threats were perceived, in their time, by two important thinkers in particular. One was that central figure of modern thought, who exerted such an influence, if rather a heterodox one, on theology, Georg Wilhelm Friedrich Hegel. The other was the "father of contemporary Protestant theology," Friedrich Schleiermacher. Until these two appeared on the scene, only Immanuel Kant, the theological sniper, was available for being "gone back to" ("Back to Kant!" the Protestant theologians loved to cry), all down the nineteenth century and beyond.

Another great questioner of Christianity took up these same challenges: Ludwig Feuerbach, whom Karl Barth was of course quite right to include in his *Protestant Theology in the Nineteenth Century*.

All these thinkers, especially Kant, Hegel, and Schleiermacher, were the heirs of a theological tradition altogether comfortable and at home in the modern new "world come of age" of their eighteenth and nineteenth centuries. And now these same scholars would provide the fillip that Protestant

Spanish original, "Los límites de la teología moderna: un texto de Bonhoeffer," first published in *Concilium*, Spanish ed., May 1979.

theology, doubtless the broadest and most far-reaching theology of modern times, would need in order to take a new and important step forward. All this was taking place while the Catholic camp kept its distance from the new world of ideas, tangling itself up in a mesh of endless, wearisome polemics with political liberalism over religious freedom and other modern liberties.

In the second half of the nineteenth century, liberal theology was even more outspoken in its acceptance of this modern, bourgeois world in which it had been born and bred. It continued the direction initiated by our three great thinkers, to be sure. But it left their criticisms and uneasiness behind. Now liberal theology would actually make the modern mentality the norm of faith, as well as of theology.

Much later, Dietrich Bonhoeffer would speak of the "easy terms of peace that the world dictated."[1] The school of Albrecht Ritschl is a clear demonstration, in Barth's view, of this spontaneous, overtly bourgeois character of liberal theology.[2] Theology is now more a culmination of the spirit of the Enlightenment than a challenge to it. By the end of the nineteenth century, liberal Protestant theology became the theology of a self-assured, middle-class Christianity.

Scholars recognize that it is only against this backdrop that the reaction of the three giants of twentieth-century Protestant theology—Barth, Bultmann, and Tillich—can be understood. Serious, rigorous, and full of courage, these thinkers' stubborn questions challenged even the thought of the trio of giants who preceded them.

Bonhoeffer, who died in the Nazi extermination camp in Flossenbürg in 1945, was a Christian theologian who sought to locate God at the very heart and center of human life.[3] He refused to see God out on its periphery. As a result he is a theologian of great lucidity vis-à-vis the limitations of modern theology. In a number of pithy and penetrating observations—particularly in a passage in a letter of his dated June 8, 1944, which will serve us as our point of departure for certain reflections on bourgeois Christianity and the systematic reflection upon the faith that this Christianity produced—he provides the counterweight in favor of what is most progressive and advanced in that theology. He criticizes all three members of our mighty trio of twentieth-century theologians, confronting them anew with the very questions of the Enlightenment that provoked their theology.

Bonhoeffer's objection to the theology of Barth, Bultmann, and Tillich is that although they indeed questioned the Enlightenment and its theology, they failed to question it squarely and radically. Their critique was doubtless the best this type of theology had ever undertaken. Yet we feel in our bones the limitations of an effort to respond to the challenges of the modern world without criticizing it in its economic bases, as on its social and ideological levels. For, as we shall see, no one ever vanquished the modern, bourgeois mentality while remaining at its heart. This, it seems to me, is what Bonhoeffer's testimony communicates to us today. As we shall also see, it may even be that he surmised this himself.

Of course by taking up this passage from Bonhoeffer's letter as the vehicle of our reflections we shall be obliged to make an approach to reality in perhaps too narrow a purview—a purely theological purview, in which the historical moorings of our material, our vehicle, will appear only by way of occasional allusion. Indeed, in order not to wander afield in our theological considerations themselves, we shall have to renounce the opportunity for detailed discussion of certain observations and criticisms by our author in other quarters of theology itself. But I trust that by taking up the penetrating reflections of this great Christian and incisive theologian, who confronted the challenges of the modern world as perhaps no one before him, we may see both the grandeur and the historical limitations of his undertaking—and thereby discern, albeit vaguely at first, another path to take.

THE WORD OF GOD IN A TIME OF CRISIS

The First World War (1914 to 1918) challenged the facile optimism and security of bourgeois society. The Belle Epoque was brusquely and brutally at an end. During these same years the socialist movement, which had been on the point of absorption and assimilation by bourgeois democracy, came to power in Russia and was radicalized elsewhere. Shortly after, the rise of fascism threatened all the liberties of modernity.

One of the results of these massive ideological readjustments was that the modern world, as it began to be deprived of its smugness and self-sufficiency, began to moderate its assaults against the world of religion. The first theology developed within the framework of a bourgeois social order began to lose its vitality. In fact it began to be accused by a new generation of theologians of having capitulated to modern thought. Now the way was open for new theological approaches, whose concern would be to meet the new challenges—to reaffirm the presence and judgment of the word of God in a world of crisis.

Among the efforts to break with the immediate theological past and blaze new trails for the proclamation of the gospel and the life of the church the names of Barth, Bultmann, and Tillich stand head and shoulders above the rest. And yet Bonhoeffer thinks that none of them actually took the bull by the horns, none of them actually responded to a "world come of age." He thinks that none of them really faced up to a world that was the result of a lengthy historical process, rooted in the late Middle Ages—a process that Bonhoeffer considers it important to bear in mind.[4] He is aware of the audacity of his critique and proposal, and is at once fired with what he has discovered and dismayed by the inadequacy of his new formulations.[5] Let us, then, follow along the course plotted for us by his letter of June 8, 1944.

Paul Tillich

Bonhoeffer rejects the theological undertaking of Paul Tillich—who takes up Schleiermacher's thread to weave a tissue of his own—by reason of its emphasis on a religious interpretation of the world:

> Tillich set out to interpret the evolution of the world (against its will) in a religious sense—to give it its shape through religion. That was very brave of him, but the world unseated him and went on by itself.[6]

Indeed, Tillich made the notion of religion into a key to understanding the human being and confronting the onslaughts of the modern world. The central place in Tillich's theology is occupied by the philosophy of religion. This is how Tillich thought he had come to grips with the questions Bonhoeffer is asking. Tillich felt that both Bonhoeffer and he were seeking a solution to the conflicts between religious tradition and the modern spirit.[7] But in Bonhoeffer's judgment they were at work on different projects.

Tillich rejects a conception of religion based on a heteronomy over the human being that would leave humanity's adulthood out of account. But neither does he accept the autonomy of those who, he says, by estranging themselves from God, deny themselves as well. Hence Tillich postulates what he calls a "theonomy"—a conception of religion that, while recognizing and accepting the advances of the human spirit, asserts that this spirit may be fully realized only in a relationship with God.

To Bonhoeffer, Tillich is only "trying anxiously in this way to reserve some space for God."[8] Tillich may have been correct that he and Bonhoeffer were dealing basically with the same theological problems. But it is equally clear that the paths they took to a solution were miles apart.

Karl Barth

Tillich's approach also differs from that of Karl Barth. Tillich himself often insisted upon the difference. Barth begins "from above," from the Trinity, from revelation, and from there descends to the human being. Tillich, just the other way, purports to begin with human beings' own questions, to which revelation thereupon makes reply.[9]

Bonhoeffer could not applaud this approach of Tillich's, notwithstanding the apparent similarity in their points of departure, and indeed the prevailing interpretation of Tillich's thought. Bonhoeffer—to simplify a bit—begins not with "human beings" precisely, but with *God become a human being in Christ*. Hence of course Barth's "descent from above" leaves him as uneasy as Tillich does. Bonhoeffer praises Barth for having undertaken the critique of religion, but feels he has not gone far enough with that critique.

Immediately after his observations on Tillich, Bonhoeffer writes:

Barth was the first to realize the mistake that all these attempts (which were all, in fact, still sailing, though unintentionally, in the channel of liberal theology) were making in leaving clear a space for religion in the world or against the world.

He brought in against religion the God of Jesus Christ, *"pneuma* against *sarx."* That remains his greatest service. . . . [But] in the nonreligious interpretation of theological concepts, he gave no concrete guidance, either in dogmatics or in ethics. There lies his limitation, and because of it his theology of revelation has become positivist, a "positivism of revelation," as I put it.

The Confessing Church has now largely forgotten all about the Barthian approach, and has lapsed from positivism into conservative restoration.[10]

Here Bonhoeffer is leveling a very basic criticism at Barth—and a paradoxical one. We must not allow the differences in their terminology to camouflage it. Barth, in spite of his protestations to the contrary, never managed to make a clean break with Christianity's traditional religious interpretation of the world—including the modern world.[11] He falls back into it, Bonhoeffer holds, when he makes of faith more a law than a gift.[12] This is why, according to Bonhoeffer, Barth fails to give us an adequate orientation toward the nonreligious interpretation of theological concepts. The result is a certain "positivism of revelation," and from here it is but a short step to a "conservative restoration"—that is, to an attempt to ignore the situation created by the modern mentality. And this, we read, is what the Confessing Church has done.

In fact, Bonhoeffer's judgment has been even more severe. Only a few weeks before, he had written that this view of Barthianism was not a matter of the interpretation of a handful of Barth's disciples, but of a "positivism of revelation" that is, in itself, *"essentially* [such] restoration."[13]

Barth always felt Bonhoeffer's judgment to have been unjust in this regard.[14] And indeed what Barth is often reproached with is precisely too radical a separation between faith and the world. He leaves the world to its own devices, runs the objection, in order thereby the better to safeguard the transcendence of God's word.

Bonhoeffer's particular contribution is of course anything but the denial of a distinction between faith and religion. On the contrary, he complains that Barth has not carried his critique of religion to its ultimate consequences.

In order to appreciate the entire scope of these observations of Bonhoeffer, we shall have to have some precisions with respect to his notion of religion, and we shall say something on this point a little further on. For now, however, we shall merely take cognizance of the fact that, for Bonhoeffer, not even Barth's theology goes to the root of the modern world's challenges. Instead, it "carries on the great concepts of Christian theology; but it seems as if doing this is gradually just about exhausting it" (speaking precisely of the Confessing Church).[15] Indeed, in spite of all, Barth's theology, in the view of Bonhoeffer, "is still influenced by [liberal theology], though negatively," to be sure.[16]

Rudolf Bultmann

Still less does Rudolf Bultmann escape this same reproach. Bultmann's undertaking, according to Bonhoeffer, is more than under the shadow of liberal theology; it is an out-and-out continuation of it:

Bultmann seems to have somehow felt Barth's limitations, but he misconstrues them in the sense of liberal theology, and so goes off into the typical liberal process of reduction—the "mythological" elements of Christianity are dropped, and Christianity is reduced to its "essence."[17]

Here, according to Bonhoeffer, is where Bultmann mistook his way. But it is not that demythologization is going too far. On the contrary, it falls short of the mark. It is doing too little.[18] An "existential" interpretation of the Bible is not a nonreligious interpretation, and therefore it is not what is needed today. A ferreting out of the "essence of Christianity" is too feeble a response to the real questions of a world come of age. Bultmann's perspective is akin to Tillich's and unlike Barth's: Bultmann begins with the hearer of the word. His is the modern spirit, molded by scientific reason and conscious of its capacity for free decision.

Here again, it seems to me, Bonhoeffer is doing something else. When he asserts that the approach adopted by Bultmann is "fundamentally still a liberal one," this is harsh criticism indeed.[19] Although recognizing the merit of liberal theology's refusal to "try to put the clock back," Bonhoeffer accuses it of "conceding to the world the right to determine Christ's place in the world."[20] Taking his position over against Bultmann's point of departure, Bonhoeffer defines "thinking theologically" as thinking from a point of departure in the "incarnation, crucifixion, and resurrection of Jesus Christ."[21]

Here we have the three great efforts to respond to the challenges of the modern mentality. And in Bonhoeffer's view, they all fall short. The first fails because it has recourse (however brilliantly and creatively) to a notion that the modern mentality has invalidated. The second fails because it goes halfway down the road and stops (of course it at least had the lucidity to start). The third fails for want of daring—as in the case of the second—and for its resumption of a worn-out old exercise in reductionism (in spite of new trails it blazes along the way).

And yet, within the very insufficiency of his approach, Barth, felt Bonhoeffer, pointed the way to a more fertile reflection upon the faith. Barth's theology had inspired Bonhoeffer's own first steps. Now it would become "home base" for him when, in prison, he began to move into uncharted territory. Thus for Bonhoeffer Barthian theology was inadequate, but at least it was a beginning. (Indeed, it was even more inadequate, and even more of a beginning, than Bonhoeffer would ever suspect.)

HOW MAY ONE SPEAK OF GOD IN A WORLD COME OF AGE?

As it had been for Barth, the proclamation of the gospel is Bonhoeffer's central preoccupation. His theological reflection was always bound up with his pastoral ministry. Surely all great theologies are sprung from this same union. The intense degree of Bonhoeffer's political commitment during the last ten years of his life only served to sharpen his concern for the proclamation of the Christian message, lead him onto new terrain, and lay out before him a whole new problematic vis-à-vis his discourse on the faith.[22] The question "How may one speak of God in a world come of age?" points up two themes he will concentrate on in his writings during his time in prison in Tegel: the world come of age we live in and the God we believe in.[23] Ultimately what this question asks (and here Bonhoeffer broaches a third subject as well, one that spans the first two) is: "What is Christianity really?" That is, "Who actually is Christ for us today?"[24] This is the question "theological thinking" asks—that is, nonreligious thinking.

For Bonhoeffer, Christian theology had become lost in misunderstandings, polemics, and apologetics with the modern world. There can be no doubt that he is thinking even of the great theological undertakings we have cited above—the work of our three twentieth-century giants. The basic reason, to Bonhoeffer's mind, for the failure of all these attempts is that humanity's adulthood had not been taken for what it was. Its real questions have not even been heard, let alone answered.

The expressions "world come of age" or "adulthood of the world," which Bonhoeffer began to use in his June 8 letter,[25] are of course an allusion to the celebrated passage in which Immanual Kant takes cognizance of the new situation obtaining in his own eighteenth century.[26] Bonhoeffer proposes to take on the entire problem—to face squarely the fact of a humanity come of age, to accept this new world without reserve, to come to grips with its questions right in the middle of the field of battle, instead of heading rabbitlike for the bushes or the shadow of a massive old wall, to reason upon the faith without any nostalgia for what is no more—in short, to do everything that modern theology has not managed to do. This is the task to come, and Bonhoeffer feels he is in virgin territory now.

Nevertheless, at no time in the course of his attempt to come to grips with a grown-up world just as he finds it does our author suggest that the historical agent of modern society and ideology will be the bourgeois class. The fact that one social class has wrested economic and political power from the grasp of more traditional sectors, and inaugurated a mode of production that is generating new forms of exploitation, does not suggest to him that this new dominant class will now determine the course of history in the West. There is no question, for Bonhoeffer, of humanity's attaining its majority by trampling underfoot the writhing mass of the poor and the despoiled. It is only the facts and events marking the mastery of nature and society by reason that figure in his account of the historical process leading to human autonomy. Concretely, these facts and events will be the great milestones in the ascent of the bourgeoisie.[27]

The protest movements of the poor, from the late Middle Ages on, find no place in Bonhoeffer's historical focus, nor does the contemporaneous labor movement.[28] It is significant that the phenomenon of Nazism, against which he struggled so courageously, did not lead Bonhoeffer to a deeper analysis of the "crisis in today's society." It was the Nazi phenomenon that seems to have provoked his judgment upon the ultimate values of modernity. Perhaps the explanation is that, taken up as he is with the fascist enemy and its attacks on liberal society from the rear, Bonhoeffer was less sensitive to the world of injustice upon which that society was built.[29]

We must come to understand this new world, this world come of age. Of this Bonhoeffer is convinced. It is true that some of his expressions could lead one to believe that he postulated a mundane self-complacency instead. But no, he writes: "The world *must* be understood better than it understands itself, . . . [namely] on the basis of the gospel and in the light of Christ."[30]

Bethge is right when he says that it is the christological perspective that is basic for Bonhoeffer. He is right again that Bonhoeffer's reflections on humanity's adulthood are neither philosophy, nor phenomenology, but theology:

> The recognition of the world's coming of age is, with Bonhoeffer, neither philosophy nor phenomenology, but the knowledge of God, i.e. "theology," and that is a knowledge that seeks to follow God where he has already preceded us. That is why Bonhoeffer's statement about the world come of age is first and last a theological statement.[31]

It is this attempt to "follow God where he has already preceded us" that requires us to reject the religious interpretation of Christianity—that we cease at last "to speak on the one hand metaphysically, and on the other hand individualistically."[32] Both ways lead us out of the world—the former by locking God up in categories of "absolute" and "infinite," the latter by "the displacement of God from the world, and from the public part of human life," in order to relegate him to the "sphere of the 'personal,' the 'inner,' and the 'private.' "[33] Here once more we have a criticism of theology's attempts to respond to the sudden attacks of the modern mentality by merely falling back instead of making a frontal assault.[34]

For our author, when all is said and done, to seek to save the faith through religion is to fail to see that religion is always partial, whereas faith is global.[35] It is an attempt to reduce the whole to one of its parts.

A comparison with Barth at this point is inescapable, and it will enable us to understand just what Bonhoeffer means by "religion." Bonhoeffer always recognized his debt to Barth, but there are clear differences between them as well. The first point of divergence is that, for Barth, religion is a necessary product of human striving. Of course, if this is what you begin with, holds Barth (and this is what his "friendly enemy," Schleiermacher, began with), you will never arrive at the God of the Bible. For Bonhoeffer, on the other hand, the religious interpretation of Christianity is something historically conditioned. It is a Western phenomenon, now fallen prey to the maturation of humanity. For Barth, religion is something inherent in human nature; for Bonhoeffer, it is a stage of history.[36]

But there is a second, more important, difference. For Barth, religion is a way of gaining control of God. For Bonhoeffer, religion is a way of understanding God as dominator of the human person. Which of the two is it—the human being's power over God, or God's power over the human being?[37] It is the latter notion that is Bonhoeffer's recognized adversary. Ultimately, he holds, the question facing us is not, "What is the modern spirit and what can it accept in the Christian faith?" The question now demanding our response is much more radical: "Who is God?"

The answer is, God is the God of Jesus Christ. That is, God is a God who saves us not through his domination but through his suffering. Here we have Bonhoeffer's famous thesis of *God's weakness*.[38] It will make its mark in theology after he is gone.[39] It is of this God, and only of this God, that the Bible tells us.[40] And it is thus that the cross acquires its tremendous revelatory potential with respect to God's weakness as an expression of his love for a world come of age.

Here is a concept charged with force and power. "It is not the religious act that makes the Christian, but participation in the sufferings of God in the secular life."[41] This is conversion. This is what it is to believe in the gospel. What makes a Christian a Christian is "being caught up into the messianic sufferings of God in Jesus Christ."[42]

But here we strike bottom, too. Here we are at the very heart of things. The cup of humanity's maturity must be drunk to the dregs. The correct response to modernity is not to place God beyond the limits of reason, or drag him into history from the outside, or domesticate him in "religious sentiment," or bottle him up in bourgeois mentality by making belief in him a human excellence. Nor again is it the answer to assert that to move away from him is the destruction of the root of all human culture. Nor, finally, is the answer to make of him the object of a free personal decision. God in Christ is a God suffering, and to share in his weakness is to believe in him. This is what it means to be a Christian.

But where is suffering today? Who are those who suffer? Thus Bonhoeffer finds himself driven to a question full of consequences. "What does this life look like, this participation in the powerlessness of God in the world?"[43]

"FROM BENEATH"

Bonhoeffer has walked, without fear and without reserve, down the road of the recognition of a world come of age—the world encountered by modern theology. And he walked it to the end, to full acceptance of that world. This is what enabled him to point to a new way of understanding God.

But now of course he will need a new way of understanding God's presence in history. And here there is a fork in the road, and it is for us to make the choice. We may simply emphasize the world's adulthood, and keep on enthusiastically pulling out the consequences, without an analysis of the historical bases upon which this phenomenon has been erected—and then we shall have entered a blind alley, fruitless for any meaningful theology. Or we may understand this last theological effort of Bonhoeffer's as having led modern theology to a collision with its own dialectical demand for a change in perspective.

It will no longer do simply to continue to think in the modern mold, refusing to accept the theological datum that that mold, that mentality, has accompanied and justified the historical process that creates this new world of spoliation and injustice. Turning our backs, in our theological reflection, on the fact that the so-called modern spirit, which is the interlocutor of progressivist theology, is in large part the reflection of a capitalistic, bourgeois society will lead us merely to a few skirmishes with the rear guard of a world in decomposition. Or at most—and Bonhoeffer saw this himself—it will permit us to forge a discourse upon the faith for the "bourgeois, petty, and grand." Bonhoeffer's courage led him to a mountaintop, and from that mountaintop he could discern, through the mists, other roads to follow, even though he would be unable forthrightly to stride down them.

Indeed, the theme of God's suffering, to which Bonhoeffer was led by his analysis of the modern world, came to him another way as well. In an earlier text, composed before any of the letters of his prison experience, he speaks of an "apprenticeship" with which he had been favored in recent years:

It is an experience of incomparable value to have learned to see the great events of the history of the world from beneath: from the viewpoint of the useless, the suspect, the abused, the powerless, the oppressed, the despised—in a word, from the viewpoint of those who suffer.[44]

It is doubtful just to what extent this "apprenticeship" influenced Bonhoeffer's later theological reflection. But it is evident that it could not have influenced it at all, had it not first enabled him to look at the history of humanity in a new way.

It would be unwarranted to attempt to deduce from Bonhoeffer's use of terms such as "poor" and "oppressed" that we are in the presence of a critical analysis of modern society on grounds of that society's injustice and oppression. But there are weighty indications that Bonhoeffer had begun to move forward in the perspective of "those beneath"—those on the "underside of history."

To cite just one example, Bonhoeffer wrote: "Jesus calls men, not to a new religion, but to life."[45] This is a statement that calls for a frank acknowledgment of its total content. We dare not "water it down" with a spiritualistic interpretation explicitly rejected on several occasions by Bonhoeffer himself.

Indeed, as he progressed in his reflections Bonhoeffer became more sensitized to the concrete, material things of human life: health, good fortune, and so on—the very things often missing from or denied to the fringes of modern society. For example, he was led to an examination of the notion of "blessing" in the Old Testament and its applicability today. He found that it includes the good things of earth, and that in it "the whole of the earthly life is claimed for God."[46] One must appreciate the whole meaning of the passage in Luke that tells us that when Jesus' disciples were with him "they 'lacked nothing.' "[47]

Thus Bonhoeffer's thesis that God suffers on the cross leads him to deplore the unjust suffering of the outcasts of society, and he proclaims the right to life in all its dimensions as an exigency of the Bible itself. Once more in the history of thought a profound sense of God has led someone to a new sensitivity to the plight of the poor. Their deprivations, and even the particular expressions of their faith in God, now become the object of Bonhoeffer's attention.[48] True, he never really made this insight the center of his theological discourse. It remains focused first and foremost on the great challenges of modernity. But he did manage to engage these challenges directly, and this led him to sense the limitations of his own theological enterprise. His reflection is taking a tack whose origin is very deep in his personal experience, and this is why his testimony, and the paths he opens up, are charged with such potential for further advance.

Actually it was Barth who had broken the way for Bonhoeffer here. A great deal has been written recently about the influence of Barth's pastoral experience with the working classes on his theological positions, and it is a matter of record that this experience led him at one time to a frank political militancy. Whatever may have been his precise political options, it is certain that his sensitivity to the new forms of spoliation and exploitation created by a capitalist society did play a role in his theological thinking: it made him attentive to the deterioration of God's word into a "bourgeois gospel" and alerted him to the need for a theology accommodated to the underclasses.[49] It led him to a notion of God as taking sides with the poor against the powerful.[50] It even led him to envision a role for the church in the struggle for social justice in the world of the oppressed.[51]

Barth's thinking offers an example of the irruption of the perspective of the poor into the modern problematic—where, despite all, Barth's theology remains. But something very important is stirring at the theological limits reached by a Bonhoeffer, and even more at those reached by a Barth. Each of them discerns the glimmer of a dialectic in the history of the Christian faith. The modern, bourgeois mentality is not overcome in ideological dialogue, but in a dialectical opposition to the social contradictions this mentality represents in the real world of history. Only from beyond the frontiers of this modern bourgeois world will it be possible to respond to the challenges of that world. That is, only from within the world of poverty and exploitation that the bourgeois world produces can that same world be confronted and overcome.

It may be that the absence of social analysis prevented Bonhoeffer from carrying his intuition to its mature theological implications. But he had made a beginning. He had moved toward a perspective "from beneath"—not in the sense of proceeding from the human being to God (as in the expression, "christology from beneath," or "low christology," for example), but from a point of departure in the universe of oppression, and of aspirations for deliverance, in which the poor are languishing. He had moved toward a theological outlook whose point of departure is in a faith lived by exploited classes, condemned ethnic groups, and marginalized cultures. The heretofore "absent from history" are making the free gift of the Father's love their own today, creating new social relationships of a communion of brothers and sisters. This is the point of departure for what we call "theology from the underside of history."

NOTES

1. Dietrich Bonhoeffer, *Letters and Papers from Prison,* Eberhard Bethge, ed. (New York: Macmillan, 3rd ed., 1967), 6/8/44, p. 180 (all subsequent references to this work will be in this fashion—i.e., letter-date and page-number).

2. See Karl Barth, *Protestant Thought: From Rousseau to Ritschl* (New York: Harper, 1959), p. 391.

3. Bethge, *Letters and Papers,* 4/30/44, p. 155.

4. Ibid., 6/8/44, p. 178.

5. Ibid., 4/30/44, p. 152.

6. Ibid., 6/8/44, p. 180.

7. See Paul Tillich, *A History of Christian Thought* (New York: Harper & Row, 1968), p. 359.

8. Bethge, *Letters and Papers,* 4/30/44, p. 155.

9. See Paul Tillich, *Perspectives on Nineteenth and Twentieth Century Protestant Theology* (New York: Harper & Row, 1967), p. 241. See also his *A History of Christian Thought* (New York: Harper & Row, 1968), pp. 123, 240, 243, 263, 293; and his *Systematic Theology* (University of Chicago Press), vol. 1 (1951), p. 61; vol. 2 (1957), p. 14; and esp. vol. 3 (1963), p. 285.

10. Bethge, *Letters and Papers,* 6/8/44, pp. 180-81.

11. It is interesting to note that, commenting on the second edition of Barth's *Epistle to the Romans,* Bultmann situated Barth's work in the line of modern attempts to demonstrate a "religious *a priori*" of faith—to Barth's no little dismay. See T. F. Torrance, "Introduction," in Barth, *Theology and Church: Shorter Writings 1920-1928* (New York: Harper & Row, 1962), pp. 14-15, 21-23; see also Günther Bornkamm's article, "The Theology of Rudolf Bultmann," in Charles W. Kegley, ed., *The Theology of Rudolf Bultmann* (New York: Harper & Row, 1966), pp. 4, 18.

12. Bethge, *Letters and Papers,* 5/5/44, p. 157.

13. Ibid., 4/30/44, p. 153—italics added.

14. See Eberhard Busch, *Karl Barth* (Philadelphia: Fortress, 1976), p. 381.

15. Bethge, *Letters and Papers,* 6/8/44, p. 181.

16. Ibid., p. 182.

17. Ibid., p. 181.

18. Ibid., 5/5/44, p. 156.

19. Ibid.

20. Ibid., 6/8/44, p. 180.

21. Ibid., 5/5/44, p. 156.

22. On his motivations for this option, see the definitive biography by Eberhard Bethge, *Dietrich Bonhoeffer: Man of Vision, Man of Courage* (New York: Harper, 1970).

23. Bethge, *Letters and Papers,* 4/30/44, p. 153.

24. Ibid.

25. Ibid., pp. 178–79.

26. As Bethge observes, Bonhoeffer had previously spoken only of an "autonomy" (*Dietrich Bonhoeffer,* p. 770).

27. Bethge, *Letters and Papers,* 6/8/44, p. 178; 7/16/44, pp. 193–95.

28. Henry Mottu has called attention to this in his "Critique de la religion et religion populaire," *Bulletin du Centre Protestant d'Etudes* (Feb. 1977), p. 27.

29. Georges Casalis speaks of a certain "sterilizing effect" of Nazism on Barth's theology: "Théologie et socialisme: l'example de K. Barth," *Etudes Théologiques et Religieuses* (1974), p. 173.

30. Bethge, *Letters and Papers,* 6/8/44, pp. 180, 182.

31. *Dietrich Bonhoeffer,* p. 771.

32. Bethge, *Letters and Papers,* 5/5/44, p. 156.

33. Ibid., 7/8/44, pp. 190–91.

34. Would it be too audacious to suspect that Tillich and Bultmann are themselves not exempt from these reproaches of metaphysical language and individualism?

35. Bethge, *Letters and Papers,* 7/18/44, p. 199.

36. See Bethge, *Dietrich Bonhoeffer,* and Claude Geffre, "La critique de la religion chez Barth et chez Bonhoeffer," *Parole et Mission* 8 (1965), pp. 567–83.

37. See Bethge, *Letters and Papers,* 7/16/44, pp. 196–97.

38. Ibid.

39. See Jürgen Moltmann, *The Crucified God* (New York: Harper & Row, 1974); K. Kitamori, *El sufrimiento de Dios* (Salamanca: Sígueme); in English see *Theology of the Pain of God* (Atlanta: John Knox, 1965).

40. Bethge, *Letters and Papers,* 7/16/44, p. 197.

41. Ibid., 7/18/44, p. 198.

42. Ibid., p. 199.

43. Ibid., pp. 199–200.

44. Bonhoeffer, *Gesammelte Schriften* (Munich: Kaiser, 1965), vol. 2, p. 441.

45. Bethge, *Letters and Papers,* 7/18/44, p. 199.

46. Ibid., 7/28/44, p. 205.

47. Ibid.; cf. Luke 22:35.

48. Of special interest here are the perceptive reflections of Henry Mottu on Bonhoeffer's respect for the wholesome kernel in popular religion (Mottu, "Critique"). The gospel's call to life has been the subject of recent emphasis in Fernando Belo, *A Materialist Reading of the Gospel of Mark* (Maryknoll, N.Y.: Orbis, 1981), and Franz Josef Hinkelammert, *Las armas ideológicas de la muerte* (San José, Costa Rica: DEI, 1977).

49. See the challenging thesis of F. W. Marquardt, *Theologie und Sozialismus: Das Beispiel Karl Barth* (Munich: Kaiser, 1972). See also the excellent collection, G. Husinger, ed., *Karl Barth and Radical Politics* (Philadelphia: Westminster, 1976); and see Mottu's fine observations in his "Le Pasteur Rouge de Safenwill: Réflexions sur le socialisme du premier Barth," *Bulletin du Centre Protestant d'Etudes* (Geneva), Aug. 1976. For the meaning Barth accorded his own political commitment it is most interesting to read a letter that he wrote to Tillich in 1933 (in Husinger, *Karl Barth,* pp. 116–17).

50. Barth, *Church Dogmatics* (New York: Scribner's), II/1 (1957), p. 386.

51. Barth, *Against the Stream* (New York: Philosophical Library, 1954), p. 41, cited in Robert McAfee Brown, *Theology in a New Key* (Philadelphia: Westminster, 1978), pp. 111–12. See also what I have written on Barth and Bultmann in chap. 7 of the present volume, in the subsection entitled "The Other History: The History of the Other," pp. 201–6.

Index

20-21, 206; of the poor, 20, 90, 105, 153, 201; to reread and remake, xii, 20, 21, 50, 201; theology of, 29, 36, 37, 90; as subversive, 21, 202
Hope: of the poor, xiii, 107; overpowering repression, 200; and Puebla, 160; springs eternal, 72
Human endeavors, in the eighteenth century, 171
Humane sciences, 58
Human rights, xiv, 87, 211
Hunger, 207
Ideological apparatus, and oppression, 79
Ideology, bourgeois, and Christian values, 39; description of, 68, 86, 124, 165n.44; dominant, 18, 46, 80, 192-193; misuse of, 69, 156; *see also* Bourgeois ideology; Liberal ideology; Marxist ideology
Indians, in Latin America, 77, 137, 185, 186, 189; *see also Mestizos*
Individualism, 174, 177
Individual liberties. *See* Liberties, individual
Industrial decline, in the US and UK, 85
Industrially developed countries, companies in, 84
Industrial revolution, 48, 49, 171-172
Industry, freedom of, 175
Injustice: institutionalized, 132, 134, 161n.11; and sin, 9; *see also* Social injustice
Institutional violence: increase of, in Latin America, ix, 28, 191; and Puebla, 161n.10; and repression, 41, 87
Integral development, in *Populorum Progressio*, 163n.34
Integral liberation: and Puebla, 145, 148, 163n.32; and reductionism, 144; relational planes of, 145-146, 147
Internal colonialism, in Latin America, 28
Intellectual, the, 103
Intraecclesial theology, description of, 41
Jesus Christ: death of, 15, 96; as a hermeneutical principle of faith, 60-61; as the manifestation of God, 12-13, 15; and the poor, 13, 162n.23, 197, 211; proclaiming justice and liberation, 206, 209; and Puebla, 137; resurrection of, 15; theological interpretation of, 104
John Paul II, Pope, x, 129, 155, 161n.7, 163n.33
Joy, of the poor, 105, 107
Justice: in the Bible, 7, 8, 10; as definitive, 14; as a global human question, 207; in political science, 50; demands of, as seen by Puebla, 164n.40
Justification, religious, and social injustice, 89
Just society, 46
Kant, Immanuel, 172, 173, 179
Kingdom of God: arrival of, 21; on earth, 14, 96, 104; and the poor, 14, 32, 105
Knowledge, 59, 175; of God, 8; theory of, 64; *see also* God, to know
Labor: devaluation of, 85; industrial division of, 49; of justice, 146
Las Casas, Bartolomé de, 77, 94; critique of, 196; theology of, 194, 195, 196-197

Latin American Bishops Conference at Medellín. *See* Medellín
Latin American Bishops Conference at Puebla. *See* Puebla
Latin American church. *See* Church, the, in Latin America
Leo XIII, Pope, and liberal Catholicism, 181
Liberal ideology, and the Enlightenment, 179
Liberation: and communion with Christ, 10, 51, 63, 207; demand for, in Latin America, 145; Jewish, from Egypt, 6; nontheological factors in, 104; opposed to developmentalism, 191; and polemics, 64, 144, 145; praxis of, 64 105; process of, 29, 38, 162n.30, 201; spirituality of, 53, 144; and struggles, 65, 78; and theology, 144; *see also* Integral liberation; Theology of liberation
Liberty: bourgeois movement for, and its effects on the poor, 186; and the individual, 87, 172, 174; religious, 177
Life situation, in Latin America, 28
Love, 18, 20; of God, 146, 147; in the language of political science, 50; limitations of, 44
Magnificat, the, interpretation of, 139
Maritain, Jacques, 188
Marketplace, the, and religion, 177
Martyrs, and Christian witness, 89, 153
Marxism, fear of, 164n.44-165n.44
Marxist ideology, misuse of, 156
Masses, the: awareness of, 97, 150, 191; exploitation of, 187-188
Medellín (Conference of Latin American bishops), viii, 28, 112; and the church, 34, 158-159; documents from, 26, 34, 35; faithfulness to, 120; and the poor, 116, 120, 199; and popular religiosity, 123; on poverty, 123, 128; power and prophecy of, 81, 122-123, 127, 199
Media, the public, and domination, 79
Memory, 12, 80
Messianic practice, 32, 96
Mestizos, 187, 189; *see also* Indians
Methodology, 100, 104
Metz, Johannes Baptist, 182-183
Mighty, the, and misuse of the gospel, 103
Militancy, 205; for Barth, 232
Modernity, 186, 230; ideology of, and the bourgeoisie, 176, 213
Modernization, in Latin America, 132
Modern spirit: influence on theology, 178, 198; subject of, 212
Moltmann, Jürgen, 185
Multinational corporations. *See* Transnationals
Narrative, language of, and theology, 184
National security, ideology of, 86
Neighbor, Christian understanding of, 44
Neto, Henrique Pereira, fate of, 70
New Covenant, the, 11, 15, 22
New liberal theology, as criticized by Metz, 183-184
Nicaragua, popular movements in, 82
Nonbeliever, the, viii, 92
Nonperson, the, and liberation theology, viii, 92, 193, 213